S0-AOC-113

The Strategy of
the Italian Communist Party

The Strategy of the Italian Communist Party

From the Resistance to the Historic Compromise

Donald Sassoon

Foreword by
E. J. Hobsbawm

St. Martin's Press, New York

JN
5657
.C63
S27
1981

© Donald Sassoon 1981

All rights reserved. For information, write:
St. Martin's Press, Inc., 175 Fifth Avenue, New York, NY 10010
Printed in Great Britain
First published in the United States of America in 1981

ISBN 0-312-76478-2

Library of Congress Cataloging in Publication Data

Sassoon, Don.
    The strategy of the Italian Communist Party.

    Bibliography: p.
    1. Partito comunista italiano.   2. Communism − Italy.   3. Communist strategy.
I. Title.
JN5657.C63S27   1981   324.245075   81-5733
ISBN 0-321-76478-2   AACR2

APR   7 1983

To Anne

CONTENTS

Foreword

Considering the political significance of the Italian Communist Party and the constant international interest in its affairs, the number of serious books about it in the English language is surprisingly modest. It has never ceased making the flesh of western government politicians creep, since its sheer size and popular support have persistently called for its association with the national government of Italy, from which it has been excluded since 1947. It is, after all, with 1.8 million members probably the largest non-governmental communist party in the world, and even today more than half of all Italians, including the inhabitants of most of its major cities from Naples northwards, are living under regional, provincial or city administrations which are led by or include the Communist Party. Its achievement in the cities and regions long governed by it are impressive, and it possesses the, among Italian parties unique, quality of never having been seriously associated with scandal. It is the only honest party of any size in the country. Whether these are legitimate reasons for considering it as a special threat to the western way of life — it cannot even be plausibly accused of rationing its criticism of the USSR —, they are certainly reasons why the political right should keep an eye on it.

Conversely, the political left outside Italy has admired the party for its success and promise, not to mention its association with Antonio Gramsci, the most original political theorist in western marxism, who is himself the subject of a by now ample bibliography in English; probably a longer one than the party he once led and still inspires. Alternatively, it has been seen on the further edges of the left — inside Italy perhaps more so than outside — as a betrayer of revolutionary hopes, and a party now little different from social democracy. In all these quarters interest in its affairs, while fluctuating, never ceases.

Donald Sassoon's book is a valuable addition to the literature about Italian communism, for three reasons. In the first place his view of the Italian C.P. is neither starry-eyed nor panic-stricken, and his presentation of its post-war history is therefore judicious. He has resisted the temptation to see this history as either progress or retreat, or to play down the Party's miscalculations, failures, setbacks and internal divisions. Thus he provides notably clear statements of the 'generational' structure of both party leadership and membership, of its failure to keep pace with the changes in the structure of Italian society during the 1950s and 1960s — and of the degree of its success in regaining (or failing to regain) ground lost during various periods. On specific and vexed questions of party history he is both concise and balanced. There are, for instance, few better and briefer accounts of the debate on whether the Party considered an insurrectionary bid for power in 1945, what the prospects for such a bid would have been, what factors influenced the situation at the time (e.g. the Greek experience of December 1944) and how the much later retrospective debates on this question are to be judged. In short, nobody interested in the history of the P.C.I. can fail to benefit by the author's combination of knowledge, lucidity and judgment.

Secondly, he has set out to write not the history of the Party and its role in post-war Italy (though he throws much light on both), but a study of its objectives and strategy. I know of no other book in English which does so. The exercise is of more than local interest, since it illuminates the predicament of communist parties elsewhere in the west founded in the expectation of a 'world revolution' inspired by the Bolshevik Revolution and modelled on it, which did not take place; and which have sought for alternative strategies for achieving social transformation and, increasingly, alternative models for socialism. On the other hand the book is of specific Italian interest, since the Italian Party, both in theory and practice, has been by far the most conscious of the need for such strategic rethinking, and since this rethinking took place in terms of the peculiar conditions in one country.

The experience of the P.C.I. is particularly interesting because it includes both phases of advance, as in the period of resistance and liberation and in the middle 1970s, and of retreat, as under fascism and in the 1950s, and combinations of advance in one part of the country and retreat in another, as when the Party grew in the South and fell back in the North in the 1950s, and the other way round in the later 1970s. It also includes moments, as in the later 1960s, when it was temporarily outpaced by events. Sassoon guides us through the complexities, difficulties and debates of the past four decades of strategic thinking. Both political scientists in general, and political activists in parties committed to social transformation, will read his book with advantage.

In the third place, his book is a study of one of the most intelligent, remarkable and formidable political leaders in twentieth century Europe. Not for nothing is the title of the Italian version of this work 'Togliatti and the Italian Way to Socialism'. Politicians who never make the leap from opposition to power are often the forgotten men and women of history; or at the very least, their merits and significance tend to be underestimated. In his own country this is unlikely to be the fate of Palmiro Togliatti, the last great figure of the Third International, the chief architect of the P.C.I's postwar policies, and the person responsible, almost singlehanded, for the survival and political fortunes of the writings of Antonio Gramsci. Elsewhere, almost twenty years after his death, he is more likely to drop out of sight. In this book he appears neither as hero nor villain, if only because this is not a study of heroes or villains, or indeed one which gives much scope for portraits of individuals. He carries his share, which must be large, of both praise and blame for the strategy, achievements and errors of his party. Nevertheless this book is largely about him. It should help to do justice to an extraordinary figure, an extraordinary career, and a contribution to the development of international socialist thinking which is likely to be overlooked because it produced political practice rather than books of theory.

In conclusion, it is perhaps worth mentioning that Sassoon's book is based not only on an impressive command of the sources and literature, but also on a considerable first-hand knowledge of both Italy and its Communist Party, and on an understanding, based on first-hand observation, of the complexities of both. Specialists will know this already, but readers less familiar with the subject may be assured that the author's qualifications for writing it, command respect.

July 1981, E. J. Hobsbawm

Introduction

The functionalist tradition in sociology and political science has favoured the study of the internal organization of political parties, their sociological composition, the characteristics of their members and the psychological behaviour of their electorates; it has established categories such as 'pro-system' and 'anti-system' parties, 'broker' party, 'catch-all' party, etc. In an essay published in 1957 on the party in mass society, Otto Kirchheimer distinguished the so-called 'mass totalitarian party', defined as a party which composes and adjudicates, or, if needs be, suppresses conflicting claims according to programme and goals, from the so-called 'mass democratic party', which is both the custodian of a liberal ideological tradition and the mechanism for the distribution of 'services' and the satisfaction of needs. The crisis of this latter form of political rule has given way to the 'integral' party (a party which is so identified with a particular political system as to lose its own autonomy) and the protest party.[1]

We could go on delving into taxonomy, but here all we are interested in doing is to show that the study of political parties has been strongly influenced by the construction of models and that the ideological origin of such mode of investigation — the works of Weber, Michels, Ostrogorski and, more recently, Duverger, Almond and Selznick — unveils a vision of the political party as a pure instrument of organization and mediation.

American studies on political parties which have had considerable influence in Germany, Britain, France and, more recently, in Italy, are not only marked by the Cold War but, more importantly, by the realities of the American political system. As Apter has correctly pointed out:

> American political parties are not centres of passion. Today they are part-time organizations . . . Parties do not appear to stand for anything very meaningful. Perhaps their most outstanding characteristic is their very lack of ideology.[2]

The kind of study of political parties in which the strategic and programmatic moment was left unexamined could be located in the ideology of 'the end of ideology'. Before the war the study of political parties was mainly concerned with a conventional history of the party's fortune. But in 1951 Duverger's text, *Les partis politiques*, was published in France. This pioneering work classified systems of parties and party organizations and provoked a remarkable development of studies, particularly in the UK where within three years the following books appeared: *Political Parties and the Party System in Britain* by Sidney Bailey (1952), *The Party System in Great Britain* by Ivor Bulmer-Thomas (1953) and the classic text by Robert T. McKenzie, *British Political Parties* (1963).

It is worth pointing out that McKenzie, in the Preface to the first edition of his study, wrote that the purpose of his book was 'to examine the distribution of power within the two major political parties. It is not concerned with party ideologies or programme, nor does it deal in any detail with the minor parties.'[3] In the Preface to the second edition McKenzie explains that his lack of concern for ideologies and programmes only meant that he was not going to attempt a 'systematic history or analysis of the ideologies, philosophies or programme of the two parties' and adds '. . . but, of course, this book is deeply concerned with the ideological issues and policy disputes which have racked the parties, and the ways in which they have debated and resolved these controversies'. These controversies, however, are examined only 'for the light they throw on the policy–decision process in the parties'; hence they are of little interest in themselves.

Although we are not here questioning the intellectual legitimacy of studies such as McKenzie's, it is nevertheless significant that there is a widely-held view that it is perfectly possible to examine political parties without paying too much attention to their programmes. This may reflect the opinion that programmes as such are designed mainly to ensure an electoral victory and hence are little more than propaganda exercises. This opinion hides the unfortunately popular belief that politicians are no more than able manipulators of public opinion and that a healthy disregard of what politicians say is the hallmark of the intelligent citizen.

We find here, once again, that fear and suspicion that the liberal tradition has always had towards the big political parties, these creatures of a mass society which provoked the anxiety at the beginning of the century of the two principal theoreticians of the political party: Michels and Ostrogorski.

Beyond these polemical motivations, the idea of a history of the strategy of a political party is based on the hypothesis that when the programme of a political party is established it acquires a dimension which cannot be reduced to the intentions of its makers and that, besides, the programme itself reveals something of the nature of politics of the country in which it is born, of the aspirations of its people and of the problems facing it.

This study has as its object this kind of programme. Its ambitions are hence limited. I do not think, however, that this limit is such as to obliterate either the historical dimension or the legitimacy of studies of other aspects of political parties. In underlining the importance of the programme of a political party we have in mind a definition of the political party which appeared in the first number of the daily *Ordine Nuovo* (1 January 1921). Its author, Antonio Gramsci, wrote:

> An association can be called a 'political party' only in so far as it possesses a constitutional doctrine of its own, in so far as it has succeeded in concretizing and promulgating its own notion of the State, and in so far as it has succeeded in concretizing and promulgating among the broad masses a government programme of its own — a programme which would enable it actually to organize a state in practice, i.e. in concrete circumstances, using real men and not abstract phantasies of humanity.[4]

Gramsci thus situated himself in a line of continuity with the Leninist rupture which, after *What Is To Be Done?*, substituted the thematic of the problem of the organization of the party with that of the *political direction* of the party. In fact the Leninist text has been considered for a long time as the central one for the development of the Communist doctrine of the political party as a group of 'professional revolutionaries'. However, a rigorous reading of the text itself would show the contingent and functional character of the elements of 'secrecy', 'discipline' and 'professionality' which Lenin, on the basis of the very particularities of the Russian situation, counterposed to Menshevik proposals which amounted to a rigid imitation of the model of the German Social Democratic Party. Lenin's 'rupture' entailed a theoretical revolution which would become the necessary basis providing the Russian masses with that political leadership and that programme of government which would enable them to effectuate the transition from 'subordinate masses' to hegemonic national class. It follows, then, that the political programme of the party will have greater or lesser importance to the extent that that party aims to 'become state' in the 'enlarged' Gramscian sense and not a mere functional organiza- tion for the administration of things.

Communist parties tend to be more conscious than others of the need to connect their strategies to a set of political–theoretical principles. Consequently they tend to produce a body of writing which is far larger than that of their more pragmatic social-democratic and conservative counterparts. This is all the more striking if we were to compare the Italian Communist Party's intellectual production to that of the British

Labour Party. The Labour Party, an authentic party of government which can rely on the electoral support of millions of people has no daily newspaper, has not had a theoretical journal, rarely organizes conferences on political or cultural themes, has no publishing house and now has few intellectuals who could be described as 'Labour Party intellectuals'.

The Communist Party we are examining has a considerable amount of political power which is in part derived from its mass membership (1.8 million members). It is not only the largest Communist Party in the non-socialist world, but it also possesses instruments for the diffusion of its strategy far in excess of any other party in the West. Its daily paper is one of the most widely read in Italy and its publishing house one of the largest. It has several research institutes and a variety of party schools. Its intellectuals are among the most prestigious in Italy. Its influence is widespread in all walks of life and in all the institutions of civil society. Its cultural activities attract large numbers of people. It publishes journals dealing with historical studies, philosophy, the law, the cinema, the economy, etc. It is a mass party not purely in terms of its actual electoral support, but in terms of its ability to mobilize masses of people. Its strategic pronouncements can thus be found in a wide number of publications and constitute a vast body of texts available for analysis.

This mass party was born out of a very specific situation: the Second World War. Unlike the French Communist Party, one of the few other Western Communist Parties with a significant mass following, the Italian party was a negligible force in the pre-war years. It was then a small and persecuted sect numbering a few thousand militants. The Italian Resistance provided the terrain for a real rebirth: the sect of 6,000 activists became a mass party of nearly 1,800,000 members.

In a speech to the Communist Federation of Reggio Emilia (25 September 1946), Togliatti pointed out that the decision to become a mass party had been historically determined by a pre-existing mass mobilization. In a sense fascism had needed to organize the Italian mass in order to construct a new form of state. This organization of the masses had been achieved from on high and in an authoritarian manner. Nevertheless it had contributed to the political regimentation of a considerably large proportion of the population. The political organization of the fascist state had necessitated the previous 'disorganization' of the masses, i.e. the destruction of their autonomous organizations. In these circumstances, Togliatti explained, it was not possible to follow the example of the French Communist Party and to recruit only those members who had proved themselves to be 'reliable' Communists. It was necessary to open the doors of the party to all those who wanted to join it, and even to mount extensive campaigns for the rapid development of a mass membership. The specificity of the Italian situation was precisely the fact that, having undergone the experience of fascism, the Italian population was, so to speak, already politically mobilized. After the war they would have passed under the influence of those organizations which had been able to maintain a legal existence under fascism: the Catholic organizations. It was thus necessary for the Italian Communists to create and develop not only their own political party, but a whole range of organizations from sporting clubs to cultural circles so as to penetrate into civil society at all levels and challenge Christian Democracy.

It is in the years of this rebirth that our investigation starts.

The most immediate methodological question we had to face was how to isolate from the mass of documents, articles and speeches those which could be said to constitute the 'party line'. One possible approach would have been to consider 'official' only those statements which emanate directly from the leading organs of the party: from the Executive Committee, from the Central Committee and from the party congresses. Such a legalistic approach would have had the advantage of clearly restricting the choice of documents. But a party policy is more than the resolutions it passes at its congresses. We have thus decided to include articles and speeches by leading party spokesmen and intellectuals which appear in its journal. Because of this lack of rigour the dividing line between the 'official' and the 'unofficial' is at times blurred. Nevertheless no single major strategic guideline has been imputed to a single spokesman, nor to a single article, with one exception: the pronouncements of the party leader, Palmiro Togliatti, are usually considered to be sufficiently authoritative as not to warrant further supporting evidence.

More than anyone else Palmiro Togliatti shaped the policies of the Italian Communist Party in the post-war period and he is thus to bear most of the burden of praise or blame. His death, in 1964, can be taken to symbolize the end of a phase of Communist history. He was the last great figure of the Third International (Mao Tse-tung, who survived him by twelve years, never had an important role in the Comintern). When Togliatti died, he left behind him a generation of Communist leaders who owed their political outlook and style to him more than to anyone else. Thus our object of investigation is very much Togliatti's mass party and this is amply reflected in the space which is devoted to analysing his contribution.

This study has thus a strong chronological element. Only in that way would it be possible to reveal the continuity amid the shifts which characterize the development of the strategy of the Italian Communist Party.

It will become apparent that the most important date in this development is 1956, the year of de-Stalinization. This is reflected in the structure of the study. While the first part, consisting of five chapters, covering the years from the Resistance to 1956, is strictly chronological, the second part (chapters 6–10) consists of five essays each containing an analysis of relatively distinct aspects of the strategy in the period 1956–64: its international dimension, its relation to the question of socialism and democracy, the nature and characteristic of its project of structural reforms, the alliances it envisages and the reflection it conducts on the internal structure of its party organization.

The third part brings the study up to date and is delineated into two sections. The first, entirely devoted to foreign policy with a strong emphasis on European affairs, examines the development of the policy which came to be known as 'Eurocommunism'. The second examines the development of the strategy of the 'Historic Compromise'.

For reasons of space I have had to eliminate various sections dealing with the Party's cultural sphere. This would have involved an examination of the PCI's historical writings and its considerations on the Italian political tradition and on Marxist theory in the forms in which it was developed in the international Communist movement and by Antonio Gramsci.

I cannot thank all those whose written work has been a source of inspiration and of intellectual stimulation. Among those whose direct advice has improved this book I have to thank first of all Eric J. Hobsbawm and Bernard Crick who have discussed various aspects of this project from its inception. In particular special thanks are due by the reader to Bernard Crick: without his suggestions the book would have been heavier and more jargon-ridden. I have had the opportunity to discuss various aspects of this work with Italian scholars, in particular with Ernesto Ragionieri who died when he had so much more to do.

I would also like to thank Giuseppe Vacca and Christine Buci-Glucksmann who have read the original manuscript and to whom I am grateful for their perceptive advice. My particular gratitude goes to Anne Showstack Sassoon without whose intellectual and moral help I could not have written this book.

Notes

1. O. Kirchheimer, 'The Party in Mass Society', in *World Politics*, October 1957–July 1958, pp. 289–94.
2. D. Apter, *Comparative Politics* (D. Apter and H. Eckstein, eds.), New York, 1963, p. 327.

3. R. T. McKenzie, *British Political Parties*, London, 1963, pp. v and ix.
4. A. Gramsci, *Selections from Political Writings 1910–1920*, London, 1977, p. 368.

PART I 1944–1955

1 The Resistance Strategy

The strategy of the Italian Communist Party (PCI) during the Resistance was based on the unity of all anti-fascist forces against the invading German armies and their fascist allies. This strategy subordinated all other political objectives to the victory of the anti-fascist coalition.

When Togliatti returned to Italy in 1944 after a long exile, he directed the party to postpone 'the institutional question' (that is the question of the monarchy) until the aftermath of the war. These directives became known as the 'Salerno turning-point' ('la svolta di Salerno'), from the southern town where Togliatti landed.

Critics of the PCI of both left-wing and right-wing persuasion have understood the 'turning-point' to signify a radical departure from 'traditional' communist objectives. But the Salerno turning-point constituted neither a break with *real* 'traditional Communist objectives' nor a betrayal of previous policies. The policies elaborated by Togliatti in 1944 were a direct continuation of the political line which triumphed at the Seventh Congress of the Comintern in 1935. This line, narrowly defined as 'frontist', adopted then by the PCI, was never abandoned, except by some senior party cadres during the disorganization caused by the Soviet–German Pact and the beginning of the Second World War.

One can distinguish between two main trends in the communist movement. One trend, exemplified by the strategy adopted during the so-called 'Third Period', considered all struggles as being immediate struggles for socialism and not for some intermediate objectives.[1] This line implied a situation of 'class against class' for the immediate implementation of the socialist programme. It was a situation where social-democratic forces were considered to be the 'left-wing of fascism' (hence the epithet 'social-fascism': socialists in words, fascists in deeds) and the objective defenders of the bourgeois order. They were, therefore, enemies of the proletariat at the same level with the most reactionary forces. In fact they were worse enemies because by pretending to be socialist they confused the issues and impeded the development of a clear-cut class struggle.[2] This line triumphed at the Tenth Plenum of the Comintern in 1929.

The second trend prevailed at the Seventh Congress of the International. It was put forward by Dimitrov and Togliatti. It advocated collaboration with all forces against fascism. It stressed the importance of bourgeois democratic institutions for the working class in the period of capitalism. It urged Communists to work even in fascist mass organizations in order to reach the working class. It emphasized for the first time the need for revolutionaries to adapt to national conditions. The line of the Comintern in 1935 has prevailed with interruptions in most Communist Parties since then. As such it was not simply a tactical move, to be abandoned once fascism was destroyed. It became the fulcrum of communist strategy. It showed the way to the creation of a system of alliances for the attainment of limited objectives which, it was argued, though not constituting a socialist revolution, would pave the way to socialism.

The line of the Third Period was formulated on the basis of a view which presupposed the impending crisis of world capitalism. The economic crisis was thought to be the crisis of the 'system', hence a crisis which could not be solved within the existing international social order. From this a set of simplistic equations followed: capitalism equals fascism; economic crisis equals political crisis; political crisis equals revolutionary crisis. The struggle was essentially one of class against class with no intermediate goals and no tactical and strategic alliances. The subsequent stabilization of world capitalism and particularly the rise of Nazi Germany and the quasi-elimination of the German CP destroyed the optimism of the Third Period and gave way to a re-thinking whieh produced the adoption of the Dimitrov–Togliatti line at the Seventh Congress of the Communist International.

The popular front strategy has been called 'Stalinist'. In the mind of many this involved a policy of class collaboration in the West which was objectively counter-revolutionary and which guaranteed the Soviet Union the possibility of continuing a policy of peaceful coexistence with the capitalist world. According to this view the 'national' interests of the USSR were in total contradiction with those of the workers' parties in the capitalist world. The leaders of these parties are therefore accused of putting the interests of the Soviet Union above those of the class they purported to lead.

However, Stalinism can be understood to mean an international working class strategy based on the application of the doctrine of 'socialism in one country' thus defined:

> . . . that the proletarian revolution will not spread rapidly and evenly over the world from one or two centres, but on the contrary will make geographically localized advances followed by temporary stabilization and even retreat, over a long period; that socialist states will therefore

have to survive for considerable periods in coexistence with an imperialist world itself riven by shifting internal contradictions, and that therefore socialist governments will be faced with a relatively autonomous arena of socialist struggles at the diplomatic level, defined by its own changing conjuncture, to which they have to adjust their external policies.[3]

In this sense the Seventh Congress of the Comintern represented a historical turning-point in which the most fruitful contents of the Stalinist strategy were highlighted: the self-sufficiency of the Soviet revolution and the autonomous development of the revolution in the West according to new and original paths. Paradoxically the 'polycentric' logic of the Stalinist analysis was never carried to its wider theoretical implications.[4] Ironically, these could be explicitly drawn only after 1956, that is after the initial stages of the ideological process known as 'de-Stalinization'. If this interpretation is accepted, then it follows that the sort of compromises socialist governments are forced to make by prevailing international and national conjunctures is not necessarily binding upon the communist parties in other countries.[5] It assumes the uneven development of the revolution and therefore the relative autonomy of its development in every country. The strategy and tactics of the revolutionary party must therefore be determined by the relations of forces prevailing in the country within which they are operating. It is true that these principles were not observed during the period of the Third International. The doctrine of socialism in one country, understood as a declaration of independence from the vanguard state, still coexisted with the subservience of the Third International to the Communist Party of the Soviet Union (PSU). The subservience of the strategy of national roads to socialism does not imply its non-existence.[6] At the Seventh Congress Dimitrov proclaimed:

> Comrades, proletarian internationalism must, so to speak, 'acclimatize itself' in each country in order to sink deep roots in its native land. National forms of the proletarian class struggle and of the labour movement in the individual countries are in no contradiction to proletarian internationalism: on the contrary, it is precisely in these forms that the international interests of the proletariat can be successfully defended.[7]

Along the same lines Togliatti stated in his report:

> The fact that there is an identity of aims between the policy of peace of the USSR and the policy of the working class and of the Communist Parties in the capitalist countries is, for us, beyond discussion. This identity of aims cannot be an object of doubt within our ranks. Not

only do we defend the Soviet Union in general, but we support concretely its policies and each of its actions. But this identity of aims does not mean at all that for every act, in every moment and on all questions the tactic of the proletariat and of the Communist Parties which are still fighting for power must coincide with the actual tactical position of the Soviet proletariat and of the Bolshevik Party who are in power in the Soviet Union.[8]

Hence there had to be an identity of aim and a common general strategy between the Soviet Union and the workers' parties, but not a similarity of tactics and therefore no subordination of the tactics of one party to those of another. This, of course, sanctioned the right of the Soviet Union to follow a 'national' foreign policy independent from the requirements of the Communist Parties:

> From the theoretical point of view the possibility of an agreement which would envisage, in determinate circumstances, even the military collaboration between a workers' state and a capitalist state is not open to doubt.[9]

The popular front stategy can be seen in two ways. It can be seen as a mainly defensive struggle against fascism where fascism is the principal enemy of the working class and against whom all forces including some bourgeois forces can be mobilized.[10] It can also be seen as a stage in the struggle for socialism, the stage of the elimination of the social basis of fascism, that is, according to Togliatti, agrarian and monopolistic interests.[11] Linking the strategy of the Seventh Congress to the policies pursued by the PCI in the 1950s and 1960s, Togliatti asserted that the working class and its organized vanguard, in its struggle against any possible 'reactionary degeneration' is aware of the fact that it is necessary to act on the very structures of society by isolating:

> . . . the most reactionary and chauvinist bourgeois groups and not merely expel them from political power, but destroy their privileges and their position of dominance of the economic sphere. A new conception of democracy is therefore implicit in the policy of unity of the working class . . . *The defence against fascist and reactionary threats becomes a positive action of social change* [my emphasis].[12]

It is perfectly true that the continuity between the line of the Seventh Congress of the International and the strategy of the Italian road to socialism has been stressed by PCI leaders such as Amendola for ideological reasons. There is the attempt to show that the strategy of the party is not based on opportunistic twists and turns, but is perfectly consistent with its own past. Amendola in particular was to remain for a long time the principal exponent of this unilinear view of history. This approach would also be adopted by those critics of PCI strategy who wanted to trace the alleged contemporary reformism of the party to the triumph of a centrist and reformist tendency in the party's past.[13] With hindsight it is always easy to read into past declarations the origins of present directives. However, it is clear that both the Italian road to socialism and the popular front strategy imply a differentiated analysis of capitalism. This analysis recognized that capitalism never offers the situation of a straightforward head-on clash between the bourgeoisie and the proletariat, but that on the contrary it is the task of the proletarian 'vanguard' to find allies among the other classes and strata such as the peasants and the middle classes in order to isolate and split the ruling class.[14] It recognized that the 'vanguard' party cannot limit its action to the tasks of propaganda and agitation until the 'crash' comes, but it must use all the possibilities of the situation to open up a favourable conjuncture. As Dimitrov put it at the Seventh Congress of the International:

> We want our parties in the capitalist countries to come out and act as real political parties of the working class, to become in actual fact a political factor in the life of their countries, to pursue at all times an active Bolshevik mass policy, and not confine themselves to propaganda and criticism and bare appeals to struggle for proletarian dictatorship.[15]

The political party of the working class must be ready to accept limited gains and even to retreat if necessary. It must be willing to compromise. It must retain under all circumstances a readiness to accept swift tactical changes and to move from a position of legality to one of illegality and vice versa. In order to achieve this condition it is necessary for the revolutionary party to be able to operate without being tied to the requirements of any other revolutionary party or revolutionary state. The Seventh Congress opened this possibility. It did not grant it. The Third International still existed and the PCI was still known as the 'Communist Party of Italy, Section of the Third International'. For political and ideological reasons the policies of the Soviet Union guided and determined the policies of the single parties, but it cannot be denied that the Seventh Congress ended with the recognition of the possibility of every party to decide in an autonomous manner the way in which it would contribute to the realization of the common political line.

The decisions of the Seventh Congress were not arrived at independently of Stalin's will. It is clear that it was then impossible for any communist leader to take a position which did not meet with the approval of the CPSU without breaking all ties with the international communist movement. This, however, does not mean that the policies of the Seventh Congress did not represent, as far as the PCI was concerned, the beginning of an 'Italian road to socialism'.

The style of Togliatti's report to the Seventh Congress was noteworthy for the absence both of dogmatic phraseology and of lengthy quotes from Marx, Engels, Lenin and Stalin. This is not merely a reflection on Togliatti's personal style, but it is an expression of an intention to disengage Marxism from the sclerotic dictatorialness of the Third International and from a dogmatism which it had partly inherited from the Second International. It was a conscious attempt to use a language which could be understood by Italians and an effort to adapt Marxism to the cultural characteristics of Italy.[16] Of course, Togliatti at the Seventh Congress sent his greetings to 'Comrade Stalin, the leader, teacher and friend of the proletariat and of all oppressed people'. This was no contradiction, but the recognition that Togliatti was conscious that the struggle against fascism could not be separated from the defence of the only country where the workers had taken power. Therefore Communism, in 1935, to Togliatti as to many others, meant Stalinism.

The principal themes of the Seventh Congress were developed by Togliatti in a fruitful manner in the report he devoted to the Spanish Civil War. We can find here a number of propositions which are characteristic of the strategic perspective which was presented more explicitly at Salerno.

First of all Togliatti rejected the concept of a revolutionary 'model':

It would be incorrect to establish a complete identity between the Spanish revolution on the one hand and the Russian revolutions of 1905 or 1917. The Spanish revolution has its distinct, original features, which derive from the particularities of the situation of the country as well as from the international conjuncture.[17]

Secondly, Togliatti poses the objective of a new and specific transitional stage of the socialist revolution and that is a new type of democratic republic and not a 'democratic dictatorship of workers and peasants'.[18]

Thirdly, the class sign of this new transitional phase is given by the elimination of the material base of fascism and this also implies the creation of new democratic institutions which could facilitate the reunification of the masses:

. . . this democracy of a new type could only be, in case of a victory of the popular forces, an opponent of any form of conservative spirit. This democracy would possess all the conditions for its further development. It would offer a guarantee for all the developments of further economic and political conquests of the Spanish workers.[19]

The PCI of Togliatti developed the political line of the Seventh Congress on the basis of the interpretation of the Spanish experience. This entailed the re-grouping of all anti-fascist forces against Mussolini's regime. This meant that it was necessary to initiate a unitary policy between the PCI and the PSI, the party from whom the PCI split in 1921. The basis of this move was the view that the success of fascism was partly due to the division of the working class. This view, and the consequent emphasis on working class unity became one of the principal points of PCI strategy. The pact of co-operation with the PSI was signed in July 1937. It stressed that:

In the present period of political struggle the two parties propose to educate and organize the entire Italian people towards a struggle for the conquest of liberty and democracy and for the establishment of a democratic republic, presided over by the working class, which will guarantee bread, peace and freedom to the people, which will take all necessary action for the destruction of the economic basis of reaction and fascism at their very roots (nationalization of industrial and finance monopoly capital, destruction of every form of rural feudalism, etc.) and which will open the road to socialism.[20]

This declaration is important because it is a clear indication that many of Togliatti's speeches in 1944 were not the beginning of a new strategy and did not constitute a break with the prevailing strategic orientation of the PCI. Certainly the pact with the PSI declared that both parties would organize the whole people (not only the working class) for the struggle for liberty and democracy and for a *democratic republic*; but in fact even the call for a republic was tactically 'negotiable'. In answer to the radical group *Giustizia e Libertà*, which had declared that it would not enter any agreement with the left unless the goal of an Italian republic was accepted by all parties to any future coalition, the journal of the PCI, *Stato operaio*, declared:

The institutional form of the future Italian state and the necessary measures to be taken to link the popular masses with the State will be decided by the free people in free consultations, without excluding the convocation of a Constituent Assembly.[21]

This was written in February 1939, more than five years before the turning-point of Salerno where Togliatti made a similar utterance. In 1939 as in 1944 the PCI was for a democratic republic, but its actual immediate aim was the unity of all popular forces against fascism. Socialist or even republican slogans were thought to be divisive, hence they were dropped.[22] The immediate struggle was neither for socialism nor for a republic but for the overthrow of fascism. This was the primary task. After the political destruction of the fascist state, the democratic republic would be the best possible weapon for the destruction of the socio-economic roots of fascism. The tasks of the democratic republic would be to destroy monopolies and feudal remnants, not private property as such. This is what was meant by the destruction of the social basis of fascism. The state would hence remain a capitalist state, but one where the proletariat would be the presiding force. This formulation is not as unorthodox as it sounds. The possibility of a bourgeois state where the proletariat would be the dominant force had already been envisaged by Lenin (in what were, however, completely different circumstances).[23] Later the PCI did not find it difficult to show the coincidence between this formulation of working class dominance in a democratic bourgeois country and the Gramscian concept of hegemony which presupposes the proletarian conquest of hegemony prior to the actual conquest of state power.[24]

The response of the Communist Parties to the Soviet–German pact shows that the lessons of the Seventh Congress had not been assimilated. Quite apart from the elements of historical necessity which may justify the pact from the point of view of Soviet interests, it must be noted that the ideological way in which the pact was presented by the CPSU casts doubts as to the extent to which the implications of the Seventh Congress had been understood. Whereas international fascism had been the main enemy in 1935, it now became one imperialism among many. The new logic was: if there has to be a war among imperialist states, it is better to let them fight it out.[25] Thus there are no differences among imperialist powers, just as in 1929 democratic and fascist parties were all enemies. The differentiated analysis on which the popular front strategy was based was consigned to oblivion — until 1941. The USSR had justified the pact in terms of the foreign policy interests of the Soviet State. Molotov had declared on 31 August 1939, in a speech to the Praesidium:

The non-aggression pact between the USSR and Germany marks a turning-point in the history of Europe and not of Europe alone. Until yesterday the German fascists had a hostile policy towards us. Today, however, the position has changed and we are no longer enemies. The art of politics in the sphere of foreign relations does not consist in increasing the number of the enemies of one's country but on the contrary in reducing the number of these enemies.[26]

The Comintern adapted its line to the foreign policy of the USSR and Togliatti followed the turn as he had followed the line of the Third Period, presumably with as much reluctance. However, according to Ernst Fischer, Togliatti, after having accepted the Comintern line on the pact, never considered it more than a purely temporary situation.[27] Yet the substance of the strategy changed entirely, though not for long. The slogan of a united front was changed into a slogan for a united front from below, the polemic against the Social Democrats was renewed with vigour and the slogan of a workers' and peasants' government was put forward.

However, in the issue of 25 August 1939 of the *La Voce degli italiani* there appeared a 'Declaration of the Communist Party of Italy' written by Togliatti. The declaration attempted to provide an anti-fascist interpretation of the Pact:

> . . . the action undertaken by the USSR in accepting to discuss a non-aggression pact with Germany is a powerful contribution given to the peoples who are now under the yoke of the fascist dictatorship.

This was followed by what was an obvious attempt to remain faithful to the line of the Seventh Congress of fascism as 'the principal enemy':

> Today, even though the governments of Rome and Berlin are forced to bow before the firmness of the Soviet Union, the international situation continues to be very serious and the peoples of Europe are still under the threat of war. In this situation the Communist Party reminds all the workers of Italy, reminds all Italians who want to save their country from catastrophe, that their duty is to intensify this struggle . . . to contribute in any way possible — on the basis of the desire for peace which pervades the overwhelming majority of the Italian people — to stop fascism from beginning a new war. If war were to break out in spite of everything, we repeat that we would fight without hesitation so that from the war itself would ensue the military and political defeat and the end of fascism, for this is one of the conditions for a future of freedom, peace and social progress for the peoples of capitalist Europe.[28]

Furthermore, in a document of 1941 (written before the end of the Soviet–German pact) one can detect again a change in emphasis and a certain continuity with the Seventh Congress analysis. Some of the elements of this document will become the principal components of the Salernò policy. The document, written by Togliatti for the Comintern, examined the contradictions of Italian fascism and first and foremost the beginning of the disintegration of the social forces the fascists had relied upon (monarchy, Church, bureaucracy, army, middle strata). The task of the Communists in this situation was:

> . . . to create a link, a kind of bridge between the old anti-fascist elements of the working class and the currents of dissatisfaction appearing within the masses influenced by fascism on the one hand and the Catholic masses on the other. This bridge must have the object of channelling the general dissatisfaction of the people towards a unitary objective: the struggle against Mussolini and against fascism, that is, against those responsible for the war and for the situation the Italians find themselves in.[29]

This line was elaborated in the years of 'revolutionary defeatism' when the Soviet–German pact seemed to have destroyed the policy of alliance and of intermediate objectives of the popular fronts. The German invasion of the USSR paved the way for the re-establishment of the pact between the PCI and the PSI. In October 1941, it was extended to the radical group *Giustizia e Libertá* (which later became part of the Partito d'Azione or Action Party). Togliatti was then in Moscow and used his radio broadcasts to guide the policy of the PCI in Italy. Thus the Communist leaders in Italy did not have to wait until Togliatti's arrival for guidance. In 1941, Amendola, then in France, was renewing the links between the anti-fascist forces and the unitary policy was pursued during the whole war according to Togliatti's strategy. But this strategy and that of the party did not always coincide.

After the Armistice of 8 September 1943 the direction of the PCI was divided into two sections: the northern section was led by Secchia and Longo from Milan and the southern section was led by Scoccimarro and Amendola (among others) from Rome. The two sections had different views about the new Badoglio government appointed by the King after the ousting of Mussolini on 25 July 1943. This difference was partly a reflection of the different political situation facing the two centres. The Milan centre was faced with the prospect of a lengthy and costly military struggle against the Germans and the new northern fascist Republic of Saló. Their chief priority was the proper conduct of the war and the strengthening of the unity of all anti-fascist forces. Milan was therefore ready to accept an 'open' interpretation of Togliatti's directives.

The Roman centre of the PCI was not in favour of making any

concessions to Badoglio which might weaken the position of the anti-fascist front, that is, the CNL (Comitato di Liberazione Nationale; the Socialists and the Actionists were particularly anti-monarchist). The exchange between the two centres was at times quite harsh and it seems that the Milan centre felt that the Roman group was more concerned with political intrigues and the scramble for future ministerial posts than with the conduct of the war.[30] The Milan centre felt that they were the true centre of the Resistance, for it was in the North where the real work of organization, propaganda and struggle was being done.

When Togliatti arrived in Italy (27 March 1944) his order was clear and coherent with his political priorities: the leading cadres should stop indulging in sterile polemics and should devote themselves entirely to the Resistance effort.[31] A few months later, on 6 June, in his 'Instructions to All Comrades and to All Party Cadres', he declared:

2. . . . . The insurrection we are aiming for must not be that of a political party or of a section only of the anti-fascist front. It must be the insurrection of the whole people of the whole nation.

3. Always remember that the aim of the insurrection is not the imposition of political and social transformations in the socialist or communist sense. Its aim is national liberation and the destruction of fascism. All other problems will be solved by the people through a free popular consultation and the election of a Constituent Assembly when the whole of Italy will have been liberated.[32]

When Togliatti arrived in Italy on 27 March 1944 the political situation had reached a dead end. The parties of the CLN could not agree to form a government with Badoglio because of what was then known as 'the institutional question', that is, the question of the monarchy.[33] The left-wing parties wanted 'guarantees' that the monarchy would be abolished. Togliatti's proposal, that is, a postponement of the whole matter and co-operation with Badoglio, created a new situation: the deadlock was broken. In so doing Togliatti was carrying to its logical conclusions the strategy chosen by the PCI since 1941, but he was also influenced by international considerations. Both the Allies and the USSR had already agreed to recognize the Badoglio government.[34] This political fact coupled with the military development of the war must have made Togliatti realize that future socio-economic boundaries would have to conform to the realities of military advances and control. It was quite clear, one year before the Yalta Conference enshrined it formally, that Italy would fall within the Western sphere of influence. Under those circumstances the

Italian Communists would have to adapt themselves to these military facts with all the flexibility they could muster.[35]

Stalin explained the position with his characteristic bluntness: 'This war is not as in the past. Whoever occupies a territory also imposes on it its own social system. Everyone imposes his own system as far as his army has the power to do so. It cannot be otherwise.'[36]

The National Council of the PCI met in Naples on 30–1 March and approved Togliatti's proposal to work towards a government of national unity. The resolution adopted pointed out the contradiction between a mass movement excluded from political power (the CLN) and a government without authority because unsupported by the mass parties. The resolution posed four conditions for Communist entry in the government:

1. To maintain and strengthen anti-fascist unity.

2. To postpone the 'institutional question' until the convening of a Constituent Assembly elected by universal suffrage.

3. To create a government strong enought to conduct the war.

4. To maintain as open as possible the anti-fascist front and to guarantee to all its participants a democratic future in Italy.[37]

On the whole the Rome and Milan directorates of the PCI accepted the 'turning-point'. This was partly due to the fact that Togliatti's prestige was considerable, partly to the sense of discipline which was deeply rooted in the habits of Communists who, for many years, had followed all the previous directives emanating from the national and international leadership of the Communist movement and partly due to the fact that Togliatti had taken upon himself the responsibility for such a move. In the case of Milan, the Communists were already in agreement with the principles of the 'turning-point'.

The response in Rome to Togliatti's initiative was not one of complete approval. When Amendola read Togliatti's cable to the Roman centre, Scoccimarro exclaimed 'You'll be the ones to carry these policies out!'[38] The rest of the party accepted the new directives.

Togliatti intervened to re-establish discipline: the polemics subsided and Scoccimarro withdrew his objections.[39] What had become obvious was that the full implications of the PCI strategy during the Resistance were not completely clear to not only the great majority of party activists, but to some of the leaders too.

Togliatti, in a series of speeches and articles, elaborated these implications and transmitted to the Italian Communists a set of strategic guidelines, inspired by Gramsci's writings, which were to become deeply rooted in the party and which represented the first coherent formulation of what came to be known as the 'Italian road to socialism'. It was only later that it would become obvious that these strategic elaborations were Togliatti's interpretations of the theoretical notes elaborated by Gramsci in his prison cell. In 1944 Gramsci meant little more to the Italian Communists than the name of their most glorious martyr. The notes he had written in jail had not been published and had not been circulated. They were in the hands of Togliatti who had read them and tried to master them. He was thus better able to present to his party a novel and 'national' way of thinking and developing a national strategy. His speeches and ideas may have sounded new to a party whose leading cadres had developed their political Marxism through Stalin's *Principles of Leninism* and *The History of the CPSU(B)* (Short Course).

On 11 April 1944, Togliatti, in his speech to the Naples Communist organization, indicated the immediate tasks facing the party. Sectarian attitudes were to be abandoned. The policies of the party had to be such that they would permit an ever greater co-operation with the PSI, possibly a fusion. Furthermore, particular attention had to be paid to the need of forging close ties with the Catholic masses, that is, the middle strata, but particularly the peasants.[40] Thus was established the basic 'bloc' upon which the future Communist strategy would depend: the unity of Communists, Socialists and Catholics represented by three mass parties: PCI, PSI and the Christian Democratic Party (DC). The PCI and the PSI were both representing the working class, hence their fusion into a new party of the working class was considered to be a feasible proposition. The alliance of the new party with the DC would form a workers' and peasants' bloc which would be strong enough to initiate a wide and thorough set of reforms in co-operation with the middle strata. The unity of the Resistance would be based on three conditions: a government of national unity, the guarantee of the formation of a Constituent Assembly and a programme of uncompromising struggle against the Germans and the fascists.[41]

By October 1944, although the conduct of the war remained the dominant objective to which all others were subordinated, Togliatti had begun to emphasize demands which would become fundamental after the end of the war: the elimination of fascism and the democratization of the country.[42] In Naples, in April, he had explained that the objective of post-war reconstruction was to be a democratic and progressive system based on pluralism of parties, basic democratic freedoms, and the destruction of the roots of fascism. This objective would be implemented by banning any reconstruction of a fascist party and by an agrarian reform and anti-monopoly legislation.[43] These demands were to be put forward on the basis of Togliatti's analysis of the social basis of fascism: a 'bloc' of the most reactionary section of the ruling class: monopolistic and agrarian interests. The Resistance was a political struggle for the expulsion of fascism from the arena of political power. The tasks of post-war reconstruction were to be the elimination of its socio-economic roots. A grand unity of Socialist, Communist and Catholic forces, that is, a unity of proletarians, peasants and middle classes could be forged against the monopolistic–agrarian bloc. What Togliatti wanted the PCI to struggle for was:

> . . . a fighting democracy which will defend freedom by destroying the objective bases of fascist tyranny thereby rendering impossible any reactionary rebirth. We want a democracy which will be actively anti-fascist and anti-imperialist and hence really national, popular and progressive.[44]

The elimination of the social basis of fascism did not entail the elimination of capitalism. The sectarian view which identified capitalism and fascism had been politically defeated at the Seventh Congress of the Comintern. What Togliatti was calling for was not the dictatorship of the proletariat, for this slogan would once more isolate the working class from its potential allies and encourage the rebirth of fascism:

> I know, comrades, that today the problem facing the Italian workers is not that of doing what was done in Russia . . . The most conscious elements of the working class must avoid being isolated . . . The democratic forces must avoid being divided.[45]

The call for an anti-monopoly and anti-agrarian bloc was:

> . . . an original development of the proposal to create governments of national unity against fascism which had been made within the ranks of the communist movement since 1935.[46]

Although the principle of capitalist accumulation would not be touched, the regime of progressive democracy would abolish monopolies and large agrarian landholdings. Progressive democracy was not meant to be a social truce but a struggle between the bloc of democratic and progressive forces and the most reactionary groups of society. The introduction of the concept of progressive democracy raises all sorts of questions for Marxist–Leninist theory. Togliatti's progressive democracy cannot be understood in purely reformist terms. The reforms which give the state its progressive character are not functional to capital. On the contrary they undermine it, they eliminate or weaken its concentration. They break its historical alliance with agrarian elements. The reforms are wrested from the capitalist state by a democratic government with wide popular support, where state and government cannot be mechanically identified according to a simple scheme whereby to a capitalist base inevitably corresponds a capitalist government.

A progressive democracy entails a new position for the working class. The working class, maintained Togliatti, had to become the 'directive class' or the 'national class'.[47] Togliatti uses the word 'directive' in the Gramscian sense: the directive class is that class which has been able to assert its hegemony (both cultural and political), but not necessarily a class which has been able to take over political power and exert its dictatorship. The working class must become the directive class, maintained Togliatti, because the old ruling class which has ruled Italy before and during fascism has completely failed in its task:

> This class has failed not only to defend the immediate interests of the workers, but has proved to the whole country that it is unable to direct the country even after having led it to the catastrophe we are witnessing. It has therefore failed in its task of national directing class.[48]

This reactionary class, which claimed to be the depository of the concepts and ideals of the nation, had in fact betrayed it. Togliatti put forward his own concept of nation, 'a Marxist concept' he said; the nation is composed of the working class, the peasants, the majority of the intellectuals, white collar workers and the professional strata.[49] It is in the context of the betrayal of the old ruling class and of the national catastrophe which ensued that the working class demands the right to become the vanguard force which will defend the interest of the whole nation. As Togliatti declared:

> The working class must abandon the position of opposition and criticism which it occupied in the past and intends to claim, with the other democratic forces, a directing function in the struggle for national liberation and for the construction of a democratic regime.[50]

This analysis depended on a particular view of the peculiarities of the Italian bourgeois revolution: the Italian Risorgimento. Togliatti's analysis was the result of his reading of Gramsci's prison notebooks. Togliatti's analysis in 1944–5 was his first mediation of Gramsci. For many years Gramsci in Italy would be seen through Togliatti and the debate on

Gramsci was always characterized by the strategic implications of the debate himself. To challenge Togliatti's mediation of Gramsci was never a purely academic question: it was a deeply political challenge striking at the core of the strategy known as the Italian road to socialism.

For Gramsci the Risorgimento was the Italian bourgeois revolution, but it was an interrupted and unfinished revolution. Its failure to unify the country by solving the southern question was due to the weakness, stupidity and provincialism of the class which directed it. Gramsci had written:

> Those men in effect were not capable of leading the people, were not capable of arousing their enthusiasm and their passion . . . Did they at least attain the end which they set themselves? They said that they were aiming at the creation of a modern state of Italy and they in fact produced a bastard. They aimed at stimulating the formation of an extensive and energetic ruling class, and they did not succeed; at integrating the people into the framework of the new State, and they did not succeed.[51]

Togliatti developed this analysis. The class which was not able to fulfil its own historical tasks produced fascism and led Italy to ruin. A new bloc had to be formed around the working class, the only class which could now direct the nation. Its hegemony had to precede its actual conquest of political power, for the period of hegemony had to be a period of consolidation and strengthening. It is a period during which the working class comes to dominate civil society, that is the area of consensus upon which the repressive state apparatus relies in order to dominate the nation. Gramsci had written:

> . . . the supremacy of a social group manifests itself in two ways, as 'domination' and as 'intellectual and moral leadership' . . . A social group can, and indeed, must already exercise 'leadership' before winning governmental power (this is indeed one of the principal conditions for the winning of such power); it subsequently becomes dominant when it exercises power, but even if it holds firmly in its grasp, it must continue to 'lead' as well.[52]

Togliatti saw the war and the Resistance as opening up a situation where the working class would have the possibility of conquering the area of consensus of the bourgeois state. This was a new historical situation for the Italian working class and this task entailed a 'party of a new type'. In October 1944, in Florence, Togliatti had declared:

The reality of the situation is that we, Italian Communists, first among all the Communists in Western Europe, find ourselves facing a new problem, never faced before either during the years of legality or during the hard years of illegality and persecutions. We Italian Communists, first of all the Communists in the whole of Western Europe, are faced with the new and serious task of creating a Communist Party with completely new and different tasks from those which faced our party in the past.[53]

This was a radical departure from the Kautskyist view of the role of the revolutionary party as an organization which should build its institutions independently of the prevailing social order and whose political tasks consisted in building up its own strength through propaganda and agitation until the time was ripe for a political take-over. This Kautskyist view had survived the Second International and had acquired a dominant position in the international communist movement. Togliatti wanted to change this concept of the party which he considered outdated:

. . . the new party is the party of the working class and of the people, a party which no longer limits itself to criticism and propaganda but intervenes in the life of the country in a positive and constructive way; [this process] starts in the factories and in the villages and must arrive at the central committee and those whom we delegate as representatives of the working class and of the party in the government. . . . At the same time the new party we are thinking of must be a national Italian party, that is, a party which poses and solves the problems of the emancipation of labour within our national life and liberation in claiming for itself all the progressive traditions of the nation.[54]

These crucial concepts are reiterated and expanded in most of Togliatti's speeches of 1944. The party had to become a mass party and had to open its doors to as many activists as possible. The Communist organizations had to be as decentralized as possible. The mentality of a 'sect' typical of the years of clandestinity had to be eradicated. Even those who had been members of the Fascist Party could become Communists (in many cases in order to hold State employment, for instance, in the railways, one had to join the Fascist Party).[55] The directive to transform the PCI into a mass party was entirely fulfilled. It is estimated that the party had 5,000–6,000 members in July 1943. By the Fifth Congress of the Party (19 December 1945–6 January 1946) the numbers had increased to the remarkable level of 1,770,000 members.

It is important to bear in mind that the new concepts introduced by

Togliatti in the Italian political arena in 1944–5 were not given theoretical status by him in those years, nor was the link with Gramsci made explicit. There was no attempt to justify these concepts with reference to the writings of Marx, Engels, Lenin or Stalin. Togliatti proclaimed them as original Italian contributions to proletarian strategy. A theoretical debate on what came to be known as the 'Salerno thematic' did not take place in the post-war years. It is precisely on this point that the PCI was less than adequate and had eventually to pay a heavy price: the failure to understand the new developments of Italian capitalism in the early fifties and the loss of its monopoly on Marxist culture in the early sixties.

Notes

1. The Sixth Congress of the International (1928) had broken down the political and economic development since 1918 as follows: 1. Post-war capitalist crisis; 2. Relative stabilization of world capitalism. The Congress announced the opening of a 'third period' which would be characterized by an explosion of all the contradictions of capitalism.
2. See in particular Kuusinen's report to the Tenth Plenum (3 July 1929) in *Protocolle del Plenums des EKKI*, Karl Hoym, Hamburg, 1929; reproduced in parts in *Critica Marxista*, No. 4, 1965, pp. 143–6.
3. Ben Brewster, 'Communication' in *New Left Review*, No. 70, Nov.–Dec. 1971, p. 110. See also Colletti's critique of 'socialism in one country' which sees the entire question in terms of a 'declaration of independence from the West, a proclamation which re-echoed some of the old Slavophile Russian tradition. It did not represent an economic analysis, programme, or a long-term political strategy' in 'The Question of Stalin', *New Left Review*, No. 61, May–June 1970, p. 74.
4. See Lucio Magri, 'Il valore e il limite delle esperienze frontiste' in *Critica Marxista*, No. 3, 1965.
5. This principle was explicitly formulated in the following manner by Mao Tse-tung in 1946: in discussing the compromise occurring at the international level between the USSR and the Western powers he wrote: 'Such compromise does not require the people in the countries of the capitalist world to follow suit and make compromises at home. The people in those countries will continue to wage different struggles in accordance with their different conditions' from 'Some Points in Appraisal of the Present International Situation' in *Selected Works*, vol. IV, Peking, 1961, p. 87.
6. The emergence of the strategy of national roads to socialism at the Seventh Congress does not mean that the Congress was in any way a challenge to Stalin's dominance. In the summer of 1934 Dimitrov submitted his new views on social democracy and on the united front to Stalin as well as to the commission in charge of preparing the thesis for the Congress. See Ernesto Ragionieri, 'Palmiro Togliatti e il VII congresso dell'Internazionale', PCI publication, Rome, 1973, p. 59.
7. Georgi Dimitrov, *Report to the VII Congress — For the Unity of the Working Class Against Fascism*, London, Red Star Press, 1973, p. 102.
8. Palmiro Togliatti, 'La preparazione di una nuova guerra mondiale da parte degli imperialisti e i compiti della Internazionale comunista' in *Opere scelte*, Rome, 1974, p. 227.
9. Ibid., p. 225.

10. This is the view of Trotsky and of others which characterized and criticized the popular front strategy as the strategy of a defensive unity. For a different position see E. J. Hobsbawm, '. . . the Popular Front strategy . . . was more than a temporary defensive tactic, or even a strategy for eventually turning retreat into offensive. It was a carefully considered strategy of advancing to socialism' in 'Forty Years of Popular Front Government', *Marxism Today*, July 1976, p. 223.

11. See in particular Togliatti's analysis of fascism of 1935 published with the title *Lectures on Fascism*, London, 1976. Of the various interpretations of this text see E. Sereni, 'Fascismo, capitale finanziario e capitale monopolistico di stato nelle analisi dei comunisti italiani', *Critica Marxista*, No. 5, 1972, pp. 42 ff, and Giuseppe Vacca, 'Il contrastato approccio dei giovani a Togliatti' in *Rinascita*, No. 33, 24 August 1973.

12. P. Togliatti, *Il partito comunista italiano*, Rome, 1971, pp. 72–3.

13. This interpretation is characteristic of Bordigist views. Bordiga, the first leader of the PCI, was fundamentally sectarian and rejected any idea of alliance with other parties. Bordiga lost control of the party to Gramsci in the years 1923–6. His contemporary followers trace the alleged reformism of the party to the triumph of Gramsci's 'centrist' tendency. See in particular: A. De Clementi, *Amadeo Bordiga*, Turin, 1971 and 'La politica del P.C.d'I. nel 1921–22 e il rapporto Bordiga–Gramsci' in *Rivista storica del socialismo*, No. 28 and No. 29, 1966; Luigi Cortesi, 'Alcuni problemi della storia del Pci' in *Rivista storical del socialismo*, No. 24 1965; S. Merli, 'I nostri conti con la teoria della rivoluzione senza rivoluzione di Gramsci' in *Giovane Critica*, No. 17, Autumn 1967; and 'Le origini della direzione centrista del P.C.d'I' in *Rivista storica . . .*, No. 23, 1964.

14. For a general analysis of the significance of the popular front strategy, see Milos Hajek, *Storia dell'internazionale comunista (1921–1935)*, Rome, 1975 (original title in Czech: *Jednotna fronta.K. politicke orientaci Komunisticke internacionaly v letech 1921–1935*), particularly the last chapter; Franco De Felice's introduction to *Fascismo, democrazia fronte popolare*, Bari, 1973; and P. Spriano, *Storia del PCI*, Vol. III, Turin, 1970, pp. 118–40.

15. G. Dimitrov, *Report to the VII Congress . . .*, London, Red Star Press, 1973, p. 112.

16. See also Dimitrov: 'We want to find a common language with the broadest masses for the purpose of struggling against the class enemy, to find ways of finally overcoming the isolation of the revolutionary vanguard from the masses of the proletariat and all other working people, as well as overcoming the fatal isolation of the working class from its natural allies in the struggle against the bourgeoisie, against fascism . . .', op. cit., p. 113.

17. P. Togliatti, 'Sulle particolarità della rivoluzione spagnola' in *Opere scelte*, Rome, 1974, p. 256.

18. Ibid., p. 265.

19. Ibid., p. 266. See also the interesting analysis of Giuseppe Vacca in his *Saggio su Togliatti*, Bari, 1974, pp. 256–62.

20. Quoted in G. Amendola, 'Insegnamenti dell' VII Congresso dell' I.C. (Rileggendo Dimitrov)' in *Critica Marxista*, No. 4, July–Aug. 1965, p. 29.

21. See 'Sulla parola d'ordine della repubblica' in *Lo stato operai* (15 February 1939) and r.g. (Ruggero Grieco), 'Pregiudiziale repubblicana' in *Lo Stato operaio* (30 March 1939) quoted and discussed in P. Spriano, *Storia del PCI*, Vol. III, Turin, 1970, p. 302.

22. According to Cortesi (1965), op. cit., p. 169, in the 1937 PCI–PSI pacts too the socialist perspective was dropped altogether. This was inevitable, the author comments, once the anti-fascist and capitalist struggles were no longer seen as parts of an indivisible conjuncture but as separate stages.

23. See, for instance, Lenin's *Two Tactics of Social Democracy in the Democratic Revolution*, written in 1905.
24. A. Gramsci, *Selections from the Prison Notebooks*, London, 1971, pp. 57–8.
25. Mario Alighiero Manacorda, 'L'azione sovietica nel 1939 per evitare la guerra' in *Rinascita*, Vol. 20, No. 31, 3 August 1963. Dimitrov himself wrote an important article on the imperialist nature of the war 'on both sides', 'The War and the Working Class in the Capitalist Countries' reprinted in *The Communist International 1919-1943*, Documents selected and edited by Jane Degras, Vol. III, London, OUP, 1965, pp. 448–59. Amendola, then in Paris, recalls the divisive effect of the new line and of Dimitrov's article in particular, see *Lettere a Milano*, Rome, 1973, pp. 19–21.
26. P. Spriano, *Storia . . .* , Vol. III, Turin, 1970, p. 318.
27. Ibid., p. 331.
28. The full text of the declaration appears in M. Pistillo, *Giuseppe Di Vittorio 1924-1944*, Rome, 1975, pp. 196–8.
29. P. Togliatti, 'La situazione economica e politica-sociale dell'Italia', reprinted in *Critica Marxista*, Vol. 6, No. 1, Jan.–Feb. 1968, p. 101.
30. Some of the most important documentation on this dispute can be found in P. Secchia, *Il PCI e la guerra di liberazione 1943-45*, Milan, 1973, pp. 182–200; Amendola, *Lettere . . .*, pp. 118–249; Luigi Longo, *I centri dirigenti del PCI nella Resistenza*, Rome, 1973, particularly chapter 3; see also P. Spriano, *Storia del PCI*, Vol. V, Turin, 1975, pp. 110–37 and Ragionieri, *Il Partito comunista*, in *Azionisti cattolici e comunisti nella Resistenza*, Istituto nazionale per la storia del movimento di liberazione, Milan, 1971, pp. 325–35. Togliatti's Salerno policies vindicated somewhat the position of the Milan centre. I find F. Catalano's view that Togliatti's policy 'was firmly rejected by the Communists in the still-occupied North of Italy, who were more interested in finding a way of eliminating the old ruling class and of replacing it by the proletariat' totally unsubstantiated (see his 'The Rebirth of the Party System, 1944–48' in S. J. Woolf (ed.), *The Rebirth of Italy 1943-50*, London, 1972, p. 60.
31. Amendola wrote: 'Togliatti wanted to terminate a useless debate. It was a severe recall to discipline, the end of a regime of freer discussions. This regime had had some inconvenient aspects but it had taught us the value of a frank exchange of ideas which we would not easily find again', in *Lettere . . .* p. 323.
32. Quoted in Secchia, op. cit., p. 509.
33. For a discussion of the deadlocked CLN Bari Congress see Franco De Felice, 'A proposito del Congresso di Bari dei Cln e la Resistenza' in *Il 1943 — Le origini della rivoluzione antifascista — Critica Marxista*, Quaderno No. 7, 1974. See also Velio Spano 'I comunisti e il Congresso di Bari del 1944' in *Cronache meridionali*, No. 4, 1964.
34. The USSR recognized the Badoglio government in March 1944. Togliatti arrived in Italy shortly afterwards and proposed a government of national unity which would include the monarchists. The coincidence of the two events has led to a prolonged debate about the degree of independence of Togliatti's initiatives. On this question see C. Pinzani's interesting essay 'Togliatti e L'Unione Sovietica' in *Rinascita*, No. 15, 11 April 1975, and Antonio Gambino's well researched *Storia del dopoguerra. Dalla Liberazione al potere DC*, Bari, 1975, in particular pp. 34–45.
35. P. Togliatti in 'La politica di unitá nazionale dei comunisti' in *Critica Marxista*, No. 4/5, July–Oct. 1964, p. 31. For a survey of the impact of international politics on Italian political development see G. Warner, 'Italy and the Power 1943-1949' in S. J. Woolf (ed.) *The Rebirth of Italy 1943-1950*, London, 1972.
36. M. Djilas, *Conversations with Stalin*, Harmondsworth, Penguin, 1962, p. 90.
37. A. Lepre, *La svolta di Salerno*, Rome, 1966, pp. 97–8.

38. G. Amendola, *Lettere* . . ., p. 300.
39. Ibid., p. 323.
40. P. Togliatti, 'La politica di unità nazionale dei comunisti' in P. Togliatti, *Opere scelte* (hereafter cited as *OS*), Rome, 1974, pp. 306–7.
41. Ibid., pp. 312–14.
42. P. Togliatti, 'I compiti del partito nella situazione attuale' in *OS*, p. 350.
43. P. Togliatti, 'La politica di unità nazionale dei comunisti' in *OS*, pp. 322–3.
44. P. Togliatti, 'Partito nuovo' in *Rinascita*, No. 4, Oct.–Nov.–Dec. 1944 (now in *OS*, p. 372).
45. P. Togliatti, 'La politica di unità nazionale dei comunisti' in *OS*, p. 304.
46. P. Togliatti, 'Classe operaia e participazione al governo' in P. Togliatti, *La politica di Salerno aprile-settembre 1944*, Rome, 1969, p. 45.
47. I have used the word 'directive' for the Italian 'dirigente' despite its strange ring in English because the Hoare-Nowell-Smith translation of Gramsci's *Prison Notebooks*, London, 1971, uses this term in a similar context throughout the text.
48. P. Togliatti, 'I compiti del partito nella siuazione attuale' in *OS*, p. 343.
49. Ibid., p. 346.
50. P. Togliatti, 'Che cosa é il partito nuovo' in *Rinascita*, No. 4, Oct.–Nov.–Dec. 1944.
51. A. Gramsci, *Prison Notebooks*, p. 90.
52. Ibid., pp. 57–8.
53. P. Togliatti, 'I compiti del partito nella situazione attuale' in *OS*, pp. 341–2.
54. P. Togliatti, 'Che cosa é il partito nuovo' in *Rinascita*, No. 4, Oct.–Nov.–Dec. 1944.
55. P. Togliatti, in *Il partito*, pp. 47–51.

2. The Mass Party

The Italian Communist Party emerged from the successful insurrection which defeated the Germans in April 1945 as a powerful political force. It was able to present itself to the Italian masses as the hegemonic centre of the Resistance. Its moral and political prestige had grown enormously for it could speak with the authority of a party which had never ceased to fight against fascism. That the working class and the Communists had a leading role in the Resistance is not left-wing rhetoric. It has been estimated that at least 40/50 per cent of the participants in the armed Resistance were in the Communist 'Garibaldi' brigades, while of the 300,000 armed participants enrolled by the end of the fighting at least half were workers or peasants.[1] Out of 70,000 partisans killed, 42,500 were Communists. Moreover, to concentrate exclusively on the figures of the armed Resistance can be misleading, for one of the peculiarities of the Italian Resistance is that it operated in conjunction with a movement of strikes and sabotage in the factories. The strike of more than 500,000 workers in March 1944 was the largest strike which ever took place in Nazi-occupied Europe.[2].

As we have seen the PCI had used this strength and this great prestige to support not a socialist take-over but a reconstruction along democratic lines. This strategy, accepted with discipline by the majority of the rank and file, was, however, far from being understood in its entire complexity. A great number of cadres believed that Togliatti, with his 'Salerno' strategy, had wanted to deal with the Germans and the Fascists first and to reserve his strength in order to deal with the bourgeoisie immediately afterwards.

This meant that within the party two political lines co-existed. The first, accepted by nearly the whole leadership and by a majority of the rank and file, conceived the objectives of the Resistance and of post-war reconstruction to be in terms of intermediate political goals: a progressive democracy, structural reforms, etc. The second political line, which represented the view of an important sector of the rank and file, thought that Togliatti's strategy was merely a tactical move which rested on the proposition that a struggle on two fronts (against both fascism and the anti-fascist sector of the bourgeoisie) had to be avoided at all cost. This second line was seldom politically articulated precisely because it was held by a section of the rank and file with little access to the party press and little propensity for political writing. It is important to note that this second line had the same view of the PCI that the opponents of Communism had: a popular conception of the activities of the Communists as being character- ized by political cunning, double-dealing and a single-mindedness which put them into an advantageous position when dealing with their supposedly more squeamish liberal allies. Togliatti was aware of the problem when he warned thus the party's cadres in August 1946:

> Whenever we delve into the minds of our comrades, we find the strangest conceptions of what Communism and our party should be, conceptions which are difficult to reconcile with our party line. Acceptance of this line is often superficial or formal, or is justified by the same stupid epithets as our opponents use regarding us ('tactics', 'trickery', 'secret plan' and so forth).[3]

Many proletarian activists would of course welcome cunning and single- mindedness particularly when used to 'trick' the bourgeoisie. The para- doxical situation was reached when Togliatti's words were believed neither by bourgeois politicans not by an important segment of his own working class supporters.

This 'duplicity', as Togliatti himself called it in 1956, manifested itself at the Fifth Congress of the party which took place between 29 December 1945 and 5 January 1946. At the Congress some of the delegates expressed the opinion that, having defeated fascism, the Communists should take up once more the flag of the class struggle and call for a definitive clash with the forces of the bourgeoisie. It was up to the Scoccimarro (who had been far from welcoming Togliatti's Salerno policy) to explain that the party line, that is, the policy of collaborating with the Government under the banner of national solidarity and reconstruction, was not a mere tactical decision but a strategic objective of the working class.[4] In August 1945, Scoccimarro, then Minister of Finances, declared: '. . . in the present economic situation of our country, even if all the subjective conditions were favourable, one could not achieve a socialist economy on the entire national scale.'[5] The call of the dissenters for a 'return to the class struggle' implied that, in their view, the Resistance had meant a suspension of the class struggle and that the partisan warfare against the Germans and the fascists had nothing to do with 'class'. They saw the class struggle only in terms of a political extension of the trade union struggle between workers and employers.

For instance, in August 1944, an unknown party member wrote from

Turin to the headquarters of the Piedmont Communist Party. In his letter he expressed his fear that the party was sacrificing its 'Communist conceptions' for the sake of anti-fascist unity, he added:

> The Communist Party must express the historical interests of the proletariat; it cannot fulfil this task unless it maintains its full political independence irrespective of its relations with any other party. I find that the Party press does not fulfil the tasks of a 'proletarian press'. In fact Party press and Party propaganda seem to stress solely the struggle against the Germans at the expense of what should be its principal aim: the Communist education of the masses.[6]

It is not within the scope of this work to attempt to quantify in any way the extent of 'left-wing' dissent within the PCI. What is of interest here is to study how the party's strategy on the political as well as the cultural level had to cope with these internal problems. One must appreciate that the transformation of the PCI from a party of 6,000 members to a mass party with more than two million members had radically changed its internal physiognomy. Some of the old cadres, reared under the iron discipline of the underground could not help being seriously worried that the 'new party', swamped by two million politically unprepared members, would inevitably lose some of its 'Bolshevik toughness'.

The most serious problem pressing the leadership of the PCI was to hold together this great mass of workers and peasants and to give it purpose and a sense of political direction such as it had had during the Resistance. Guidance and control are part of the fundamental tasks of a Leninist party; hence the evidence of the party restraining the masses does not necessarily prove that the party is pursuing reformist policies. The locus of criticisms can only be at the level of political analysis of the practice of a revolutionary party in a given conjuncture. The simultaneous existence of two political lines set off a debate which, though often conducted as political shadow-boxing, centred on the question: was a socialist insurrection possible? This debate took place in the immediate post-war years, but it was never in the forefront of internal Communist political strife. It was used in a polemical vein in order to attack not so much the policies of the PCI during the Resistance, but the way in which the party was tackling the new problems which were emerging in the period of reconstruction. The debate re-surfaced in the 1960s. Again its purpose was primarily political. The new leftist extra-parliamentary 'vanguards' used the debate as a weapon with which to attack the alleged reformism of the PCI.

There were two fundamental reasons for not calling for a socialist insurrection in 1945, one internal and one external. The internal reason was that the partisan movement was fundamentally weak and it could not be used in a socialist direction.[7] Even though the Communists had a dominant position within it, it is calculated that 50 per cent of the partisans were not Communists, and therefore they would be unlikely to support a socialist insurrection. Even if the prestige and the strength of the PCI could have acquired the control of the overwhelming majority of the partisans, these were still, at their peak, only 300,000. If, it was argued, only 300,000 men could be relied upon to carry on armed warfare against the Germans, presumably even fewer and certainly no more would continue an armed fight against Italian bourgeois forces. Furthermore, practically the whole strength of the Resistance was located in the North and Centre and in particular in the industrial sections of the North and in the Emilia, but not in the Veneto. The movement became really strong only when the victory of the Allies was certain. A civil war would have split the country into two. It is unlikely that the South, with its large masses of peasants untouched by socialist ideology and with its lack of experience in partisan warfare, would have in any way supported a socialist solution.[8] On the contrary, the South would have provided a strategic enclave for the regrouping of the counter-revolutionary and fascist forces.

The second reason against was external: Italy was under military occupation. The Anglo–American forces had already attempted to favour the non-communist elements during the Resistance. After its conclusion they continued to support, at times quite openly, the more moderate elements in the anti-fascist coalition.[9] Their presence strengthened enormously the supporters of a return to pre-fascist democracy.

These, then, were the reasons put forward by the PCI to defend itself from the accusation of having failed to move immediately from the 'stage' of the anti-fascist struggle to the 'state' of a workers' government.[10] As Gian Carlo Pajetta, one of the foremost Communist partisan leaders, pointed out:

> The alternative could not be and never was in any way a new insurrection. We would have had to undergo the Greek experience, in fact, as it had already taken place, it would perhaps have been impossible even to attempt it along similar lines.[11]

Thus it would seem that the fundamental reasons for the 'missed opportunity' of a socialist insurrection were due to questions of national and international relations of forces. The texts of the period would suggest a reading in this sense, also because in the course of political controversies against the advocates of a socialist insurrection a justification of the party line which relied on tactical considerations could be more easily understood and accepted. To the activist who wanted to do 'what they did in Russia' it was always possible to explain that that was not possible because there was not enough consensus or because of the American presence, etc. However, by remaining anchored to contingent considerations one remained also prisoner of the same optic which saw the Resistance as a 'missed opportunity' or, worse, as a 'Resistance betrayed'. To those who say that the revolution was not undertaken because Stalin did not want to, one is left to answer with the argument that Stalin had nothing to do with it, that the problem was that of the unfavourable relations of forces. It is obvious, however, that in a debate of this nature both parties share the same 'insurrectionist' mentality.

There is no doubt that a good section of the leading group of the PCI thought along these lines and there is no doubt that Togliatti — whose starting-point was quite different — was happy to guarantee the unity of his leading group by accepting the above justifications which rested on national and international strategic considerations.

It is, of course, difficult to deny the validity of these motivations. One should add, however, that the main reason why the socialist insurrection did not take place was because Togliatti was already advancing a conception of the revolution 'as a process', and this conception implied a socialism quite different from the Soviet model and quite remote from any insurrectionist temptation.[12] The objective which — as we shall see — Togliatti had posed to the war of liberation was that of a stage in the anti-fascist revolution: the creation of a republic of a 'new type' in which the process of reorganization of the working class into a directing or leading class could take place. In other words, Togliatti was substituting for the concept of revolution as a momentous rupture the concept of 'progressive democracy' as an intermediate and transitional form of state. This conception of politics, however, took a long time before it could dominate the party and its leading group. Reading the recently published 'diaries' of Pietro Secchia, it is difficult not to note the remarkable ideological differences which existed then in the leading group of the PCI. This 'silent' (because never 'official') political struggle between positions typical of the Comintern mentality and the conceptions that Togliatti was developing would become ever more complex with the growth of the mass party within which coexisted three generations of activists.

The first generation was that of the founders of the Italian Communist Party, those who had joined in the years 1921–6. It included the most senior elements: Togliatti, Secchia, Longo, Grieco and the trade union leader Di Vittorio.

The second generation had joined the party during the 1930s. They were first and foremost anti-fascists who had come to consider the Communist Party as the major force in the opposition to Mussolini's regime. A typical representative of this generation was Giorgio Amendola.[13] This generation spent the years 1929–43 in clandestine activities; many of them were jailed or sent to confinement, some took part in the Spanish Civil War and in anti-fascist activities in France and other countries. They learned how to infiltrate fascist trade unions, newspapers, cultural groups, etc. Some of them, who had become acquainted with each other in and around the University of Rome, were to provide the Resistance with some of its best organizers. Their names, Ingrao, Pajetta, Guttuso, Lombardo Radice, Alicata, were to become influential in Communist political and cultural activities in the 1950s and 1960s. The cadres who led the Resistance were not new recruits but seasoned veterans of the Spanish Civil War and of clandestine activities in the 1930s and 1940s.[14]

While the first two generations shared a fairly similar outlook and had undergone relatively similar experiences, the third generation exhibited some special traits. This generation, by far the largest, had joined the party in the years 1943–5. For them the Communist Party was the Party of the Resistance, but they were also attracted to Communism by the example of the Soviet Union in the war and by Stalin. What we now know of Stalin and Stalinism must not obscure what the name of Stalin then meant to the Italian working masses. To them during and after the war Stalin possessed a mythical quality: he was the invincible leader of the heroic Soviet workers, the conqueror of Europe and the annihilator of fascism, the man who would bring the Soviet paradise to the Italian masses. 'Ha' da veni' Baffone' was the rallying cry of the southern workers; in Milan it was 'Arriva Barbison' (Big Moustaches is going to come), 'Baffone' would come and free them all. 'We'll do what they did in Russia' was another popular expression.

This, of course, caused endless problems to the PCI leadership. First of all they had to make it very clear that 'we would *not* do what they did in Russia', the objective being a 'progressive democracy', not a proletarian one. Secondly, the slogan 'Ha' da veni' Baffone' had serious implications for the Resistance. For, if Stalin was going to come and liberate Italy, why fight at all? Better to consolidate one's forces and await the entry of the Red Army for a final Communist take-over. The Stalin myth could take, therefore, two contradictory aspects: on the one hand it was a manifestation of proletarian consciousness, on the other an aspect of the 'wait-and-see' attitude characteristic of the more backward elements of the Resistance.

It was obviously necessary to unite and mould the party into a force which would be able to tackle the tasks of the reconstruction. Togliatti recognized this need and in a speech in Florence, in 1947, he said: 'We are already a mass party; now we must also acquire the principal qualities of a cadres party.'[15] He underlined the need for theory:

> Without a revolutionary doctrine a revolutionary party cannot exist. Without an advanced doctrine a vanguard party cannot exist. In our party these truths have been a little forgotten. From this attitude it follows that today we do not read enough, study enough and do not develop theory sufficiently.[16]

The implications were that the lack of theoretical preparation meant that the sort of Marxism which existed at the level of cell and section was a 'gut' Marxism characterized by the repetition of sectarian formulae. This, of course, was a general problem of the international communist movement for which Stalin's conception of ideological propaganda with its didactic and catechistic features bore a share of the responsibility.

Part of the problem facing Togliatti and the leadership group of the PCI was to dispel the commonly-held view that the revolution in Italy would follow the pattern of the Soviet revolution. Togliatti declared:

> International experience teaches us that in the actual conditions of the class struggle in the whole world, the working class and the advanced masses, in order to reach socialism — that is, in order to develop democracy to its extreme limit which is precisely that of socialism — must discover new paths different, for instance, from those which had been chosen by the working class and the labouring masses of the Soviet Union.[17]

Here Togliatti was openly saying what had been the implicit content of his entire policy during the Resistance: the rejection of the October 1917 model as a universal path for revolution. His statement was a declaration of independence from the USSR and from the model it represented. We shall see how this declaration could not survive the impact of the Cold War and the birth of the Cominform and how the PCI would have to wait until the period succeeding the Twentieth Congress of the CPSU in order to re-introduce openly all the problematic elements of the 'Italian road'.

The question of the extension of democracy into socialism, coupled with the related problem of the link between reforms and revolution, would be discussed endlessly by the party in the years to come. In the 1940s, it was accepted with relative ease and with little controversy.

Togliatti pointed out that Yugoslavia had not followed the Soviet road, but had chosen an 'advanced democratic regime which is developing in the direction of socialism'.[18] Italy too, said Togliatti, could have developed in the same way if the CLN could have been used as organs for a mass struggle for the democratization of the country. This had been impossible, he added, not so much because of the weaknesses of the movement for national liberation but because of international reasons.[19] Togliatti did not expand on the international aspects, yet these were extremely important for he considered them to be the chief motive for the inability of the Resistance to become the spring-board for a popular democracy.

But whether Togliatti had foreseen the Cold War or had imagined a long period of international anti-fascist co-operation, the main strategic component of his political line could not be affected. This component, which overrode all other considerations, was the creation of the mass party, mass not only in terms of membership but in terms of its effective presence in the Italian political system; a presence which could not be removed easily and which would be sufficiently entrenched to survive any difficulty. This, above all, was his real political objective and this he achieved.

From the period of the Resistance to the onset of the Cold War, the Communists did not explain or denounce the international constraints which existed, but it is clear that they understood the strategic relevance of the new international order. Togliatti had drawn these conclusions:

> We understand that in every country the road to socialism and demo-
> cracy assumes particular forms in accordance with the diversity of the
> development of capitalism, with its national characteristics and tradi-
> tions and with the position that country has taken during the Great
> World War. This seems to me the most interesting aspect of the present
> situation and of the way in which the class struggle develops inter-
> nationally. If this is true — and I think it is — it follows that our task
> is to acquire that ideological preparation, those policies and that
> organization which will allow us to find our road, the Italian road,
> the road which is shaped by our particularities, traditions and con-
> ditions . . .[20]

This was the first time Togliatti mentioned the 'Italian road to socialism'. He would not use this expression again until 1956.

An important element in the reconstruction of the new state was to be the new 'directing' function of the working class and Togliatti insisted that the working class could not direct the nation without allies.

To its traditional ally — the peasantry — was to be added a new important element: the middle strata. The most elaborate analysis of this new

element in the alliance strategy of the PCI was made by Togliatti in a speech at Reggio Emilia on 24 September 1946.

It was no accident that Togliatti had chosen the Emilian region as the place for such analysis. The central regions of Emilia, Umbria and Tuscany had traditionally been strongholds of radicalism. The anarchists had scored notable successes in the nineteenth century and, afterwards, the Socialists had been able to become the dominant political force. After the Resistance the PCI had become the most important party in what had come to be known as 'the red belt' of Italy. Yet these regions were chiefly agricultural with a greatly differentiated population in the countryside. It was obvious that the PCI would not be able to obtain any support in these areas if it adopted a policy of proletarian intransigence. It was precisely in the 'red belt' that the strategy of alliances, in particular with the middle strata, acquired a specific importance.

Togliatti defined the middle strata in a negative way:

> 'Middle strata' . . . are a socialist group which is in between two extremes of the social ladder, which include those who are 'in the middle' between the wage-earners and those who own the means of production, that is the capitalists . . . the concept of middle strata, so explained, is clear enough; it is, however, very rich in content [for] between wage-earners and capitalists there is a large number of social groupings.[21]

According to Togliatti, sharecroppers were to be included in the middle strata, for sharecroppers do not own their land (but rent it) and do not receive a salary. The small and middle farmer are part of the middle strata as well, for, although they own their land, they do not exploit farm labour.[22] Togliatti went on:

> Then, there are the urban middle strata . . . from small and middle merchants to shopkeepers and artisans, to the entrepreneurs of small and middle firms. Finally there are the intellectuals, from the school-teachers and the priests to the various categories of professional people and to the men of great culture such as poets, artists, scientists and writers.[23]

Of course, all these social groups did not constitute (and should not be considered) a uniform bloc. Togliatti claimed that the party was already representing important sectors of the middle strata as its electoral successes in the Emilia as well as the social composition of its membership amply demonstrated.[24]

It seems evident that Togliatti had rejected the Kautskyist doctrine of the proletarianization of the peasantry and the middle strata.[25] According to this view, the development of capitalism would sooner or later transform the peasantry and other social strata into wage-earners. Once this transformation was over, the former middle strata would acquire a truly proletarian consciousness. They were therefore considered in terms of their future socio-economic position and not in terms of their present interests and their existing relationship to the capitalist mode of production.

For Togliatti, in the present situation, there were no fundamental contradictions in interests between the proletariat and the middle strata.[26] The close unity of these groups with the proletarian vanguard was indispensable if a radical programme of reforms was to be adopted. This was so because the existing conjuncture was characterized by the attempt of reactionary groups to divide the movement which had liberated Italy from fascism.

This view was at the centre of the Communist analysis and underlined the decision not to attempt a programme of socialist reconstruction. Togliatti explained:

> It seems clear that we do not propose a reconstruction of our economy according to socialist or Communist principles. For such a transformation the country, taken in its entirety, is not yet ready even if some of its sectors are already mature [for socialism] . . .[27]

Togliatti realized that Italy was not facing a revolutionary conjuncture for international as well as internal reasons. Two choices then really faced Italian society: not social revolution or capitalist development, but capitalist development under the direction of the working class or capitalist development under the dominance of the bourgeoisie. The PCI chose the former course of action. The theoretical underpinnings of this policy was never explicitly elaborated by Togliatti and it is even possible that he would not accept it as a realistic assessment of the Communist strategy. After all, in addition to an agrarian reform, part of the programme of the Communists was a campaign for the destruction of capitalist monopolies. Such campaign would certainly weaken the development of capitalism. However, the anti-monopolist end of the Communist strategy was never pushed forward with much vigour. The dominant concern was the Southern question. Togliatti frequently stressed the agrarian component of the Communist programme. The development of agriculture would have to be undertaken according to a general plan determined 'by permanent common interests and not by the transitory interests of private speculation'.[28]

This could only be done with the support of a mass movement of workers in the countryside. This movement would take part in a struggle for the elimination of the 'latifondo' and for the revision of all agrarian contracts. Large capitalistic landholding would have to be broken up and distributed to the peasantry or changed into some form of co-operative farming. The duty of the Communists would be to lead a vast movement of organized rural labourers (who were already favourable to co-operative farming) and of sharecroppers and peasants who wanted their land liberated from excessive debts and rents.[29] The Emilia speech of 1947, on the problem of the middle strata and on the question of the formation of a new bloc, constitutes one of the central statements on Communist policy in the period 1945-7, a statement which forcefully put forward the particularity of the 'Italian road to socialism'.

It is relevant to note that these controversial views were aired by Togliatti to an audience of party workers (during the Organization Conference of the Communist Federation of Reggio-Emilia) and that at no time did he feel the obligation or the need to quote or even mention Marx, Lenin or Stalin as if to establish further his independence from the classical texts of Marxism and, indirectly, from October 1917. It would be up to other Communists to establish the orthodoxy of the Italian road, particularly when the beginning of the Cold War and the birth of the Cominform would seriously endanger Togliatti's analysis.

Notes

1. See the evidence in L. Valiani, 'La Resistenza italiana' in *Rivista storica italiana*, Vol. LXXXV, Fasc. 1, 1973.
2. P. Spriano, *Storia del PCI*, Vol. V, Turin, 1975, pp. 257 ff.
3. P. Togliatti, 'Istruzioni per le Conferenze provinciali di organizzazione' in *La politica dei comunisti dal V al VI Congresso*, Rome, n.d., p. 107.
4. M. Scoccimarro, 'Una discussione sulla nostra politica' in *Rinascita*, Vol. 2, No. 12, December 1945. Amendola, in *Lotta di classe e sviluppo economico dopo la Liberazione*, Rome, 1962, confirms that not all of the PCI was convinced of the strategy of a 'democratic advance to socialism', p. 43.
5. Quoted in S. J. Woolf, 'The Rebirth of Italy, 1943-50' in S. J. Woolf (ed.), *The Rebirth of Italy 1943-50*, London, 1972, p. 226.
6. P. Secchia, *Il Partito comunista italiano e la guerra di liberazione 1943-45*, Milan, 1973, p. 631.
7. P. Secchia, *Il Partito Italiano . . .*, Milan, 1973, p. xxxiii.
8. G. C. Pajetta, 'Alle origini del partito nuovo' in *Rinascita*, Vol. 30, No. 35, 7 September 1973.
9. The influences of the events in Greece cannot be underestimated. Harold Macmillan, in summing up the negotiations between the Resistance, the Allies and the Italian Government, wrote: 'The lesson of Greece was that we had to get control over these movements right from the start. Assuming that the campaign might end in the early summer [of 1945], now was the time to have a clear understanding and to infiltrate the partisans with British officers and reliable Italians . . .', quoted in G. Warner, 'Italy and the Powers 1943-49' in *The Rebirth of Italy 1943-50*, p. 43.

10. In his report to the Tenth Congress of the PCI (1962), Togliatti claimed that one should not interpret the Allied occupation of Italy as an element which acted as an obstacle to a socialist insurrection, because a socialist insurrection was not on the agenda in any case (in P. Togliatti, *Nella democrazia e nella pace verso il socialismo*, Rome, 1963, p. 187). For a different analysis see the Sereni-Secchia debate: E. Sereni, 'La scelta del 1943–45' in *Rinascita*, No. 5, 29 January 1971 and P. Secchia, 'La Resistenza: grandezza e limiti oggettivi' in *Rinascita*, No. 8, 19 February 1971.

11. G. C. Pajetta, 'Dalla liberazione alla repubblica' in AA.VV. *Problemi di storia del Partito Comunista Italiano*, Rome, 1971, p. 94.

12. On this point see Togliatti's comments in his Report to the Tenth Congress of the PCI, in *Opere scelte*, pp. 1073–4.

13. See Amendola's interesting autobiographical account of the events which led him to join the PCI. Amendola was the son of an influential liberal leader, Giovanni Amendola, who had tried to oppose fascism, albeit in an ineffective way. It was the failure of the liberal opposition to fascism which contributed to Amendola's decisive 'choice of life'; see *Una scelta di vita*, Milan, 1976.

14. P. Secchia, in an Appendix to his *Il partito comunista italiano e la guerra di liberazione 1943–45*, provides a list of 1,673 partisan leaders and shows that most of them had been politically active before the Resistance. Out of the 1,673 partisans listed, 1,003 had been condemned by the Special Tribunal, 718 had been under confinement and 130 had fought in Spain.

15. P. Togliatti, 'La nostra lotta per la democrazia e il socialismo' in *Il Partito*, Rome, 1973, p. 56.

16. Ibid., p. 57.

17. Ibid., p. 58.

18. Ibid., p. 58.

19. Ibid., p. 59.

20. Ibid., pp. 59–60.

21. P. Togliatti, 'Ceto medio e Emilia rossa' in *Opere scelte*, p. 458.

22. Presumably the middle peasant employs a small number of labourers, however, he lives primarily off his own labour and not on surplus-value.

23. P. Togliatti, 'Ceto medio . . .' in op. cit., p. 459.

24. According to Togliatti's figures of party membership in Reggio Emilia, 17 per cent of members were rural proletarians whereas sharecroppers and farmers represented 29 per cent of the membership.

25. See Karl Kautsky, *La Question agraire*, Paris, 1970.

26. P. Togliatti, 'Ceto medio . . .' in op. cit., p. 460.

27. Ibid., p. 464.

28. Ibid., p. 480.

29. Ibid., pp. 480–1.

3 The Communist Compromise

It is now possible to begin to visualize the main problems of Italian society in terms of the Communist analysis. Italy is seen as a social formation characterized by the co-existence of several modes of production and several social relations belonging to earlier phases of capitalist production. It is therefore a highly stratified society with a profoundly uneven pattern of development.

Revolutions do not take place because a country has or has not reached a particular stage in economic development. Revolutions take place because of the particular articulation of a set of contradictions of which the economy represents only one aspect, albeit the determinant one.

A concrete analysis of Italian society would show that the dominant role was held by monopolistic elements. Given the particularities of the Italian social structure, the Communist strategy, in practice, was centred around the construction of a new bloc, led by the working class, by splitting the old ruling bloc (destruction of the agrarian ruling class) and by the re-building of Italy along democratic lines with a working class government.

It is in this context that State intervention (and the need for working class control over it) acquires a new meaning: the instruments of the State would be used in order to plan and direct the development of the economy in a 'democratic' direction. This proposal was called by the Communists 'il nuovo corso' (the new course). As Togliatti declared:

> We are accused, when we speak of a 'new course', of wanting to suppress private initiative. This is not so. We want to leave a large area to the development of private initiative, particularly to that of the small- and medium-sized entrepreneur. At the same time we maintain that the state must intervene in order to direct the whole work of reconstruction, in order to co-ordinate private firms, to guide them, to tie them organically to each other according to national needs, and ensuring that healthy private initiative is not suffocated and eventually destroyed by the prevailing of plutocratic groups and by speculation.[1]

Before examining the 'new course' proposed by the Italian Communists, we must look at the programme with which the party confronted Italians prior to the elections for the Constituent Assembly and the referendum on the monarchy, which took place on 2 June 1946. The programme was elaborated at the Economic Conference of the PCI of August 1945 and at the Fifth Congress of the party (January 1946). Togliatti, as late as 1958, had this to say about it:

> This programme, which we presented to Italy in 1946, has, on the whole, substantially kept its great value. We developed and applied it to new conditions and to new events, but we have remained faithful to it.[2]

The programme of the Congress proposed the constitution of a democratic republic based on a representative parliamentary system. The new regime would pursue a 'policy of peace'. The Communists declared themselves opposed to international blocs and spheres of influence. The PCI was against a federal organization of the State although it recognized the need to give Sicily and Sardinia some form of regional autonomy. It demanded the democratization of the police and the army as well as the election of judges.

On the economic front, the Communist proposals were characterized by *realpolitik* and by the repeated refusal to adopt a political line which would endanger the unity of the tripartite coalition.

In his intervention at the Economic Conference of August 1945, Togliatti insisted that the PCI did not want a crisis but that it was 'orientated towards constructive solutions in both the political and the economic field'.[3] The crux of the Communist policy would be production and productivity: 'our policy must be one of production and not of subsidies except in exceptional cases'. There was no question of economic ('Utopian') planning and in so far as the PCI demanded control over production, it was not control of the type used by the Bolsheviks in 1917, but more like that already in existence in the USA and Great Britain. Togliatti was also not very interested in nationalization which was to be used only 'after having studied the situation with care and with a sense of responsibility'. He even criticized the trade unions for not being sufficiently interested in the problems of production. His only appeal to the workers was that 'whenever they are working they should increase their productivity'.

Is the conclusion to be drawn from this that Togliatti's moderation had reached an excessive level?[4] A more fundamental criticism would be that the Italian Communists had realized the hazards of following a classical Soviet-type strategy, but could offer no alternative except a progressive Keynesian one.

It is quite clear that Togliatti was conscious of the dangers involved through the presence of the PCI in the government, which could inspire the workers to take over factories and disrupt production at a time when the economy was in ruin and when the newly-established democratic order could easily be destroyed. Yet one reads the economic programmes of the Italian Communists without finding anything particularly original. A traditional disregard for economic questions and twenty years underground had demanded a price which the PCI had to pay.

The confusion existing in the various programmes can be exemplified by comparing Togliatti's timid references to nationalization in August 1945 with the resolution approved on 6 January 1946 by the Fifth Congress of the PCI which stated that the party 'proposes the nationalization of all large monopolistic firms, of the big banks and of the insurance companies, the beginning of economic planning, etc.'[5]

The trade union movement too favoured some forms of national planning. At the Conference of the Confederazione Generale Italiana del Lavoro (CGIL), held in January 1945, it was declared that national reconstruction had to take place on the basis of a plan which would establish national priorities after consultations, through local committees, with the working population.[6] Politically, this was a very significant event, for the CGIL represented a united front at the trade union level corresponding to the tripartite coalition.[7]

The Rome Pact of 3 June 1944 which enshrined the rebirth of a united trade union movement was characterized by a high degree of politicization. This was both its chief strength and its weakness. It was its strength because it connected the economic organization of the labour movement to the principal ongoing struggle — against fascism. Significantly its Communist co-secretary, Di Vittorio, in his report to the CGIL Conference (January 1945, Rome), stressed that the economic rebirth of the country should be conceived as a great mobilizing process of vast masses of people which should represent the highest synthesis of the 'national interest'.[8]

Its main weakness, however, resided precisely in its close identification with the three leading political parties, the PCI, the PSI and the DC. The secretariat of the CGIL was formed of three general-secretaries, each representing a definite political tendency.[9] Clearly this sort of situation could last only as long as the three parties co-operated together. Furthermore, there was a profound division in the objects and aims of the left tendencies and those of the DC. For the PCI, and to a lesser extent for the PSI, the CGIL had to achieve the re-unification of the working class at the economic level, while the party could accomplish the task of political synthesis which would have allowed it to become the hegemonic force

in the country. For the DC the trade union movement would have facilitated its project of ideological penetration in those working class strata
which had hitherto escaped its influence and the renewal of its severed
connection with agricultural workers.[10]

This ideological division entailed a general subservience of the trade
unions to the political parties. Thus the economic debate within the
CGIL reproduced the economic debate within the political parties. Neither
the PCI nor the DC had an original economic theory. The PCI put as its
foremost priority the maintenance of the tripartite alliance and could
not develop anything but the productivist line already mentioned. The
DC was itself divided between an interventionist policy of the reformist-
social-democratic type and a frankly capitalist path which coincided with
the proposals emanating from the Liberal Party and particularly from
Luigi Einaudi, then the leading economist in Italy. Interventionist Christian
Democrats and 'productivist' Communists were able to find a common
terrain in the trade unions and that is why the CGIL could formulate, at
its first congress, economic proposals which were relatively close to those
of the PCI. Thus the PCI had already established a widespread working
class basis for its anti-monopolistic programme.

At the beginning of 1946 this programme seemed to rely for its implementation on two main weapons: economic planning and nationalization.

The Communists also demanded that national production be controlled
through the recognition and the extension of the system of the 'consigli
di gestione' or 'workers' management councils'; these were workers'
organizations which had taken over the running of the factories during
and after the Resistance.

In the agrarian sector the Communists proposed the elimination of the
large estates of absentee landlords and the limitation of capitalist farms.[11]
Thus the 1946 Communist programme dealt with three aspects:

1. The necessary legislation to democratize the country.

2. Anti-monopolistic legislation.

3. Agrarian reform.

In the next two years this general programme would not be consistently
presented. The struggle for a democratic social system would take place
principally in the Constituent Assembly where the impetus of Communist
pressures was limited by the desire to preserve the tripartite coalition. The
struggle for anti-monopolistic reforms could never seriously be carried out.

The real centre of Communist strategy in the politico-economic sector
(as opposed to the social and institutional sector) was in its Southern

strategy. This is not to be understood in terms of a separate and autonomous arena of struggle: the agrarian strategy was part and parcel of the Communist strategy. If it was privileged *vis-à-vis* the anti-monopolistic strategy, it was not solely due to contingent reasons of priorities and of tactics, but because the effective relation of forces in Italy pre-empted, in practice, the implementation of both simultaneously.

In essence the Southern strategy was an attempt to alter radically the relations of classes in Southern Italy. The first priority of the PCI was to establish itself in the South as the leading organization of the peasantry. It attempted to do so by turning to the peasants' co-operatives which had emerged from the occupation of the lands of 1943–5.[12] The PCI, which could count on the presence of a Communist, F. Gullo, as the minister in charge of agriculture, was able to obtain the promulgation of a law in 1944 which authorized the distribution of uncultivated land and the reform of agricultural contracts.[13] The peasants' co-operatives were the agencies officially designated to receive the expropriated land. As expected, most of the 414,000 acres of land conceded became the property of individual peasants. Only 10 per cent of the distributed land was cultivated collectively.[14]

The initial reform was not very important and did not have any significant impact on the structure of the Southern system. It was promulgated mainly because of the occupation of the land and the peasant riots which had occurred in the period 1943–5.

The three main parties (PSI, PCI, DC) were, in principle, all in favour of land reform. This agreement was enshrined in the Constitution under Article 44:

> For the purpose of securing a rational exploitation of the soil and of establishing just social relationships, the law imposes obligations and restrictions on private property in land; it fixes limits to its extension according to the region and agrarian zones; it promotes and requires reclamation, the transformation of the latifondi, and the reconstruction of productive units; it aids the small- and medium-sized proprietor.

The implementation of this article, as that of many others, was not undertaken immediately. It was implemented to a limited extent only after 'the most revolutionary event in post-war Italian history' occurred: the struggle for the land of 1949–52.[15]

The PCI Southern strategy, an application of Togliatti's general alliance strategy, emphasized that the Communists were not against private ownership in land. Ruggero Grieco, the party's leading spokesman on the Southern question, wrote:

We do not find ourselves before the task of a socialist revolution, but rather the conquest of a popular advanced democracy . . . the middle group of peasants can be attracted into the orbit of politics in defence of their interests . . . sometimes occasional alliances are necessary.[16]

The new bloc was constituted in a negative way, that is, by the elimination of those social forces whose interests were considered antagonistic to what was judged socially necessary during the prevailing conjuncture. Thus Scoccimarro was able to declare, in 1945, that what was needed was:

. . . a system [of alliances] with the working class at its head . . . and alliance with the southern peasants first, with the petty bourgeoisie, the intellectuals and the progressive medium bourgeoisie, isolating the conservative and the upper bourgeoisie.[17]

A few months later, Fausto Gullo wrote:

We must protect the rights of the non-cultivating landowner, the professional or artisan, the employee who owns a modest plot of land. This group of small- and medium-sized bourgeois landowners, who are so much a part of Italian life especially in the Mezzogiorno . . . cannot be confused with the class of the large proprietors, merely because they own a piece of land.[18]

Although in the years 1945–7 the party did not carry out a real political battle in the South and limited itself to the enunciation of general strategic principles, it must not be assumed that there was no Communist presence in the South. The party was very active from the beginning. Togliatti had understood the danger of an excessive concentration of efforts in the Centre and in the North, where the PCI's strength lay, and had begun to form a team of young intellectual *meridionalisti* (or pro-Southerners). For their political and strategic orientation these *meridionalisti* could rely not only on the works of Gramsci and the other classics of Marxism, but also on the existing considerable corpus of theory on the Southern question – the work of three generations of scholars such as Fortunato, Nitti, Salvemini and Dorso.[19] They represented a particular trend within Italian Communism. They differentiated themselves from many of the Northern proletarian cadres for their greater emphasis on and belief in the absolute necessity for a wider alliance of workers with all the potentially progressive strata of the countryside. The *meridionalisti* were convinced that the resolution of the Southern question was the key to the Italian Revolution. One should avoid emphasizing these differences excessively: the recognition of the importance of the South was a common feature among all Italian communists. The difference between the two trends was one of emphasis.

The *meridionalisti* believed that the Communist strategy in the South should operate on two levels: at the governmental level and from below. This view was accepted by Togliatti.

> How are we to win the battle of reconstruction which is vital to the future of Italy? We see, at bottom, only one vital solution, which consists of coupling intervention from above to prevent the rebirth of the old reactionary cliques, with unremitting action from below to provide a new powerful and grandiose development of the national parties in the whole of the South. As in the whole of Italy, so in the South, indeed more so in the South than in the rest of Italy, the popular masses are today waiting and seeking with a new faith which is almost messianic, the leadership of the new parties and of the new men. Let us start, then, by solidly organizing these masses in political formations, as well as in larger economic organizations (trade unions, peasant leagues, etc.) and, supported by this force, we shall fight for the political rebirth of Southern Italy.[20]

The keynote of PCI strategy in the South in the years 1945–7 was political mobilization: the party's task consisted in an eventually successful attempt to become a real political force in the South.

The PCI had based its analysis on the assumption that only the broadest possible movement of people in the countryside would ensure the maximum possible gain in the given circumstances: an agrarian reform. Furthermore, it sought a permanent insertion in Southern politics not just as the party of the poor peasants, but as the party which most opposed the interests of the large landlords. Any critique must start with a consideration of the feasibility of such a twofold aim and of its desirability from the point of view of the transition to socialism.

The PCI strategy in the South was clearly consistent with its general strategy which sought to include the middle strata in a new 'directing' bloc. However, it has been admitted by Amendola that the attempt to organize the small-holding peasantry with the rural proletariat in the *Federterra*, instead of in an independent organization, had considerably limited the expansion of the PCI.[21] In 1947 the PCI was in a position of using its southern apparatus in a political direction. The Committees for the Land were inserted in the broader 'Movement for the Rebirth of the South'. The action of the Movement was twofold: on the one hand it organized demonstrations and congresses as well as regional assizes, on the other it prepared for the general elections of 1948.[22]

The features of the Movement were consistent with Togliatti's appeal for a 'constructive party'. From a long-term perspective, the Southern strategy was certainly a fruitful one. The PCI prepared the ground for the outburst of peasant unrest of the late forties and consolidated it in the fifties at a time when its working class basis in the North was being eroded. In the short-term, however, the two levels of the over-all strategy, the industrial and the agrarian, were not always consistent with each other: the agrarian reform, if carried out according to the Communist plan (a plan which ruled out collectivization) would of necessity strengthen the industrial area by providing a healthy agrarian sector, the indispensable condition for a rapid capitalist development.

Obviously, *in theory*, it would have been perfectly possible, at the same time, to expand the state sector by taking over the principal capitalist concentrations, but, *in practice*, this could not have been achieved: the Communist Party was not strong enough. The DC, moreover, quickly revealed itself as being dominated by strong conservative influences which were not willing to allow sweeping changes to occur and the Allied presence in Italy constituted a restraining political element — these factors were all powerful obstacles to any widespread nationalization. Furthermore, the immediate Italian problems of the post-war period — unemployment, inflation and speculation — could not be immediately tackled without a social truce on the economic front.

By September 1946 this situation was acknowledged by the Italian Communists. An editorial in *Rinascita* (certainly written by Togliatti himself) pointed out the dangers ahead in spite of the relative victories achieved by the abolition of the monarch and the promulgation of the Republic. The collapse of the Italian economy had created difficult conditions for the Italian masses in spite of the gains made in the political field:

> Thus, a real, not just an apparent, contradiction has appeared in the very body of Italian society — a contradiction between the political level and the economic level, and this, we must recognize it, is favour-able to the anti-democratic forces, to the forces of reaction.[23]

According to this view there were only two paths ahead: reconstruction along 'democratic lines' (that is, the 'new course') or 'a very deep crisis similar to the one which gave us fascism'.

So far it seems that the PCI's structural reforms in the industrial sector were based on nationalization and limited economic planning. However, the agreed objectives of the tripartite coalition which emerged from the Resistance did not include nationalization and economic planning, and, as we have seen, the Economic Conference of the PCI of August 1945 did not demand any nationalization or planning and hence did not put forward more 'advanced' demands than the CLN.[24] As Amendola wrote:

> The question of structural reforms was kept in the background as an element in the perspective of democratic development. The emphasis was entirely on the question of solving, immediately, the unemployment problem.[25]

The logic of the Communists seemed to be that, as there were important problems to be solved, the basic structural reforms could not be pushed forward and the focus of the immediate struggle had to be directed towards other burning issues. The reality of the situation was such that the party was not politically able to press forward the full programme of the Fifth Congress (which *did* include some nationalization and the beginning of economic planning). According to Amendola:

> Faced by the offensive launched by the monopolistic groups, which were playing the card of inflation, the working class attempted, through the action of the Communist Party and of the Socialist Party, to co-operate with the groups of the 'productive' sector of the bourgeoisie (such co-operation will be precarious and brief).[26]

The co-operation with the 'productive bourgeoisie' was undertaken as a response to the 'offensive of the monopolistic groups'. What is puzzling about this view is that monopolies existed in the productive sector as well, FIAT being the most glaring instance of an industrial monopoly.[27] The only way in which Amendola's statement can be interpreted is by supposing that, faced with the offensive of the monopolists, the party attempted to split them by driving a wedge between the 'productive' monopolies on the one hand and the big finance capital and agrarian monopolists on the other.

This policy was pursued particularly after the abolition of the monarchy and the elections for the Constituent Assembly (2 June 1946). As Amendola wrote:

> . . . the policy of the new course was considered to be a policy of alliance between the working class and the productive bourgeoisie for the reconstruction of the country. It developed, in particular, after 2 June, within the scope of the tripartite alliance between the Communist Party, the Socialist Party and the Christian Democratic Party, in order to accelerate industrial recovery . . .[28]

By 1947 the attempt to split the monopolist–agrarian bloc through an alliance with the productive bourgeoisie had failed, for the DC had succeeded in representing and uniting the entire spectrum of capitalist and agrarian interests.

To initiate in 1945–6 a collaboration with the productive bourgeoisie meant not solely the maintenance of the alliance with the DC, but the jettisoning of much of the industrial aspect of the PCI structural reforms.

In the post-war context, 'structural reforms' were understood to be the means by which the elimination of the socio-economic roots of fascism could be carried out. As such they were understood not as a partial structural correction of capitalism but as a blow inflicted at the core of the adversary's defence. In so far as this line involved partial nationalization of the capitalist economy, it scored some relative successes in Italy with the establishment of ENI (the state oil company) and the reorganization of IRI (the state holding company: Institute for Industrial Reconstruction).[29]

In the light of the pressures existing for a Communist compromise in the industrial sector, we have now the background for an analysis of Communist economic policy. A starting-point is provided by Rodano's important article in *Rinascita* of October 1946.[30]

Following Togliatti, Rodano put forward the view that, after 2 June, the economy had become the primary centre of attention. The 'democratic parties' had to carry out, at the economic level, the struggle which, at the political level, had found a satisfactory development in the Republic and the Constitution. Rodano pointed out that until then private initiative had been left entirely free by the government, or at least by those 'liberalistic' elements in it who, 'for particular reasons of political contingency' had dominated the key positions of the Italian economy. The private sector, forced to resort to self-financing (with hard currency), was obliged to maximize exports without any regard to the question of exchange rates. This caused a restriction of internal supply with a consequent inflationary spiral which, in turn, generated a deterioration in the terms of trade. In the short run the inflationary spiral could help the private sector for it enabled it to finance more easily its production cycles and pay back previous loans with the present inflated currency. This trend, wrote Rodano, was conducting the nation towards an enormous general economic imbalance and a pronounced tendency to inflation. Against the 'neo-liberal' conception of economic 'non-management', the 'new course' strategy was formulated thus:

. . . the content of the New Course . . . can only be defined with reference to the fundamental data of the situation which it proposes to alter in a progressive direction. The New Course is the living antithesis to the liberalistic economic policy and it is the only policy which could be concretely conducted in 1946 in Italy . . . the New Course is based, of necessity, on one essential foundation. It consists in the struggle to restore between the State and the private sector normal modern relations absolutely necessary in the exceptional conjuncture of the post-war period; this must be done by recognizing that the State has had, historically, and particularly in Italy, a pre-eminent function in production and that private enterprise is inadequate, in every sector, to the enormous tasks of reconstruction . . .[31]

This strategy was partly based on the view that whereas 'classical liberalism' was in agreement with the principle of state intervention, the neo-liberals, who were then controlling the economy, conceived the role of the State in an extreme *laissez-faire* manner. It is relevant to note at this point that, historically, Italian economic thought was far more influenced by the Bismarkian model of capitalist development (where the State actively intervenes) than by the concepts of economic liberalism which had prevailed in England. Once more the Communists would emphasize and appropriate the traditions of the Risorgimento.[32]

According to Rodano, it was the task of the State to use 'its repressive machinery' in order to hit at speculation by fiscal means and by exchange control and, also, a high wages policy would have to be entertained in order to increase purchasing power. Fiscal policy would have to be used to ensure that savings destined to speculative or unproductive usage could not be generated in order to provide the State with the necessary funds for the financing of private enterprise. Such fiscal policy would have to be coupled with a policy of income redistribution. Rodano stated that, in these circumstances and given the parameters within which the Communist strategy had to be articulated, any aspiration towards planning would be unrealistic. Not planning, but 'economic programming' was to be the path of government action.[33]

If, and only if, this strategy was to be adopted by the government, wrote Rodano, then a truce on the wages front could be considered by the working class. In fact the Communists (and the CGIL) did agree to such a truce.[34] The truce could be considered to be the compromise which the working class, through its political representatives, offered to the productive sector of the bourgeoisie.

In other words, the PCI strategy was based on a compromise with the 'productive' sector of the bourgeoisie, but, for propaganda reasons, it was not possible for the PCI to define such strategy openly. An editorial in *Rinascita*, undoubtedly inspired by Togliatti, talked of compromise for the first time and in an explicit manner:

> It was evident — and also, we must recognize it, normal — that the Italian conservatives could adhere to the policies of the most advanced sectors of the anti-fascist bloc only with solid guarantees. The Italian conservatives had to assure themselves that the political liquidation of fascism, the achievement of political conditions for a normal democratic development, did not coincide with revolutionary or even profound changes in the Italian economic structure. Hence all the conditions were present within the anti-fascist coalition for a compromise between its principal elements.
>
> The nature of this compromise could only be based on the following points: renunciation of a revolutionary economic programme; the direction of economic life (and hence of financial renewal and of the reconstruction) to be left in the hands of conservative elements; the undertaking of all parties to resolve all fundamental political questions; defence, at the trade union level, from the threateningly anti-social and anti-national consequences of a conservative economic policy which would base itself on out-and-out *laissez-faire*; hence freedom of trade union action, minimal reforms in the agrarian field and, at the same time, development of popular initiative in order to take care of the most immediate demands and to meet the more pressing needs of the masses . . .
>
> The compromise left the door open for two perspectives: that of the democratization of the country as a whole in a way which would allow the fulfilment of fundamental political objectives, and that of the democratization of the Italian conservatives themselves as a result of their understanding of the real conditions of economic life and political struggle in Italy. The compromise of the anti-fascist front was the possibility of a grand pledge, guaranteed by the presumed intelligence of the Italian conservatives. Unfortunately we must recognize that, today, never has such a pledge had such a bad guarantee.[35]

However bad the guarantee, the idea of a compromise was never repudiated by the PCI nor could it have been for it believed that no real alternative existed.

If the 'economic compromise' was relatively unsuccessful, the constitutional compromise was marked by a series of results which the PCI considered to be more than satisfactory. This compromise centred on the establishment of the Republican regime and on the adoption by the Constituent Assembly of a democratic constitution. The rejection of the monarchy was of fundamental importance because it signified a definitive break with an institution which had traditionally been the rallying point of conservative opinion; it eliminated another element of the State machinery which had supported fascism and it destroyed an ideological symbol of national unity which could not have been in any way used as a rallying element by the PCI.

The referendum on the monarchy, held on 2 June 1946, saw the narrow victory of the Republic: 12.7 million votes for and 10.7 million votes against. In the eyes of many Communists this victory constituted the most important and tangible achievement of the post-Resistance period. To a certain extent it confirmed the correctness of the decision to postpone the 'institutional question'.

The fact that the Republic won by a few percentage points demonstrated that, although the Communist Party had reached a position of enormous influence in the country, large masses of people had nevertheless been left untouched by the 'purifying' influence of the Resistance and were ready to call back the royal family which had, for twenty years, collaborated with fascism. It was significant that a large proportion of the monarchist vote came from those Southern regions which had not undergone the experience of the Resistance. This tends to support the communist assertion that a civil war would have split the country and would have undone the work of the Risorgimento.

The Republic was achieved essentially thanks to the votes of the left. However, it is without doubt that at least two million Christian Democrats voted against the monarchy while six million voted for it. Togliatti saw in these two million votes the embodiment of what was later referred to as the 'anima popolare' (popular spirit) of the DC as opposed to its 'conservative soul'. With these two million votes the PCI thought it had a foothold in the enemy camp, an instrument which it hoped to use to force the DC to continue with the tripartite coalition government.

With this strategy in mind, the Italian Communists began to prepare themselves for the work of the Constituent Assembly, the elected body which was to give Italy its first republican constitution.

Togliatti presented his conception of what a constitution should include at the First Sub-Committee of the Constituent Assembly with a report entitled 'Principles of Social Relations'.[36] Togliatti wanted the inclusion in the new constitution of principles regulating economic life alongside the constitutional guarantees of traditional rights. He saw the constitution as programmatic, and not one which embodied what had already taken place. What Togliatti wanted was a constitution which would enshrine the future right of the Communists to call for a rapid transformation of the economic system within a constitutional framework. The constitution, he declared, had to be a compromise, the confluence of two ideological currents: the human and social 'solidaristic' views of the Socialists and the Communists with the 'solidaristic' view of the Christian Democrats.[37] This compromise was incorporated in the famous Article 7 with which the Lateran Pacts between the Vatican and the fascist regime were endorsed and written into the constitution.

Article 7 was passed, thanks to the Communists. The motion was carried by 350 votes to 149, the Socialists and the Republicans voting against. If the 104 Communists had voted against, Article 7 would have been defeated by 253 to 246 votes.

A whole historiographic tradition has evolved from the study of this question. In the view of many, Togliatti's decision is to be considered as a total reversal of established Communist policies on the question of the Church and was entirely determined by the PCI intention to remain in the government. However, as an interesting and careful article by H. S. Broadhead shows conclusively, the Communist decision to vote in favour of Article 7

> was by no means as unpredictable, or out of character as has often been supposed. To see the PCI decision as a cynical departure from a firmly established anti-clerical tradition is to overlook Togliatti's long and consistent opposition to that tradition and underestimate his ability to have his way in the policy-making councils of the party. Attempts to explain that decision have been based on a stereotype of correct Communist behaviour which has never been true of the PCI, at any rate at the official level.[38]

Gramsci himself had written:

> In Italy, in Rome, there is the Vatican, there is the Pope: the Liberal state has had to come to terms with the spiritual power of the Church and the workers' state will have to do likewise.[39]

The PCI position was, to put it schematically, that anti-clericalism was a bourgeois tactic to divide the workers, and it was an attempt to isolate the Socialists and the Communists from the peasant masses.

In a speech to the Constituent Assembly Togliatti insisted on the continuity of the Communist perspective on the question of the relations between Church and State. After reminding his audience of Gramsci's position on the matter and of the declaration made by the PCI during its Fifth Congress, he proceeded to explain that the Italian Communists considered that the constitution had to guarantee freedom of worship, that the solution to the Vatican question was to be considered definitive (that is, that the Lateran Pacts had solved it once and for all) and that the Concordat was a bilateral treaty which could be reviewed only after bilateral consultations with the Church.[40] It was obvious that the Communists were not happy with the inclusion of the Concordat in the constitution, but Togliatti was aware of the costs of voting against Article 7: De Gasperi, the DC leader, had already made it clear that, if the article was not accepted, he would try to obtain a national referendum and this could re-open the institutional question. Furthermore, a referendum would have split the country along religious lines and would have jeopardized the entire Communist strategy. Togliatti made a direct reference to it when he recalled the past successes scored by the anti-fascist coalition, successes which seemed to have sanctioned a religious peace. He added:

> Not only that, but we reached a great achievement, a great victory, unity in the trade union front, when we reached a pact of trade union unity among the great traditional currents of the Italian labour movement: the Communist, the Socialist and the Catholic.[41]

It is evident how the Vatican question was tackled in complete consistency with the established strategy. It can also be said that

> Togliatti saw in the uncertain fate of the Christian Democrats' proposal to include the Lateran Pacts in the constitution the opportunity he so badly needed to demonstrate conclusively that the PCI was not hostile to religion and the Church. By delivering the PCI's vote to the Christian Democrats, he would ensure the passage of their proposal, and thus demonstrate beyond all reasonable doubts that Catholics had nothing to fear from the PCI.[42]

If Togliatti's move was for the short-term, then it obviously did not pay off, for the Communists were expelled from the government two months later. It was from outside the government and in an atmosphere of impending Cold War that the Communists prepared themselves for the battle on the remaining sections of the constitution.

This put the Communists in a difficult position: on the one hand there was a need to attack the government with the maximum possible vigour, particularly in view of the elections of 1947; on the other hand they had to contain this opposition within certain limits in order not to jeopardize the Constituent Assembly by provoking a political crisis which might have endangered the gains of the Resistance, that is, the

Republic and a progressive constitution.[43] There were several important instances of compromise between the two main streams in the Assembly, the PCI–PSI and the DC. One of these was the change of Article 1 from the communist-supported 'Italy is a workers' republic' to the present, vague 'Italy is a democratic republic founded on labour'.[44] The right to strike was limited thus: 'The right to strike may be exercised within the framework of the laws regulating it', therefore making possible numerous restrictions on it. Similarly, freedom of private enterprise was guaranteed 'as long as it does not conflict with social utility'. Presumably it could be constitutional to eliminate private property on grounds of social utility.[45] In the words of Pietro Calamandrei: 'To compensate the left-wing parties for their failure to effect a revolution, the right-wing forces did not oppose the inclusion in the constitution of the promise of a revolution'.[46] The signatories of the constitution were De Gasperi, the Communist leader Terracini, who was President of the Constituent Assembly, and De Nicola, a Christian Democrat, who was the provisional President of the Republic. This is symbolic of the compromise the constitution represented, for De Nicola was an important representative of the pre-fascist political class and had himself been a temporary supporter of fascism.[47]

Notes

1. P. Togliatti, 'Ceto medio e Emilia rossa' in *OS*, pp. 464–5.
2. P. Togliatti, *Il Partito Comunista Italiano*, Rome, 1971, p. 95.
3. P. Togliatti, 'Intervento al Convegno economico del Partito comunista italiano. 23 agosto 1945' in L. Barca, F. Botta and A. Zevi *I comunisti e l'economia italiana 1944–1974*, Bari, 1975, pp. 68–72.
4. Towards the end of 1955 Togliatti would give the following justification for the moderation of the PCI: 'In practice, our first actions had to be limited ones not so much because of the size of material disasters, but because of the presence of the Anglo-American authorities and for the positions these were defending with tenacity and harshness . . . In the initial stages until the beginning of the debates in the Constituent Assembly, it was practically impossible, unless one was prepared to enter into open conflict with the occupying powers to promote economic policies which tended to prepare, even as a distant goal, the elimination of the old capitalist groups from their positions of power', in 'Per un giudizio equanime sull'opera di Alcide De Gasperi' in *Momenti della storia d'Italia*, Rome, 1974, pp. 198–9.
5. 'Risoluzione approvata al V Congresso del PCI' in L. Barca, F. Botta and A. Zevi, op. cit., p. 81.
6. C. Pillon, *I comunisti e il sindacato*, Milan, 1972, p. 358.
7. Bianca Salvati, 'The Rebirth of Italian Trade Unionsm, 1943–1954' in S. J. Woolf (ed.), *The Rebirth of Italy 1943–1950*, London, 1972, p. 186.
8. See Adolfo Pepe, 'La CGIL dalla ricostituzione alla scissione (1944–1948)' in *Storia Contemporanea*, No. 4, December 1974, p. 615.
9. Equal weight was given to the three tendencies irrespective of their actual

relative strength. The executive committee was made up of fifteen members, five Catholics, five Socialists and five Communists, even though at the First Congress of the CGIL, the PCI 'tendency' controlled 40 per cent of the delegates, the PSI 30 per cent and the DC 15 per cent. These political tendencies were officially recognized through the designation of three General Secretaries: Di Vittorio (PCI), Grandi (DC) and Lizzardi (PSI)..

10. A. Pepe, op. cit., p. 598.
11. Extracts of the 1946 party programme are quoted in P. Togliatti, *Il partito comunista italiano*, Rome, 1971, pp. 91–5.
12. S. Tarrow, *Peasant Communism in Southern Italy*, New Haven, 1967, p. 281.
13. Ibid., p. 250.
14. Ibid., p. 282. As Tarrow points out: 'In effect, the government merely legitimized occupations already made', p. 279.
15. Ibid., p. 270.
16. R. Grieco, *I communisti e le lotte per la riforma agraria*, Rome, 1949, pp. 16-17; also quoted in Tarrow, op. cit., p. 255.
17. M. Scoccimarro, 'Dottrina marxista e politica comunista', *Rinascita*, Vol. 2, No. 5/6, May–June 1945.
18. F. Gullo, 'Suggerimenti per una riforma agraria', *Rinascita*, Vol. 2, No. 12, December 1945; also quoted in Tarrow, op. cit., p. 260.
19. P. A. Allum, *Politics and Society in Post-war Naples*, Cambridge, 1973, pp. 77–8.
20. Togliatti in *Rinascita*, Vol. 1, No. 1, June 1944, p. 16, quoted in P. A. Allum, 'The South and National Politics' in S. J. Woolf, op. cit., pp. 100–1.
21. G. Amendola, *Lotta di classe e sviluppo economico dopo la Liberazione*, Rome, 1962, pp. 45–6. The Federterra was the Communist organization for agricultural labourers; it later became the Peasants' Alliance.
22. P. A. Allum, 'The South . . .', op. cit., p. 117 and Tarrow, op. cit., p. 285.
23. 'Nuovo Corso' in *Rinascita*, Vol. 3, No. 9, September 1946.
24. The Resistance programme was, of course, very vague. It talked in terms of restructuring the economy in an anti-fascist direction, but gave no clear guidance. The PCI, during the Resistance, had not advanced a concrete programme of specific reforms. See L. Basso, 'Il rapporto tra rivoluzione democratica e rivoluzione socialista nella Resistenza', *Critica Marxista*, No. 3, July–Aug. 1965, p. 18.
25. G. Amendola, *Lotta di classe* . . ., op. cit., p. 58.
26. Ibid., p. 43.
27. For an analysis of the PCI policies and activities in relation to FIAT see: L. Lanzardo, *Classe operaia e partito comunista alla FIAT: La strategia della collaborazione, 1945-1949*, Turin, 1971.
28. G. Amendola, *Lotta di classe* . . ., op. cit., p. 37.
29. L. Cafagna, 'Note in margine alla "Ricostruzione" ', *Giovane Critica*, No. 37, summer 1973, p. 7.
30. Franco Rodano, 'Il "nuovo corso" ', *Rinascita*, No. 10, October 1946. A considerable weight should be given to Rodano's article even though it was published as part of an ongoing debate in *Rinascita* and not as an official text. Rodano was one of the closest advisers of Togliatti. His contribution to the debate should be considered as having been directly inspired by Togliatti himself.
31. Ibid.
32. The liberal economic historian G. Hildebrand wrote that the chief reason for the imbalance between the North and the South was due to the lack of state intervention: 'failing drastic intervention by the state, the South was doomed economically from the start' (*Growth and Structure of the Economy of Modern Italy*, Cambridge, Mass., 1965, p. 281). However, the fact is that the State *did* intervene but in a way which pre-empted any development of southern industry

(by abolishing internal tariffs after unification) and ruined southern agriculture (by adopting protective barriers which deprived the South of its export market), see P. Saraceno, 'La mancata unificazione economica a cent'anni dall'unificazione italiana' in *L'economia italiana dal 1861 al 1961*, Milan, 1961.

33. The semantic difference between 'planning' and 'programming' had not been clearly established (in that period) by the Italian Communists. From Rodano's article, it emerges that 'planning' is to be used in the sense of socialist planning, whereas 'programming' is similar to what is now called 'indicative' planning.

34. B. Salvati, 'The Rebirth of Italian Trade Unionism, 1943–1954' in S. J. Woolf (ed.), *The Rebirth of Italy 1943–1950*, London, 1972, p. 197.

35. 'La politica di Corbino' in *Rinascita*, No. 8, August 1946.

36. P. Togliatti, 'Principi dei rapporti sociali', in *Rinascita*, Vol. 3, No. 9, September 1946.

37. P. Togliatti, 'Per una Costituzione democratica e progressive' (speech to the Constituent Assembly of 11 March 1947) in *La via italiana al socialismo*, p. 68.

38. H. S. Broadhead, 'Togliatti and the Church 1921–1948', in *The Australian Journal of Politics and History*, Vol. XVIII, No. 1, April 1972, p. 77.

39. A. Gramsci, *L'Ordine Nuovo*, 20 March 1920, quoted in Broadhead, op. cit., p. 79.

40. P. Togliatti, 'Sui rapporti tra la Chiesa e lo Stato' (speech to the Constituent Assembly on 25 March 1947), in *La via italiana al socialismo*, p. 94.

41. Ibid., p. 101.

42. H. S. Broadhead, op. cit., p. 89.

43. G. Amendola, 'Il PCI all'opposizione. La lotta contro lo scelbismo' in AA.VV, *Problemi di Storia del PCI*, Rome, 1971, p. 113.

44. See P. Vercellone, 'The Italian Constitution of 1947–1948' in S. J. Woolf (ed.), *The Rebirth of Italy 1943–50*, p. 124. The humorous folklore version of Art. 1 is 'Italy is a democratic republic founded on promissory notes'.

45. Ibid., pp. 125–6.

46. Ibid., p. 124.

47. De Nicola, on being offered a place in the fascist national list of 1924, sent a cable to Mussolini declaring: 'The words with which Your Excellency informs me of the inclusion of my name in the National List have a meaning which extends far beyond my person because they recall the contribution of the elective assembly to the vast work of reform carried out by the government which you lead.' Quoted in P. A. Allum, *Politics and Society in Post-war Naples*, Cambridge, 1973, p. 73.

4   The End of the Tripartite Coalition

The difficulties which beset the tripartite coalition on the economic and social front, far from uniting it, tended to exacerbate the relations between the left (in this period the PSI and the PCI were substantially united on major issues) and the DC. A number of events led to the final dissolution of the coalition and opened a new period in post-war Italian history. We shall make no attempt to write the history of this crisis but will simply list the principal contributing factors.

The elections of 1946 for the Constituent Assembly had shown that the largest Italian party was the DC, but the administrative elections held in November 1946 revealed two significant trends: the constant increase of the PCI at the expense of the PSI but with an over-all increase for the left on the one hand, and, on the other, the diminution of the DC votes and the growth of a right-wing party (L'Uomo Qualunque). This result was taken by DC leaders as a warning: they interpreted it as a signal that their position slightly to the left of centre had left a void on their right, a void which any right-wing party, even one as deprived of ideas as L'Uomo Qualunque, could easily fill.

A second factor which should be mentioned is the position of the Church. On 22 December 1946, Pius XII, in a famous speech in St. Peter's which can be considered as a declaration of war against the left-wing parties, condemned those 'who deny God, who profane the divine and who worship the senses'. He concluded with an invitation to choose sides: 'Either with Christ or against Christ; either with His Church or against His Church.'[1]

This position of the Church reflected the end of an international alliance which had not only been a matter of governments and ruling groups but one which had seen, among others, Communists and Christians fighting side by side. Now that the Cold War was beginning, the Church called once more for a crusade against what it considered its historical enemy: 'materialistic Communism'.

De Gasperi too had understood early on that his party had to choose the 'right side' and in Italy this could only have been the American side. In 1946 he confided to an envoy of the American Treasury, Henry Tasca, then in Italy to collect 'economic data', that:

Once peace was signed . . . there would have to be a showdown out of which there would develop a general crisis, the main purpose of which would be to defeat definitively the Communists . . . [De Gasperi] felt there was no possibility of reaching any viable long-term agreement with the Communist Party in Italy.[2]

From the last days of 1946 until the beginning of 1947, De Gasperi was in Washington, allegedly to negotiate economic aid for Italy. Recent documentation confirms what had always been suspected. The negotiation between De Gasperi and the US government took the form of a discussion on the modalities for the splitting up of the coalition government, the expulsion of the left and the adoption of an intransigent anti-communist posture.[3]

De Gasperi was no 'American tool'. At the time American intelligence services were still in their infancy. Few people in Washington knew anything about Italian politics. De Gasperi did not go to the USA to receive orders but to inform them of the sort of pressures he required, of their timing and intensity.[4] He could not expel the left immediately. There were two important issues to be settled first: the signing of the peace treaty and the passing of Article 7 in the Constituent Assembly. It was necessary to involve the PCI in these two events.

While De Gasperi was in the USA, the Socialist Party split and an anti-communist minority, led by Giuseppe Saragat, formed what is now known as the Italian Social Democratic Party. The PCI and the PSI remained in the government although their influence had been considerably reduced: they lost the important ministries of Finance (Scoccimarro) and of Foreign Affairs (Nenni). In May 1947, after the signing of the peace treaty and the passing of Article 7, they were definitively expelled. The economy was now solidly in the hands of the main political representatives of the 'fourth party' (the party of money and economic power): De Gasperi had already provided a justification for his eventual action when he gave his Council of Ministers what amounted to a lecture in crude Marxism:

Votes are not everything . . . [because] the positions of command in such a serious economic moment are in the hands neither of the electorate nor of the government . . . It is not our millions of voters who can give the State the thousands of millions and the economic power necessary for tackling the situation. Apart from our parties, there is in Italy a fourth party which may not have many supporters but which is capable of paralysing all our efforts by organizing the sabotaging of loans and the flight of capital, price rises and defamatory campaigns. Experience has convinced me that it is not possible to govern Italy today without inviting into the new Government the representatives of this fourth party, the party of those who have money and economic power.[5]

Togliatti, of course, had protested loudly, proposing once more a compromise and recalling the moderation exhibited by the parties of the left and by the working class. In a speech to the Constituent Assembly on 19 February 1947 (hence a few months before the break with the DC) he declared:

In the last years no political strike has taken place in Italy . . . This is a country where the unions have signed a wage truce, a pact which is unique in the history of the trade union movement, because it establishes a maximum wage, not a minimum one . . . This is the striking and absurd feature of the economic situation in which we live: it is the working class and the unions which are giving the best example and taking the necessary steps to preserve the discipline of production, order and social peace.[6]

And again in June 1947, after the break with the DC, he said:

The workers . . . have moderated their action, they have restrained it, they have contained it within certain necessary limits in order not to be an obstacle to the work of the reconstruction. They have accepted the wage truce, that is the suspension of wage rises without there being a corresponding suspension of price rises. Our Communist and Socialist workers will see in the government the representatives of the rich, of the big capitalists such as Pirelli; they will not see men they can trust. It is obvious that they will have no trust in the government, or, at the very least, that such trust will be greatly reduced. This is what worries us most.[7]

The fundamental problem of 1945-7 from the point of view of the strategy of the PCI is that the party had never had the possibility of beginning a real economic policy of structural reforms and had not even had the possibility of initiating a Southern policy.[8] The compromise of the CLN parties involved the postponement of all these questions to the period following the creation of the Constitution.

The year 1947-8 can thus be considered a real turning-point in the history of the strategy of the PCI. The crisis which ensued dashed the hopes the PCI had for a permanent presence in the government and for conquering a power base at the centre of the political structure. Did the PCI expect that it would not be able to hold on to power?

The most likely hypothesis is that, quite simply, Togliatti hoped that the PCI would be able to remain in the government, but this did not inhibit him from thinking about the alternative of opposition. The PCI, therefore, tried to be prepared for both eventualities and to a certain extent it succeeded. The party was able to withstand the consequences of its eviction from power. The passage to opposition did not entail, in principle, any basic changes in strategy: the party had already given up the Kautskyist tradition of building one's strength and waiting for the crisis. Whether in the government or outside it, the party could continue with its 'constructive' policies and its attempts to influence the political life of the country in order to achieve some degree of hegemony. The 'Italian road to socialism', as formulated by Togliatti in the years 1943–7, did not necessarily entail participation in the government. Yet, as we shall see, it was *in principle* abandoned after 1947 and was re-adopted (officially) only after the Twentieth Congress of the CPSU. *In practice*, the constructive attitude was not abandoned although it became more difficult to implement. Both the break of 1947 and the changes in the PCI's strategy were largely determined by external events.

The new situation was not restricted to Italy. In France and in Belgium too the Communists were ousted from the government. At the international level the anti-fascist coalition was dissolved and the Cold War began.

A new international conjuncture was appearing and the CPSU prepared for another strategy. This was unveiled at the meeting of the Communist Parties of September 1947 in Szklarska Poreda (Poland) where the Cominform was created. Present at the meeting were the representatives of all East European Communist Parties (including the CPSU) and the representatives of the PCF and the PCI. Zhdanov, in his report, analysed the new international conjuncture in terms of the possibility of an impending world war.[9]

The new situation required a tightening in the ranks of the international communist movement. It meant that the policies based on the international anti-fascist alliance had to be changed. One of the implications of this new direction was that the concept of national roads had to be abandoned. Zhdanov declared:

But the present position of the Communist Parties has its shortcomings. Some comrades understood the dissolution of the Comintern to imply the elimination of all ties, of all contracts between the fraternal Communist Parties. But experience has shown that such mutual isolation of the Communist Parties is wrong, harmful and, in point of fact, unnatural . . .[10]

After Zhdanov's report, the other delegates gave an analysis of the situation in their respective countries. The PCI was represented by Luigi Longo and Eugenio Reale. Togliatti had decided not to go, probably suspecting that his party would be the object of attacks and criticisms.

Kardelj of the Yugoslav CP accused the French and Italian parties of 'opportunism and parliamentarism'.[11] He added that Togliatti had too many illusions about De Gasperi and that during the Resistance he had not been able to score the successes of the Yugoslavs.[12] The Hungarian Farkes, commenting on Longo's statement that a collaboration with De Gasperi was the only alternative said: 'this is parliamentary cretinism'.[13]

Cominform criticism of the PCI centred on one question: the inability of the Italian Communists to remain in the coalition government. Implicit in the whole attack was an unfair comparison between the performance of the Communist Parties in Eastern Europe and that of the PCF and the PCI. The underlying assumption was that the international circumstances which had favoured the Eastern European Communist Parties and played against the French and Italian ones were not determinant. What was criticized was not, therefore, the failure to lead a socialist insurrection after the Resistance, but the inability to follow the Eastern European model of 'people's democracies', at that time still considered transitional formations similar to Togliatti's concept of progressive democracy. The peculiarities of the 'Italian road' were overlooked and an abstract model was thrust upon the Italian Communists.

In this sense the establishment of the Cominform put a temporary end to the explicit pursuit of a truly national road. In the years 1947–53 the Italian Communists would have to face the problem of attempting to carry out their original strategy while maintaining some sort of international unity, a unity which entailed close ties with Moscow.

The impact of the Cominform strategy was clearly felt at the Sixth Congress of the PCI held in Milan in January 1948. Zhdanov's report was included in the fundamental documents for the preparation of the Congress.[14] The DC was now accused of having become a tool of US imperialism and of having abandoned the path of social reformism. Against the new 'reactionary' front organized by the DC and its Liberal and Social Democratic allies (Saragat), a new front had to be created: an electoral alliance between the PCI and the PSI, the Popular Democratic Front.[15] The Congress also heralded the emergence of what may be called the Zhadov–Togliatti line, a strategy which was internally contradictory. In practice it meant an attempt to continue the development of the principles laid down in the first formulations of the 'Italian road'; in theory it was a return to a hard line of intransigent opposition. The emphasis was on the electoral battle which was approaching and which was to take place on 18 April 1948.

Once more international events were to have a massive impact on Italian affairs and, consequently, on the strategy of the PCI. The Prague events of February 1948 culminating in the communist seizure of power put the PCI in an embarrassing position: would the PCI do what the Czech CP did? Would they neutralize the army and the police to ensure the success of the Popular Democratic Front? But all the PCI could do was to prepare for the general election. The climate was far from being calm. The Church intervened heavily in the campaign, and presented the choice facing the electorate as one between Christianity and Communist barbarism.[16] The DC played on the fear of the middle classes and the peasantry and presented itself as the only party which would be able to guarantee social peace and the reconstruction of the country within a free and democratic system. The USA publicly declared '. . . if the Communists should win . . . there would be no further question of assistance from the United States'.[17]

In spite of the background to the elections, the PCI was confident of victory but the attitude of some of its supporters, characterized by the repetition of a quasi-threatening 'When we win you will see!', did not help the results.[18] The middle strata had been presented by the left with the alternative that either there would be a left-wing government which would save Italy from the inevitable economic catastrophe or the DC with US protection would establish a repressive regime which sooner or later would take Italy into another war.[19] But on 18 April 1948 the middle strata, with the exception of the rural middle strata of the 'red belt' (Emilia, Tuscany and Umbria), voted against the Front. The results meant a total defeat for the left: the DC gained 4 million votes and obtained 48 per cent of the votes (it had 8 million votes in 1946 or 35.2 per cent). The PCI–PSI alliance dropped from 40 per cent to 31 per cent; part of this 10 per cent drop can be accounted for by the 7 per cent collected by Saragat's Social Democrats. The DC had now an absolute majority in the House of Deputies. The repercussions were immediate: at the PSI Congress of 1948 the left (Nenni, Basso and Morandi) was defeated and replaced by a centrist leadership. The Popular Democratic Front as a permanent organization was dissolved by the PSI (but the pact of action with the PCI was maintained) but temporarily kept in the South. In the South, in fact, the left strategy paid off: the Front improved its position on 1946.[20]

The general election of 18 April dashed all the hopes the Communists had of fulfilling their claim of being a government party. When they had been expelled from the ruling coalition in 1947, they had thought that they might re-conquer power by gaining a substantial majority with their socialist allies.[21] Now they seemed to be definitively condemned to opposition. What was needed now was a strategy sufficiently subtle and flexible to direct the party along a long-term oppositional path.

The PCI was not able to provide an unambiguous answer. After 1948 it continued with its strategy of broad alliances, constructive policies, intermediate goals and gradual development towards a position favourable to socialism. This strategy was adapted to its new role of opposition party and to the external constraints imposed by the Cold War and the creation of the Cominform. This modified strategy had no real alternatives, for once the PCI had decided that there were no objective conditions for a head-on collision with the State, it had no choice but to carry on with the strategy which had been so successful during the Resistance.

After the elections of 1948, we see the Italian Communists adopting a firmer posture without jettisoning the foundations of the strategy. This new posture was only partly determined by the Cominform. Having been mercilessly attacked by a Christian Democratic Party which had opted for confrontation with the Communists and an alliance with the USA, the PCI had little choice but to abandon temporarily any hope of compromise with the Catholic party. Yet this compromise constituted the keystone of the alliance system of the 'Italian road'.

The new Communist posture was firm, but solidly located within a defensive perspective: 1948 had obviously been a set-back for workers' parties and a new defensive phase was opening.

This position was not going to be altered even by the fateful event which occurred on 14 July. As Togliatti was leaving Parliament, a man, Antonio Pallante, fired four shots at him, seriously injuring him. The reaction in the country as a whole was prompt: an immediate and spontaneous general strike. Factories were taken over, local branches of government parties were attacked, transport was interrupted and roads were blocked. At FIAT the entire board of directors was locked up by the workers. The attempt on Togliatti's life had taken place at 11.40 a.m.; by 1.30 p.m. Milan was entirely paralysed by the workers.[22]

The leadership of the PCI was forced to take quick decisions. They knew, however, that the tide had already turned against them on 18 April. Secchia, years later, recalled these events:

> From the first moment Longo and I were very clear about what had to be done: to control the movement, not to break with legality. We talked about it with Nilde Jotti in the corridors of the hospital while they were operating on Togliatti. I said 'we must control the movement'.

'Yes' said Jotti, 'unless he dies.' I answered, 'no, even if he dies we cannot change our position. If an insurrection is a mistake, it will be a mistake whatever the result of the operation.'[23]

However, it is obvious now that the alternative was not Secchia's simplistic one between a socialist insurrection and a policy of maintaining the status quo.[24] The PCI could have tried to guide the workers' movement from a spontaneous expression of protest to a political direction culminating with demands for the immediate implementation of certain reforms or for new elections, or for the return of the PCI to the government. Undoubtedly the movement took the party by surprise and the results of the elections had certainly shattered the confidence of the party's leadership. The attempt on Togliatti's life and the consequent general strike had taken place when the party was undergoing a partial re-thinking of its strategy and at a time when it had no plan of how to deal with rapidly changing events.

Not long after the events Secchia wrote:

In the history of the Italian labour movement one had never seen such a spontaneous, massive and large general strike such as the one of 14–16 July 1948. One must bear in mind the fact that the general strike of 14 July had not been planned and had not been preceded by any organizational work . . . [The party] did not call for an insurrectional strike, did not invite the citizenry to arm itself and disarm the enemy, did not call for the occupation of public buildings, railways, radio, telephone exchange, army barracks, landing fields, etc.[25]

The fact that Secchia, considered a hardliner, an 'organizational insurrectionist', did not attempt to pursue a radical course seems to indicate that the leadership group of the party stood united on its estimate of the situation as a clearly unfavourable one for any but a defensive strategy.

The most immediate consequence of the general strike was the definitive break-up of the CGIL. The Social Democrats had already broken away from it and formed what later became known as the Unione Italiana del Lavoro (UIL). Now the Catholic union leaders left the Communist-dominated CGIL and formed the Confederazione Italiana dei Sindacati dei Lavoratori (CISL).[26] Thus the remaining basis for PCI unity with the Catholic workers was eliminated. The DC had split the labour movement and had driven a wedge between itself and the Communist Party thereby choosing its only alternative strategy: the isolation of Communism.

An important analysis of the events of 1948 can be found in an unsigned editorial in *Rinascita*, 'Sulla nostra politica'.[27] The author was certainly

Togliatti himself. The editorial pointed out that since June 1947 (expulsion of the PCI from the government) the leadership of the party had fully realized that a new period had opened up, a period which would be 'neither short nor easy'. However, and this was the important point, there was a gap between the slogan promulgated by the leadership and the way in which these slogans were carried out by the rank and file. This was due to the fact that:

. . . the political line proposed and approved by the Central Committee was not understood in its theoretical foundation and in all its aspects, hence when one came to apply it one did not know what to do or one acted quite differently.

The editorial added:

Our policies have not undergone nor will undergo any substantial 'correction'; but the mistakes of those who had not understood our policies are being corrected.

Among those whose mistakes needed correcting were, presumably, those Communists whose hopes for peaceful development to socialism had been dashed by the elections of 1948 and who could not see 'any alternative to passivity except in vain dreams about insurrections . . .'. This editorial seemed to distinguish two deviations in the PCI: excessive gradualism and naïve insurrectionism, the latter being the mirror image of the former. What Togliatti did not do was to locate the source of these deviations within the strategy itself. These deviations are firmly explained with reference to the low level of theoretical preparation of the majority of the membership. This fact can be partly explained and justified when one considers the enormous rise in membership during the Resistance. However, a more comprehensive assessment should have taken into account the fact that the leadership of the party itself had given the impression of believing that a long-lasting co-operation with conservative groups could have been achieved.

The definitive break-up of the tripartite coalition did not take place in isolation. A political division of Europe was occurring with demarcation lines closely resembling those established by the Soviet troops on the one hand and by the Allies on the other. The one country which was able to escape this division was Yugoslavia, the only European example of a 'national road to socialism'. The European situation was unfavourable to anyone taking an independent line. The 'logic of the blocs' determined a rigid demarcation line across Europe. This was the international setting for the dispute between Stalin and Tito which led to the expulsion of the

Yugoslav CP from the Cominform. As we mentioned above, the Yugoslavs had been the harshest critics of the Italian and French CPs at the founding of the Cominform. Djilas and Kardelj seemed then to echo Zhdanov. By 1948 the situation had dramatically changed. At the Cominform meeting of 28 June 1948 the Yugoslavs were accused of taking an anti-Soviet stand. Togliatti, who was present at the meeting, accepted entirely the Soviet thesis. In fact, he is said to have written the resolution himself.[28]

The action of the Cominform had one fundamental aim: to establish that the policy of national roads to socialism was not to be followed by any Communist Party or socialist state. It was obvious that the CPSU had never accepted polycentrism as a permanent feature of international Communism.

The PCI had therefore to decide whether to reject the Italian road to socialism or to break with the CPSU over Yugoslavia. In practice that was no choice at all. Historically, Togliatti had made his choice many years previously, in the late 1920s, when he had come to the conclusion that it was not feasible for a Communist Party in a capitalist country to be in disagreement with the first socialist state. The development of a political strategy which took into account the international relations of forces had always been a feature of the post-1926 leadership of the PCI. It was this thinking which determined the apparent rejection of a national road on the part of the PCI.

A dualism began to dominate the party: at home it would attempt to continue its exploration of an original road to socialism while in all matters directly concerning the international aspects of the Communist movement it would follow the general line.

When a new international climate, more favourable to a polycentric logic, was established, Togliatti admitted that the Cominform condemnation of the CP of Yugoslavia had been a mistake.[29]

It has been said that the constitution of the Cominform imposed on the PCI another direction during the period of the discussions on the Marshall Plan. At the founding meeting of the Cominform, the PCI had been accused of adopting an 'ambiguous' policy in relation to the Marshall Plan. Until the summer of 1947, Togliatti's policy had been favourable to accepting American aid provided no strings were attached. In fact not even the Soviet Union opposed the Marshall Plan as a matter of principle. In an article in *Rinascita* of 1948, that is, after the creation of the Cominform, Rodano wrote:

The break between the democratic European forces and the governments of Western Europe has not occurred over the question of the Marshall Plan, but over its interpretation.[30]

The PCI fundamental position over the Marshall Plan was that it should be accepted without any political conditions and that it should be used towards public investment whereas the DC (and the USA) wanted the money to be used to cover the Italian balance of payment deficit (only in the fifties would US aid be actually directed towards investment).[31] In so far as the DC used the aid towards investment, it was in the direction of the large private monopolies such as Pirelli and FIAT.[32] In so doing the DC aligned itself with Bevin and Bidault, the French Foreign Minister, in adopting the position that the Marshall Plan should be co-ordinated on the European scale with US advice. This move had the obvious aim of guaranteeing American control of European economic policy. The PCI (and USSR) reaction was to demand that the Marshall money should be autonomously administered by individual states in order to strengthen the public sector and, in Italy, to strengthen IRI. In other words, the money should be used to follow the sort of economic policies the Communists had been advocating since 1945. In the final analysis it is not, in practice, possible to separate the 'principle' of the Marshall Plan from its political reality. To have accepted the Marshall Plan as the USA interpreted it would have been inconsistent with established PCI policy and hence with the Italian road to socialism irrespective of the attitude of the Cominform.

The battle over the Marshall Plan was obviously primarily political and was fought around the central issues of the time: the control of Europe and its subsequent division into two spheres of influence. As far as Italy was concerned, the battle had already been fought and lost by the Communists once the military and geographical realities of the world war had determined that it would be the West which would be its (Italy's) liberator. Hence, the PCI fought the Marshall Plan from a defensive position, but was also able to prove to the Italians that it could be 'constructive' as well, for it based an element of its critique of the way the Plan was administered on the fact that Italy, a weak and defeated nation, would end up as the loser in the scramble for American money. As Rodano pointed out:

. . . within the group of sixteen countries (who have accepted the Plan), all subservient to powerful American monopolies, there has taken place a fist-fight for the further subservience of the weaker Western European countries to the stronger ones. In this fight, as it could have been easily foreseen, Italy has been defeated.[33]

Thus Marshall, according to Rodano, created a hierarchy within the imperialist camp: within the general dominance of the USA, the UK and France had become second-rate imperialist powers, but all were able to impose their will over Italy. Thus, Rodano pointed out, the British obtained the equivalent of 35 dollars of US aid per head, the French obtained 17 dollars, while the Italians were left with only 12 dollars per head. It was this 'practical' and pragmatic approach which would be chosen by the PCI rather than the more general question of the 'principle' of the Marshall Plan. This 'national' approach enabled the Italian Communists to present themselves once more as the true defenders of the national interests and to attack De Gasperi and his government for 'selling out' the nation to foreign powers.

Such political direction would be further emphasized in the course of the debate over Italy's entry in the North Atlantic Treaty Organization. The Communists warned of the dangers of Italy entering a military pact and of the consequences for political autonomy and independence.[34] It must be noted that the question of NATO was very controversial not just in the country at large, but also within the ruling coalition. De Gasperi himself was not entirely convinced of the appropriateness of entry and left-wing Christian Democrats such as Dossetti and Gronchi were clearly against entry. Saragat, the Social Democrat leader, was also against entry, but was outvoted by a majority of one at the meeting of his parliamentary party. The ruling coalition, however, was not free to do as it pleased. Like the PCI, but in a different manner, it was constrained by international events. Eventually the decision to join the Atlantic Alliance was taken between December 1948 and January 1949.

The entry of Italy into the Atlantic Pact definitely sealed the 'choice' of the Italian Republic, a choice which its supporters heralded as a 'choice of civilization' ('una scelta di civiltà'). The Italian Communist Party had lost the first round of its battle for the reunification of Italian society in an organic whole around a programme of structural reforms. It had now to learn the difficult art of legal opposition. It had the strength of having a mass of supporters and this, more than anything else, permitted it to withstand, at least in part, the attempt of the Christian Democratic Party to force it permanently into the ghetto of official but everlasting opposition.

Notes

1. A. Gambino, *Storia del dopoguerra. Dalla liberazione al potere DC*, Rome-Bari, 1975, p. 259.

2. From US Dept. of State, *Foreign Relations of the United States, 1946*, quoted in G. Warner, 'Italy and the Powers 1943–49' in S. J. Woolf, *The Rebirth of Italy 1943–50*, London, 1972, p. 52.
3. G. Amendola is right to warn against excessive simplifications. The end of the tripartite coalition was not decided in Washington but was the result of a complex interconnecting of pressures coming mainly from the Italian bourgeoisie, the Vatican and the USA; see Amendola, 'La rottura della coalizione tripartita: maggio 1947' in *Il Mulino*, No. 235, Sept.–Oct. 1974, p. 791. For an account of the 'negotiations' between De Gasperi and the US authorities see R. Faenza and M. Fini, *Gli americani in Italia*, Milan, 1976, particularly pp. 180 ff.
4. See Gambino's description of De Gasperi's Washington trip in op. cit., pp. 262–6.
5. This is told by Emilio Sereni, then a Communist minister, in his *Il Mezzogiorno all' opposizione*, Turin, 1948, pp. 20–1.
6. P. Togliatti, *Discorsi alla Costituente*, Rome, 1974, p. 155.
7. Ibid., pp. 194, 206.
8. This was openly admitted by Togliatti in 1947 when speaking to the pre-congressional debates of the Milan Federation of the PCI; see *Documenti per il VI Congresso nazionale del PCI, Prospettive della nostra lotta*, Rome, 1947, pp. 31–2.
9. G. Zhdanov, *Report on the International Situation* in Robert V. Daniels, *A Documentary History of Communism*, Vol. II, New York, 1960, p. 157.
10. Ibid., p. 160.
11. E. Reale, *Nascita del Cominform*, Milan, 1958, p. 17.
12. Ibid., pp. 118, 119.
13. Ibid., p. 123.
14. G. Galli, *La sinistra italiana nel dopoguerra*, Bologna, 1958, p. 12.
15. Ibid., pp. 12, 13.
16. See R. Orfei, *L'occupazione del potere. I democristiani 1945–75*, Milan, 1976, pp. 94–5.
17. There is now ample evidence to show that the USA spared no resources to influence the results of the elections. Recent revelations have shown that over and above the 227 million dollars the US government promised between January and March 1947, vast sums of money were directed towards the DC from the USA; see the documentation in R. Faenza and M. Fini, *Gli americani in Italia*, Milan, 1976, pp. 298–304.
18. G. Amendola, 'Il PCI all'opposizione. La lotta contro lo scelbismo' in op. cit., p. 116.
19. G. Galli, op. cit., p. 41.
20. G. Amendola, 'Il PCI all'opposizione . . .' in op. cit., p. 117.
21. Gambino (op. cit., p. 479) has assembled a sufficient number of sources showing that Togliatti had more or less expected these results and that he was not as sorry as his followers (he told Franco Rodano: 'These were the best results we could have obtained. This is all right.'), probably because he knew that the USA would not have allowed the 'loss' to the 'West' of the Italian domino.
22. For a description of the unrest see R. Del Carria, *Proletari senza revoluzione*, Milan, 1970, Vol. 2, pp. 388–92.
23. Quoted in G. Bocca, *Palmiro Togliatti*, Bari, 1973, p. 516.
24. Giorgio Galli's thesis is that the conditions of 1948 were favourable for a revolutionary takeover (see op. cit., pp. 205–11). Del Carria substantially agrees with Galli: 'The Party centre did not want a revolution, whereas the masses were waiting for the word "go!" ', in op. cit., p. 393. These positions are untenable.
25. Quoted in Del Carria, op. cit., p. 393.
26. For an account of the break-up of the CGIL see S. Turone, *Storia del sindacato*

in Italia 1943–1969, Bari, 1974, pp. 176–209. This break-up was actively encouraged with adequate financing by the American Federation of Labor and by the US government, see Joseph La Palombara, *The Italian Labor Movement: Problems and Prospects*, Ithaca, N.Y., 1957, p. 57.

27. See *Rinascita*, Nos. 9–10, Sept.–Oct. 1948.
28. G. Bocca, op. cit., p. 504.
29. See in particular P. Togliatti, 'Intervista a Nuovi argomenti', originally in *Nuovi argomenti*, No. 20, May–June 1956, reprinted in P. Togliatti, *Opere scelte*, Rome, 1974 and 'Viaggio in Yugoslavia', *Rinascita*, No. 5, 1 February 1964.
30. F. Rodano, 'Il piano Marshall e l'Italia', *Rinascita*, Vol. 5, No. 3, March 1948.
31. G. Amendola, *Lotta di classe e sviluppo economico dopo la Liberazione*, Rome, 1962, p. 59.
32. G. Amendola, 'Il PCI all'opposizione. La lotta contro lo scelbismo' in op. cit., p. 122.
33. F. Rodano, op. cit.
34. See the anthology of articles on the question of NATO from *Rinascita* 1946–9 in S. Galante, *La politica del PCI e il Patto Atlantico. 'Rinascita 1946–1949'*, Padua, 1973.

5   The PCI in Opposition

In a speech at the Theatre San Carlo in Naples on 22 June 1947, Togliatti, in a passage which is a clear warning to the party of the possibility of a long period of opposition, declared:

> What did people expect of us? They expected the insurrection on the day after De Gasperi had announced the composition of his government, an insurrection at an established date . . . If De Gasperi has succeeded in his plans, which were to have the government he now has, he has not succeeded in altering the feelings of the Italian people and we shall continue to be the party we have been from the struggle of '44 to today and that is an opposition party. But our opposition will be an opposition of a particular type; we shall not make the error of some former oppositions which seemed to have . . . as their motto 'so much the worse, so much the better'.[1]

This declaration is all the more significant when, with the elections of April 1948, the PCI found itself in opposition in every sense of the word and when, shortly later, it had to face its first major test: the struggles for the land.

These struggles, which began in a semi-spontaneous manner, presented a number of important features. They signalled the effective entry of the southern masses in national politics and, at the same time, they established the basis for the destruction of the 'agrarian bloc' and the slow deterioration of the Christian Democratic hegemony in the South.[2] In this sense these struggles represent the beginning of a new period.

Yet the peasant struggles were also rooted in the politics of post-war reconstruction. They represented the reaction of the South to the type of economic policies which had been put forward by the liberal-conservative tendencies in the government (e.g. Corbino and Einaudi). It was a reminder that the agrarian reform had been the objective of all the parties of the Resistance and that the end of the tripartite coalition had only increased the generally-held fears that, once again as often in the past, 'Rome' had forgotten the problem of the South.

The PCI, of course, had been active among the peasantry before it was expelled from the government, but it increased its presence in the countryside in a much more organized fashion in the course of 1947. It established Committees for the Land and 'Popular Consultative Assemblies' (*Consulte popolari*). The purpose was to devise novel forms of organizations corresponding to the new demands: demands which were to involve 'not only the relations between bosses and workers but the *ensemble* of the political relations of our society'.[3]

The focus of the movement in the South was the Calabria region:

> The movement for the agrarian reform started in Calabria, in the Marchesato di Crotone and it extended itself to Lucania, Apulia and Campania. Not only labourers and peasants took part in the movement for the occupation of the land, but all strata of the population. At dawn, columns of people would leave their villages and would march, waving red flags and tricolours, towards the land they wanted to conquer.[4]

The occupation of the lands of 1948–50 soon became part of the folklore of Italian politics. In a way it constituted the Southern equivalent of the Resistance. As in the Resistance the spontaneous movement and the organized one intertwined and fed on each other. It was a genuinely popular movement and the Communists encouraged it to become as wide as possible.

At first the government used the tactics of repression but eventually it was forced to retreat and conceded immediately 100,000 acres of land in Calabria before the agrarian reform bill was passed by Parliament. In 1950, 1.6 million acres were distributed and the *Cassa per il Mezzogiorno* (Fund for the Development of the South) was created.

It has been argued that the reform had an anti-communist function. The leadership of the DC never denied this. The PCI voted against the reform on the grounds that it was not comprehensive enough. In the first place, the reform covered only uncultivated land in the latifondo; secondly, there was still no limitation on the extent of land property; thirdly, the compensation paid to the expropriated was too high and, fourthly, the reform was not democratic: the peasants were excluded from its administration.[5] However, on the whole the reform benefited, to some extent, the landless labourer as well as the sharecropper and the small peasant.[6]

With the agrarian reform, the Christian Democratic Party had completed De Gasperi's plan: the stabilization of its newly-acquired hegemony in Italian political life. It was not, however, a total victory for the DC: the Communists had succeeded in establishing a foothold in the South. Furthermore, the right-wing forces in the South became estranged from the DC. In 1953 they voted against the Government bloc, thus causing the failure of the electoral reform, known as the 'Legge truffa' (the swindle law), which was designed to give a two-thirds majority to any group of parties which received at least 51 per cent of the votes.

The fundamental gain of the PCI was, as we have pointed out, the conquest of a position of relative strength in the South. However, it had failed to force through an agrarian reform which would effectively destroy the powers of the large landlords and lead to a democratic transformation of the Italian countryside. We have already explained that the agrarian reform was the key to Communist post-war strategy, so much so that it had dropped from its platform some of its most radical industrial reforms. We suggested that a 'democratic' agrarian reform, in the Italian situation, could strengthen the 'productive' sector of capitalism and that this would be consistent with Communist goals, if development would then take place under the dominance of a new 'historical bloc' led by the working class.

A capitalist development could take, in the Italian context, one of the following roads:

1. The Prussian-style 'Junker' road, that is, the gradual development of large-scale capitalist farming-out of feudalism.
2. The nationalization of land in the form of the public (that is, State) ownership of rent. This development is still 'capitalist' in the Marxist sense: State capitalism.
3. The destruction of latifondi and the development of small-scale farming.

In Italy, the PCI sought to intervene actively to avoid the possibility of 'Junker-like' development. One of the other possibilities, land nationalization, had already been ruled out. The Italian Communists had to choose the only other alternative path, the path of the 'free development of small peasant farming' (Lenin),[7] a path which presupposed the expropriation of the large estates. In the Leninist model this development could favour the workers and peasant masses and it is evident that the PCI had made similar calculations.

The Italian situation, however, had one specific feature: the deep penetration of finance capital into the agricultural sector. This feature, on the one hand, given the dominance of finance capital in the political life of the country, prevented the nationalization of rent; on the other, it seriously endangered the development of small peasant farming. As Ruggero Grieco, head of the agrarian section of the PCI since 1945 and, after January 1947, in charge of the special Southern Commission of the Central Committee, pointed out, failure to eliminate finance capital from agriculture and the probable inefficiency of small farming would condemn small peasants to eventual impoverishment and would lead to their gradual expropriation by capitalist farming.[8] Thus Grieco advocated a non-capitalist road as the 'only way out' for the small peasant. By a non-capitalist road Grieco can only mean co-operativism in agriculture, a movement which was indeed strongly supported by the PCI. The success of co-operativism, however, implied several pre-conditions and first and foremost State help and subsidies as well as a readiness on the part of the peasants to abandon the mentality of small entrepreneurs. Neither of these conditions existed in spite of the apparent radicalism of many small peasants and the creation of the Cassa per il Mezzogiorno. The Cassa's funds were mainly directed to the pockets of the bureaucracy and the entrepreneurial class. Thus Grieco's analysis contained a contradiction: the only possible agrarian reform was damaging to the interests of the small peasantry and at the same time the co-operativist solution was destined to fail in the South (it was, however, relatively successful in the 'red belt'). Co-operativism, to succeed, required a lengthy process of political education.[9]

However, although the party had not been able to formulate an organic policy for the South, it continued to defend the interests of the small peasants and embraced a productivist policy centred on the demand for more investment in the South and in agriculture. The starting-point of these policies and activities was substantially correct: the insistence that the problems of the Italian South were not extraneous to Italian capitalism. Industrial capital and a backward agriculture were inexorably linked in a pattern which constantly reproduced and exacerbated the uneven development of North and South.

We have mentioned the fact that the DC, in promulgating an agrarian reform, had been forced to alienate from itself some of its potential allies; the agrarian reform, however inadequate, was the death-knell of the old agrarian bloc. Not all the social strata which led this bloc became antagonistic to the DC, but, after the early fifties, they were always in a subordinate position to the now triumphant interests of Italian industrial and financial capital.

The Cassa per il Mezzogiorno, while it revealed itself to be a disaster from the point of view of the Southern economy, was able in a variety of ways, including the setting up of a system of patronage and clienteles, to subsidize the incomes of some social strata of the South and, in so doing, to provide a wider consumer market for industrial capital while stabilizing the political power of the DC.[10]

Finally, the continuous liberalization of Italian foreign trade (and eventually the entry in the EEC) changed considerably the relations of power within industrial capital: there was a decline of the large chemical industries as well as the electrical sector and a corresponding rise to dominance of the engineering industry, in particular, the automobile sector, that is, FIAT.[11] A new competitive spirit began to pervade Italian industry. This was facilitated by the particular form assumed in Italy by State intervention in the economy. The State, through IRI, limited itself to the purchase of controlling interests in a large number of firms, but allowed these to compete freely and seldom sought to direct in any way the flow of investment. Even some nationalized industries, such as the National Hydrocarbons Corporation (E.N.I.) could behave as an independent enterprise, and this was all the more evident when it was directed by Enrico Mattei, a strong-willed man who was able to maintain a certain autonomy from the government of the day.

There were, of course, other important economic factors which established the pre-conditions for the 'economic miracle', that is, the period of exceptionally rapid economic growth which occurred in Italy in the late fifties.[12] There was the growth of world trade, determined by the so-called 'Korean cycle'.

There was also an abundant labour market and an ample reserve of labour in the Italian South. Finally, the level of taxation was abnormally low because of the widespread tendency to evade taxes. This had the effect of encouraging private investment. It must be stressed, however, that the kind of economic growth which took place in Italy in the fifties (i.e. largely unplanned and dependent on the private sector) would have been impossible if the social and economic reforms demanded by the Italian Communists had been implemented. There is one fundamental reason for this: the basis of the development of Italian capitalism rests on its particular unevenness, that is, on the duality between the industrial North and the agrarian South. The PCI had demanded a set of reforms which would break the powers of private monopolies. These reforms entailed a policy of public investment and public direction of the economy. The DC had chosen the opposite path of capitalist development. Its monetary policy, however, had not been an expansionist one until the second half of the fifties. This policy eventually favoured, through a selective use of credit, the most successful (or more competitive) firms. This policy, however, had been largely determined by the realization of the dynamism of some sectors of the economy. These had mainly relied for productive investment on their own self-financing. What the State had done was to allow the development of the pre-conditions for this largely self-financed growth.[13]

The DC and its allies could pursue such a policy only by isolating the left and breaking the powers of the trade unions. As we have seen, by 1948 this dual aim had been largely achieved thanks to the unique international conjuncture which divided Europe into two rival power blocs.

The few years which followed the rupture of the tripartite coalition and the massive victory of the DC were the most difficult for the Italian left. In this conjuncture the CGIL formulated the idea of a Labour Plan with the deliberate objective of freeing itself from the isolation in which it had been forced.

The 'Labour Plan' was put forward at the Second Congress of the CGIL (Genoa, October 1949) and further elaborated at conferences in Rome (19–20 February 1950) and Milan (2–4 June 1950). The Plan consisted of four points:[14]

1. Nationalization of electricity and creation of a National Electric Board and a programme for an expansion of the electrical infrastructure.
2. Creation of a National Board for land reclamation and other public works in the agrarian sector in conjunction with the full implementation of the agrarian reform.
3. Creation of a National Board for public housing, including the building of hospitals, schools, etc.
4. Large programmes of public works with the aim of improving the economic structures of the country and to increase employment rapidly.

The leader of the CGIL, Di Vittorio, advocated a plan as the primary instrument for the development of the Italian economy. Its basic purpose, however, was to combat unemployment. Di Vittorio wrote that the Plan was the weapon with which to find a way out of Italy's economic backwardness.[15]

But what was the political status of a plan which had as its main target full employment? According to Bianca Salvati, the Plan in practice, far from being a realistic and constructive proposal, was a propaganda operation:

To propose a greater utilization of resources and their employment for purposes of accumulation was in itself extremely sensible: but it required a drastic change in the economic policy which the ruling forces had chosen and widespread public control over the process of accumulation. This need for reforms and public intervention in the economic mechanism remained obscure in the plan: indeed, it was deliberately minimized. As it is not credible that Di Vittorio and the

CGIL were not aware of this, and as they certainly knew that such reforms and interventions could not have been accepted, one must conclude that the enormous organizational effort which produced the plan was basically mounted for 'propaganda' reasons: because of the need to offer public opinion the image of a union which was concerned about national development and which desired to collaborate, which not only criticized the government's economic policy but put forward positive proposals (compatible for the market system).[16]

The logic of Bianca Salvati's analysis (and this passage has been chosen because it is typical of contemporary 'leftist' criticisms) implies the impossibility of 'constructive opposition' from a Communist perspective.

The distinction to be made in this case is clearly one between putting forward demands which are compatible with Italian capitalism and ones which are incompatible with it. In the latter case it would be a political exercise along these lines: the present problems of Italian society (in this instance unemployment) cannot be solved by Italian capitalism; only a socialist revolution will deliver the goods. In this case all talk of constructive opposition would be pure propaganda, all intermediate goals are impossible, and the only task for the revolutionary party consists in preparing for a socialist revolution. The alternative to this is the following: some of the present problems of Italian society can be solved in a way which would modify the relation of forces between the classes without necessarily destroying capitalist social relations. In this case intermediate goals are the order of the day: what is proposed would entail, at the most, a change in government, not a change of regime. Thus what is being put forth is the following: there is a realistic way out of the present impasse, the present government cannot adopt it because it follows policies contrary to the interest of the working class and the vast majority of the Italian people: hence a new type of government must be formed. Of course, the propagandistic element remains, but the proposals are not pure propaganda but actively insert themselves in an ongoing struggle. It is within this perspective that the 'Labour Plan' must be seen. Indeed, the motion passed at the CGIL Congress says in part: 'The CGIL is ready to give its support to a government which would undertake to carry out the plan.'[17]

The PCI made it clear that it regarded the CGIL plan as compatible with capitalist development. Togliatti wrote:

It is evident . . . that the very need for a planned economy demands, first of all, the existence of a [political] power which expresses the will and the interests of the whole people and of the working class, not those of the privileged class . . . [But] it would be a mistake to consider the proposals put forward by the CGIL . . . as a project for the real planning of the Italian economy.[18]

A fortnight later, after the government's rejection of the Plan, a document of the Central Committee of the PCI, dated 28 April, indicated that the proposals contained in the Plan should become part of a platform of struggles to be taken up by the trade unions as well as by the 'political organizations of the working class'. The document also specified a doctrinal point: the Plan was in no way to be considered a 'socialist plan', but what it intended to do was to 'entail a new economic, democratic and national policy in order to realize the maximum output and employment possible in the existing economic order'.[19]

The 'Labour Plan' was in the tradition of Italian trade unionism in the sense that, of all the European trade union movements, it had always been the least tied to corporative ideologies. Its struggles were often broader than particular industries, firms or categories but were rather directed towards the achievement of the unity of the working class. It is in this sense that one should interpret Di Vittorio's rallying cry at the end of the conference which launched the Labour Plan: 'Italy, at work, united!'

The Plan had a significance which went far beyond its immediate scope. It consolidated the independent image of Di Vittorio, hence the independence of the CGIL.[20] This independence would be further accentuated in 1956 when Di Vittorio took a stand over the events in Poland and Hungary which conflicted with the PCI.[21] Yet this independence was not *against* the PCI. Although many Communists did not realize this at the time, trade union autonomy (not to be confused with trade union political neutrality) had to be part and parcel of the Italian road to socialism. In fact, in so far as the 'Italian road' implied an alliance between Communists and Catholics, it implied trade union unity. The PCI had never wanted the split in the trade union movement which had occurred in 1948 and had always advocated a return to a single trade union federation. The return to a united trade union movement was the necessary precondition for the creation of a new bloc which would challenge the dominance of the old industrial–agrarian bloc. Yet one of the many elements which stood in the way of trade union unity was the fact that Catholic and Social Democratic workers were suspicious of the CGIL whom they considered to be the tool of the PCI and hence of Moscow. The Labour Plan of the CGIL, though it failed in the sense that it never became the point of reference for trade union action in the early fifties and that it was quietly dropped, can be taken as an element of that process of trade union autonomy (supported by the PCI) which could find its definitive impetus only after the Italian 'economic miracle', when the Italian economy entered a period of acute crises and the trade union movement found again force and unity in the late sixties and the early seventies.

The prospects of the Labour Plan were finally shattered by the Korean war (June 1950) and by the fact that the USA imposed on Italy a rearmament programme which was incompatible with the public investment programme suggested by Di Vittorio. Strangely enough it was difficult, in the Italy of 1950, to propose Keynesian policies without coming up against opposition from NATO and the USA.

In the post-1948 period the strategy of the PCI consisted in guiding a mass opposition around a specific set of demands contraposed to the policies of successive 'centrist' governments. Thus the PCI did not decide to withdraw into an 'uncompromising opposition' along the lines of traditional Kautskyist Social Democracy. There was no question of changing the fundamental lines of the existing strategy elaborated in the years of the Resistance.

The PCI had decided — and this was a definitive decision (definitive in the context of the general national and international situation of the Italian political system) — that the road to socialism in Italy was based on a grand strategy of alliances, on the progressive weakening of the industrial–agrarian ruling bloc, on a change in the international position of Italy (or, alternatively, on a change in the international relations of forces), and on a division in the Christian Democratic Party (or, alternatively, on a shift of the DC as a whole to the left). These conditions excluded even the consideration of armed struggle.

The Communist opposition would be of a 'constructive type' which would gear the whole Communist apparatus to think in realistic terms on a day-to-day basis: it would show to the Italian people that there could always be options to the policies of successive governments, that these options were preferable and realizable (i.e. that 'the socialist revolution' was not a necessary pre-condition for the implementation of these options).

Of course, this strategic alternative, though consistent with the thinking of the PCI in the preceding period, was not formulated in an explicit and programmatic manner. Rather, it was the result of scores of debates and discussions as well as of political battles. This 'caution' was partly determined by international considerations, particularly by the ties between the PCI and the CPSU. In the period 1950–5, the strategy of the PCI was in a period of transition: two tendencies emerged. The first, led by Secchia, advocated a 'tougher' opposition and the consolidation of the cadres' element of the party at the expense of its mass element. The second tendency (Togliatti's), representing the majority of the party, attempted to carry through to its logical conclusion the Italian road to socialism. It was this tendency which emerged successful, but such success could be confirmed only after the Twentieth Congress of the CPSU.

In this part we shall discuss this conflict and the definitive emergence of the Togliattian line in this transitional period, both at the political and at the ideological level.

The Seventh Congress of the PCI (Rome, 3–8 April 1951) was a congress of transition held at a time when the strategy of the party seemed in need of elaboration and adaptation. Yet there was little new: Togliatti's speech concentrated on international questions, while Longo's report on the class struggle in Italy centred mainly on the need to support the CGIL 'Labour Plan'.

The Seventh Congress emphasized international politics, but it also concentrated on the problems presented by the question of the relationship between the party and the trade union movement (in particular, the CGIL). Secchia, in his speech to the Congress, stated that, in his opinion one of the defects of the party was that it was still forced to develop 'directly' activities which should be developed instead by the trade union and the other mass organizations.

One of the consequences of this fact, continued Secchia, was that the present CGIL behaved very much like the pre-fascist CGIL which was dominated by Social Democrats: strikes were called by the CGIL without proper consultation with the rank and file, and without meetings of workers taking place in the factories discussing the best way of conducting the struggle.

Longo, in his report, warned the CGIL not to overlook the importance of the workers' commission (the shop-floor representatives of all the workers employed in a particular plant, whether union members or not. In the struggle for the unity of the working class it was important that the CGIL should consider the workers' commissions as the *locus* where such unity could be founded. From Longo's and Secchia's reports appears clear that the PCI was thinking in terms of a proper division labour between the CGIL and the PCI; to the former should be given the trade union work, to the party the political work. This consideration together with what we have pointed out with respect to the 'Labour Plan', constituted the starting-point for an entire re-thinking on the problem of the political party–trade union relationship. Such a re-thinking eventually involved the revision of the Leninist doctrine of the trade union as the 'transmission belt' of the party. This revision took place formal in 1956, but 1956 was simply the turning-point of a lengthy process which had clearly begun in 1949–51.

The demand that the CGIL should pay more attention to the struggle at the factory level rather than being content with formulating 'national' objectives encountered the opposition of many trade unionists including Di Vittorio. Di Vittorio warned that too great a concentration on the struggle in the single factory could constitute a grave danger: there could be a return to corporativism, the traditional 'vice' of the Italian working class.

Di Vittorio pointed out a further problem. If, as it was suggested, those CGIL members who happened to be in the workers' commission should try to represent the commission and not the CGIL, then it also followed that party members who were in the workers' commission should represent this and not the party. This was not very far from saying that party members who were in positions of leadership in the trade unions should represent their union rather than the party. This was both a declaration of autonomy and a suggestion that there was a certain incompatibility between being a trade union leader and a party leader. This suggestion was carried out only in the seventies when several trade union leaders resigned from the Central Committee of the PCI in order to facilitate the growth of trade union unity between the CGIL and the other two trade union federations.

A third theme emerged out of the discussions of the Seventh Congress: the relation between the 'cadres' character and the 'mass' character of the party. Secchia and, to a lesser extent, Longo were the main exponents of the view that the cadres characteristic of the party should be reinforced. This followed implicitly from Secchia's warning that the party could no longer fulfil the mass work which properly belonged to mass organizations such as the trade unions. Secchia explained that it was necessary to transform every party member into active Communists. This could only be a long-term task and the party could not 'sit and wait'. He proposed the objectives of increasing the number of active Communists by 200,000. All active members had to be organized into groups of ten, under a group leader. The group leaders had to be the chief instrument of the party's capillary action.[22]

In the Communist movement the question of organization can never be divorced from questions of strategy. It will suffice to recall that the original split between Mensheviks and Bolsheviks in the Russian Social Democratic Labour Party centred, at least formally, on questions of organization. Secchia's proposals were indicative of the affirmation of a more factory-based and 'proletarian' line; 'proletarian' in the sense of encouraging agitation and activity among the industrial working class at the expense of the policy of alliances with and recruitment among the so-called middle strata. These proposals brought Secchia in conflict with the so-called 'meridionalisti' around Alicata and Amendola for, in the PCI, the 'meridionalisti' were the most outspoken supporters of a creation of a peasant–worker bloc and believed that one of the party's primary tasks was to work among the Southern masses. Part of Secchia's 'workerist' attitude might also have derived from the fact that he had been one of the leading Communists responsible for the Resistance in Northern Italy. He may therefore have felt that the Northern industrial working class was infinitely more reliable than the Southern peasantry. Furthermore, in so far as Secchia was concerned about his own personal power, he must have been well aware that Milan and Turin represented his power base.[23] The position of Togliatti seemed to be on the side of the 'meridionalisti'. However, his position as a party leader was at its most unstable and he acted as a mediator between the two sides.

It can now be seen that the weakness of Togliatti's position was mainly due to Stalin's intervention. Towards the end of 1950 Togliatti was in the USSR to convalesce after a motor accident. He was received by Stalin who explained to him that, as the international Communist movement was in difficulty, he needed an experienced man to lead the Cominform and he offered the job to Togliatti.[24] It was obvious that Stalin's intention was to remove Togliatti from the leadership of the PCI in the hope that Secchia or Longo would take over. It seems now clear that Stalin was never pleased with the Italian road to socialism which he had accepted at times because it suited his purposes, at times because he had to. The impasse in which the PCI had found itself must have convinced Stalin that a change of leadership was necessary. Togliatti was obviously displeased by Stalin's offer and did not try to hide it.[25] He told Stalin that before accepting he needed the permission of the Party's Executive Committee. Togliatti remained in the USSR and the PCI Executive Committee considered the case. A majority (including all the 'meridionalisti') voted in favour of Stalin's proposal.[26] It seems unlikely that they all wished to eliminate Togliatti. The most likely explanation was that they were all trained under a school of thought which made it difficult to take an open stand against Stalin. As Amendola admitted, 'Yes . . . we were Stalinists'.[27]

In spite of the vote, Togliatti was able to convince Stalin to let him remain as Party leader until the end of the Seventh Congress of the PCI. Stalin understood that Togliatti would be able to convince the Executive Committee to re-consider and withdraw his offer. This episode, whose importance should not be overestimated, was indicative of a certain frame of mind and of the limited degree of freedom the Italian Communists enjoyed.

The complex problem of the relations between the CPSU and the PCI came to the fore mainly after Stalin's death in March 1953. This had immediate consequences for it marked the beginning of the rejection of what was called the 'personality cult'. The attack on the 'personality cult' in the Italian context was double-edged because it could be directed against both Togliatti and Secchia. It could be used against Togliatti because, even though he preferred to act only when he was sure that he could carry with him the bulk of the Central Committee and the party, he was the object of excessive adulation and praise. However, in so far as the struggle against the 'personality cult' was against tendencies towards excessive centralization, the object of the attack could be Secchia.

One of the fundamental reasons why the 'Secchia line' was able to emerge was that the Italian road strategy had not paid off in the short term, as many of the party's rank and file supporters had hoped. However, this strategy was formulated for the long term. Moreover, it was accepted by the younger leadership, people like Amendola, Ingrao, Alicata (not necessarily younger in age, but younger in terms of their years of party membership). Secchia, who had great qualities of leadership and organization, was no long-term strategist and his position in the party gradually weakened. He was eventually demoted and sent to Milan in charge of party organization there.

The party position on the question of collective leadership and 'personality cult' was expressed by Edoardo D'Onofrio in a *Rinascita* article of November 1953. This article contained an indirect attack on Secchia and his supporters:

> There are leading Communist cadres, formed in the struggle and during the partisan war, who have brought and transplanted in our organizations their fighting spirit, order and discipline. This is undoubtedly a good thing. However, at times they have brought too rigid a conception of life and organization, and too personal a method of leadership. There are party cadres, formed in jail, in confinement, in complete clandestinity, who have transferred in the life of the party and its mass organizations their greater knowledge of Marxist–Leninist doctrine but at times they have also brought with them certain limitations of political actions and a personal and oppressive method of leadership.[28]

These errors, maintained D'Onofrio, were a direct result of the past activities of the PCI, particularly of its twenty years of illegality. The implication was that this sort of method belonged to a different period and to a different condition: they had no room in Togliatti's 'Partito Nuovo' (New Party). He then added that the policies which relied on the development of disciplined cadres (along the lines of Secchia's 'group of ten activists') should be modified and, where possible, abandoned.

What is now evident is that Togliatti saw that the death of Stalin could provide the basis for a gradual re-acquisition of that autonomy the PCI had enjoyed up to the founding of the Cominform. In February 1954 he sent a note to Secchia asking him to prepare an article on the question of organization. The note contains detailed indications about the general line the article should propound:

> The study should deal with the period of illegality (briefly) but at greater length with the present situation. It should be very uninhibited, i.e., it should not hesitate to explain the novelty of what we are doing or what we have done or of what we say we are doing, which is either barely mentioned in Lenin and Stalin or not even mentioned at all.[29]

It is significant, of course, that Togliatti should have asked Secchia to be the one who would stress the differences between the PCI and the Soviet experience on matters of organization, particularly as the note goes on to specify that the nature of the PCI as a mass party needs emphasis. Secchia was known to have been less than happy with the mass character of the party preferring an élite or 'cadres' party.

These debates were the expression of a crisis within Italian Communism. This crisis, which began in 1947–8, reached a peak in 1956 with the events in Hungary and Poland and the Twentieth Congress of the CPSU. The unrest in Eastern Europe and the Twentieth Congress did not take place at a time when the PCI had emerged from a set of victorious battles, but on the contrary at a time when even the economic class struggle of the Italian working class was at a low ebb and when the party had suffered deep defeats.

It is to these we must now turn, but not before first analysing the major success of the PCI in this period: the campaign against the *Legge truffa* (the 'swindle law').

The events surrounding the *Legge truffa* of 1953 relate to the strategy of the Christian Democratic Party in Italy. The DC was the heir to Don Sturzo's *Partito Popolare*, born as a party representing the peasantry and sections of the petite bourgeoisie.[30] It was as such that the DC took a stand and played a part during the Resistance. In the period 1945–50, the DC achieved a remarkable 'transformation'. From a peasant party it became the main party of the principal Italian industrial groups who had previously supported the Liberal Party and then the Fascist Party. This transformation occurred during a crucial conjuncture characterized by four elements:

1. The Cold War.
2. The reconstruction in the North of a powerful industrial machine.
3. The entry of the Italian economy into a European market.
4. An enormous reservoir of cheap southern labour.

This transformation occurred leaving more or less intact the base of the DC. The Liberal Party, the traditional party of the Italian bourgeoisie, could not achieve its historical political tasks because it could not draw around itself (as could the DC) an ideological net containing the peasant masses, a section of the working class and most of the middle strata. The strength of the DC was that it was not a traditional bourgeois party and it offered to its supporters an ideology with a religious basis which sought to be 'outside classes' and which could have a unifying force. The possession of such an ideology, denoted by the term *'interclassismo'* ('inter-class') was then the necessary precondition for the domination of Italy by a traditional political party. Yet this strength constituted at the same time the main source of difficulty for stable rule. Because it represented popular masses and because there existed other parties (the PCI and the PSI and, potentially, a neo-fascist party) which could grow on disaffected DC supporters, it was necessary for the DC to try to be, in practice as well as in principle, a 'progressive' party, a party of reform. Furthermore, because it represented a large number of disparate sections, the DC was always plagued by an extreme factionalism. However, being the leading government party, it had at its disposal a large amount of political patronage which it distributed generously according to the relative strength of its rival factions. But because of this, a true reformist policy could not be implemented, for the entire machinery of the State was staffed by DC supporters who had no interests (or, at least, who believed they had no interest) in reforms: their jobs and positions depended on a political patronage characteristic of a backward State administration. Thus the DC had often to fight a battle on two fronts. Though most of the time its efforts (particularly during the Cold War) were directed against the left, it had to make sure that no votes were lost to the right.

Furthermore the existence of a proportional system of political representation made it very difficult, if not impossible, for the DC to rule alone. Coalitions became the pattern of Italian governments. Thus every Italian government was inherently weak because it was constituted by parties of different political bases and ideologies, and because the leading party was itself divided into important factions, each with its regional and economic support, each with its clientele. Thus the task of government became one of attempting to hold together these disparate interests. It is thus not possible to talk in terms of *the* strategy of the DC. What one can point out is that there have always been within the DC political forces which were consciously advancing a consistent political project. This project was the unification of the DC around a single historical aim: the unification of the Italian ruling class, of Italian capitalism. After De Gasperi the most consistent proponent of this project was Amintore Fanfani. It was the Fourth Congress of the DC in 1954 which brought Fanfani and his faction, *Iniziativa democratica* to a position of pre-eminence.[31]

For twenty years Fanfani would try to transform the DC into a modern political party. At times he played the left-wing card (for instance, by bringing in the ruling coalition the PSI in 1963) and, at others, he allied himself with the most traditional and clerical elements in the country. Of course, there were long periods in which he was excluded from power by some rival factions of his own party.

The relation between the strategy of the PCI and the Fanfani strategy is interesting. The PCI has always tried to found a new Italian unity around an anti-monopolistic struggle, whereas the DC (or at least the pro-Fanfani factions) have tried to do the same around the most powerful section of Italian capitalism.[32] To complicate the equation, there is the fact that Italian capitalism is greatly divided into rival interests and has none of the relative fusion and coherence that American or British capitalism has shown.

Given these considerations it would be a mistake to see all the actions of the DC as entirely determined by its anti-Communist attitudes except in the sense that, in order to remain the leading anti-Communist force in Italy, there should not be any powerful alternative on the right.

The land struggle of the late 1940s forced the DC to promulgate an agrarian reform. This reform alienated important sectors of Southern society from the DC. In 1948 the DC obtained 48 per cent of the votes, but during the local elections of 1951–2 it declined to 35 per cent.[33] Most of the DC losses were in the South. The PCI (in the local elections of 1951–2) gained votes in the South but lost some in the North, reflecting both its forceful support for the land struggles and the crisis it was undergoing among its working class supporters in the North. The main gains of the 1951–2 elections were, in the South, by the Monarchist Party, then the largest right-wing party in Italy.[34] This threat from potentially neo-fascist Southern forces forced the DC to pass in 1952 an anti-fascist law which prohibited any para-military formations as well as the dissemination of fascist ideology. The law was not, however, applied for twenty years. In this situation the DC attempted to strengthen its powers and ensure a stable majority by trying to pass the *Legge truffa*.[35] According to the law the coalition of parties which received 50 per cent plus one of the votes cast would obtain two-thirds of the seats in Parliament.

Togliatti saw the *Legge truffa* as an attempt to force the opposition parties out of any parliamentary debates thereby reducing them to what he regarded as a sterile role of pure protest and agitation.[36] The PCI fought the battle against the *Legge truffa* by parliamentary and extra-parliamentary means. It used all the possibilities offered by parliamentary rules to obstruct and delay the passing of the law. At the same time, it organized a great number of demonstrations and strikes in protest against the law. In so doing it was not acting in isolation. It had the support of the CGIL, of the PSI and of a sector of liberal and social democratic society.

However, the law was eventually passed and the elections took place in June 1953. Because the law favoured large groupings most parties entered into various sorts of electoral agreements. On the right there was a coalition of neo-fascist (MSI, Movimento Sociale Italiano) and monarchist forces; in the centre the DC was in alliance with the Liberal Party, the Republican Party and the Social Democratic Party. The PCI and the PSI entered into an electoral agreement (but not in a common list as had occurred in 1948). The left coalition was joined by two small groups: the *Unità popolare* led by the Social Democrat Piero Calamandrei and the former partisan leader Ferruccio Parri, and the *Alleanza democratica nazionale* of which the liberal economist Epicarmo Corbino was a prominent member. The *Unità popolare* represented elements which had been active in the anti-fascist movement. They belonged to the nationalist-republican Italian tradition. The *Alleanza nazionale* was made up of politicians of the pre-fascist period; liberal in outlook, they resented the increasing dominance of the USA in Italian affairs and though some of them belonged to the DC, they objected to its clericalism. The *Legge truffa* never became operative because the centrist coalition (DC–PLI–PSDI–PRI) obtained only 49.8 per cent of the votes. Only 56,000 votes were needed to give the DC and its allies the 50 per cent plus one majority required. Amendola noted the fact that the *Alleanza nazionale* and the *Unità popolare* had collected between them 500,000 votes; and this proved, he said, that a politics of alliance with strata which do not share the same political heritage as the PCI and the PSI can, in fact, work in an extremely progressive way.[37]

However, in all fairness, credit should be given to the right-wing coalition which captured 12 per cent of the votes. The fact that the DC was forced to implement a reformist policy (however tame) in the South had polarized southern politics, thereby causing the temporary defeat of the DC plan. It proved that it was difficult, if not impossible, to 'unify' Italy against both the right and left. Yet the DC could not move towards the right for reasons internal to the DC as well as because of the strength of the anti-fascist movement in Italy. It could not move towards the PCI for international reasons and because of the choices made since 1947. Thus the DC chose to remain in the middle and govern as best it could.

In over-all terms, the elections of 1953 were a considerable success for the PCI. Not only had they defeated the *Legge truffa*, but they had also increased their total votes.[38] Furthermore, in 1954 the party's total membership was at its absolute peak: 2,145,317 members. These figures hide a change in the party's relative strength in the various regions. The elections of 1953 had shown a marked Communist decline in the North coupled with large gains in the South.[39]

Once more Togliatti adapted or rather 're-defined' his strategy without altering its foundations. What did alter was the object around which the unity of all progressive forces could be achieved. This re-definition is contained in a proposal Togliatti made at a meeting of the Central Committee of 12 April 1954. He used the dramatic title of 'For an agreement between Communists and Catholics to save human civilization'. The central topic was the threat to 'civilization' posed by thermo-nuclear weapons. He said:

> The areas threatened are in practice the most populated areas of the world, those where civilization has made the greatest progress, that is the regions of the USA, the British Isles, Western Europe, the most populated and advanced areas of the Asian Continent, the Mediterranean, etc. In one word the seat of contemporary civilization.[40]

The existence of this threat determined a new field of study for the Communists. This was the field of 'human relations'. By this Togliatti probably meant that the domain of subjective factors acquired a new importance. Nuclear weapons, because they could destroy the whole of humanity, could also create a terrain for a dialogue between different ideologies. It was necessary, he said, to adopt a new frame of mind, one 'completely different' from the frame of mind with which the Italian Communists had hitherto conducted their political battles.[41]

Togliatti recognized that the world was divided into two 'extremes' (as he called them): the USSR and the USA. He then added that the Italian Communists should not simply consider these two extremes, but also other positions. He mentioned the positions adopted by Japan, India, France and by the British Labour Party. The clear implication was that there could be a position different from that of the USA which did not involve outright support for the USSR. This was important for Togliatti because if he wanted an anti-nuclear coalition he knew that he would have to adopt a position acceptable to a large stratum of people and that such a position could not coincide with that of the USSR. The new movement advocated by Togliatti would be

> a movement . . . of forces very different . . . in their nature, their political and social character. It would be, in fact, a movement for the conservation of human civilization, of humanity itself.[42]

The immediate target for this dialogue was the Catholic world. The hope expressed by the Communist leader was that such an agreement with the Catholics on a question of such importance might not be just a temporary one but the beginning of a long-term collaboration. He said he was making this proposal even though he recognized that the leadership of the Church was in complete agreement with the foreign policy objectives of the USA and that the Italian government headed by Scelba was clerical and reactionary.[43]

As it has often been pointed out, Togliatti saw Italian politics as characterized by the presence of two basic forces: on the one hand, the PSI and the PCI representing the traditions of radical, revolutionary democratic and lay Italy and, on the other hand, the Catholic movement represented by a party, the DC, which was not necessarily a reactionary party although, because of De Gasperi's strategic choice of 1947–8, it had a conservative leadership. He practically dismissed the other intermediate forces.

> Saragat does not count for very much and our remaining few liberals count for very little in front of the two enormous camps which today occupy such a great sector of the world.[44]

Togliatti's appeal had no chance of success in 1954 and he must have known it. One would be inclined to define such an appeal naïve and melodramatic, if one paid little attention to Togliatti's political complexity. Togliatti's appeal aimed at a definite political effect. The PCI sought, as often before, to present itself as the true conscience of the Italian

people, as the party which put nation before party politics, as the party
of the unity and the reconciliation of the Italian people, as the 'national'
party. In this sense the proposal simply continued an established national
policy. It should also be construed as a re-affirmation of the established
policy against the attempt by Secchia and others to question and change
it. Finally, it signalled Togliatti's intention to convince everyone within
his own party that to think of a revolution in Italy against the Catholic
masses was a dangerous dream.

If Togliatti's appeal to the Catholics was supposed to have some short-
term effect (which was very unlikely), it clearly failed to strengthen in
any way the PCI and its mass organizations.

Support among the Northern working class continued to decrease in
spite of the fact that in 1953 the CGIL had called two successful general
strikes. However, the employers were able to conduct a successful offensive against the CGIL by favouring the non-Communist trade unions, the
CISL (Catholic) and the UIL (Social Democrats).[45] The culmination of this
process was at the FIAT plants where the CGIL, which had previously
relied on the support of 65 per cent of the workers for the elections of
their representatives to the shop-floor organizations (the workers' commissions), fell to 36 per cent (March 1955).[46] This was a shattering blow
for the CGIL and for the PCI because the Turin working class had for
fifty years been the centre of Communist industrial strength (even during
the period of fascism).[47] According to Blackmer:

> The opinion was widespread, and shared by many in the union itself,
> that the CGIL's relative neglect of workers' problems and of organiza-
> tional activities at the plant level had at last caught up with it, and that
> an era had begun in which blatantly political trade unionism would no
> longer work.[48]

The CGIL also lost the election for the shop-floor committees in other
industrial combines such as Falck (steel), Innocenti (motor-cycle) and
Officine Meccaniche (trucks) — all former Communist strongholds. It
thus seems clear that the PCI had been unable to capitalize on the success
scored against the *Legge truffa*.[49]

On 5 May 1955 the PCI, in an official letter of the Executive Committee to the Turin Federation, examined the reasons for the defeat
at FIAT. It attributed the principal blame to the persecutions, the discrimination and the 'divide and rule' tactics of the management of FIAT,
but it also recognized, although half-heartedly, that 'some mistakes'
were made:

. . . at a certain point we lost touch with the most urgent and most felt problems of the factory and we conducted the struggle mainly on the basis of general, national indications no longer fully meeting the concrete conditions at FIAT.[50]

The letter also recognized a weakness in the level of political preparation of the cadres, implying that what was wrong with them was that they were too sectarian.

The full reasons for the CGIL defeat at FIAT are undoubtedly very complex. In so far as the PCI itself was responsible, there is little doubt that, as Sergio Gavarini wrote, while the PCI had been able to conduct a vast movement on general issues it had assumed that the 'national function' of the working class was won once and for all. Thus it did not pay sufficient attention to the fact that the capacity of the working class to become the directing class has a 'non-ideological' origin which derives from its specific condition of exploitation in the factory.[51] What the party had been guilty of was the disregard it held for the forms of organizations of the factory workers. The repercussions of this were to be felt even as late as in the sixties.

Pietro Ingrao's view, writing fifteen years later, was that the Italian Communist Party still had too mechanical a view of Italian capitalism. They considered it as a purely 'backward phenomenon' without distinguishing its dynamic elements from its stagnant ones.[52] Ingrao explained further that the struggle which the PCI was then conducting

. . . obscured . . . the *dynamism* that the specificity of Italian capitalism gave the big monopolies which helped them to acquire for themselves a dominant position in the economy, to subordinate to themselves the weaker sectors and the intermediate groups and to find, thus, a role in the international market through a policy of low wages, the use of the reservoir of southern and peasant labour and . . . the use of state capitalism.[53]

Thus the PCI in the middle of the fifties was in its most difficult situation since the end of the war. Italian capitalism was showing its ability to deal with a strong but divided labour movement and revealing itself not to be Malthusian and paleo-capitalistic as everyone thought it was. The chief opposition party was losing its stronghold in the very heart of Italian capitalism, in FIAT and in the large firms while not realizing that the 'economic miracle' was on its way. This was the party which, after having emerged as a leading force during the Resistance, was evicted from the coalition government it had practically forged, while its area of operation, Italy, fell within the orbit of the USA. This was the party which suffered a crushing defeat at the first general elections ever held after the war, saw the life of its most respected leader threatened, and saw its members excommunicated by a reactionary Church dominating a Catholic population. This was the party which could have been reduced to a small group of parliamentarians if only 60,000 Italians had voted differently in 1953.

It was precisely at this unfavourable conjuncture that the most important event in the post-war history of the international Communist movement took place: the Twentieth Congress of the CPSU.

Notes

1. Quoted in Franco De Felice, 'Togliatti e la costruzione del partito nuovo nel Mezzogiorno', paper presented at the 'Convegno di studio su Togliatti e il Mezzogiorno' held in Bari, 2–4 November 1975, mimeo, pp. 79–80.
2. On the gradual disintegration of the 'agrarian bloc' see G. Amendola, 'Il balzo nel mezzogiorno (1943–53)' in Quaderno No. 5 of *Critica Marxista*, Rome, 1972.
3. E. Sereni, 'Nuovi obiettivi e forme di lotta' in *Rinascita*, Nos. 11–12, Nov.–Dec. 1947.
4. G. Amendola, op. cit., p. 236.
5. P. A. Allum, 'The South and National Politics, 1945-1950' in S. J. Woolf (ed.) *The Rebirth of Italy 1943–50*, p. 118. This seems to confirm the harsh reaction of the PCI to the agrarian reform; see the resolution of the Executive Committee of 1 May 1949 in L. Barca, F. Botta, A. Zevi (eds.), *I comunisti e l'economia italiana 1944–1974*, Bari, 1975, pp. 133–6.
6. Tarrow, *Peasant Communism in Southern Italy*, New Haven, 1967, p. 295.
7. Lenin, *The Development of Capitalism in Russia, Collected Works*, Vol. 3, p. 33.
8. The need to favour industrial capital over finance capital was generally accepted by the Italian Communists. See R. Grieco, *Problemi di politica agraria*, Rome, 1950, pp. 18–19.
9. For a criticism of Grieco's position, see F. De Felice, op. cit., pp. 32–5.
10. M. D'Antonio, *Sviluppo e crisi del capitalismo italiano 1951–1972*, Bari, 1973, p. 236.
11. Ibid., p. 32.
12. It should be said that such rapid growth was largely unplanned and unforeseen as Michele Salvati has pointed out: 'At the beginning of the 1950s very few government economists (and still less those of the opposition) expected the exceptional economic development which in fact characterized the decade' in 'The impasse of Italian Capitalism', *New Left Review*, No. 76, 1972, p. 5.
13. M. D'Antonio, op. cit., p. 222.
14. S. Turone, *Storia del sindacato in Italia 1943–1969*, Bari, 1974, pp. 229–30.
15. G. Di Vittorio, 'L'industria italiana e il piano del lavoro' in *Rinascita*, Vol. 7, No. 6, June 1950.
16. B. Salvati, 'The Rebirth of Italian Trade Unionism, 1943–1954' in S. J. Woolf, *The Rebirth of Italy 1943–1950*, London, 1973, p. 205 n.
17. *VII Congresso Nazionale del PCI. Documenti politici di organizzazioni democratiche di massa*, Rome, 1954, p. 34.

18. P. Togliatti, 'Il piano del lavoro', *Rinascita*, No. 2, February 1950.

19. In *La politica economica italiana 1945-1974. Orientamenti e proposte dei comunisti*, Rome (n.d.), pp. 61-2. Di Vittorio too made it clear that he was not envisaging a general economic plan, possible only, or at least so he thought, in a socialist society; see S. Turone, op. cit., p. 230.

20. Di Vittorio's personal appeal should not be underestimated. Of him J. La Palombara wrote: 'A gifted orator, he shuns the arid, sterile language of the doctrinaire Communist. He speaks of bread, housing, schools, electrification, farm implements, wages, pensions, and so on. And he usually manages to slip into his speeches a few inflections which reveal his southern origin and which endear him to the workers and peasants', in 'Left-Wing Trade Unionism: the Matrix of Communist Power in Italy', *The Western Political Quarterly*, Vol. VII, No. 2, June 1954, p. 218.

21. S. Turone, op. cit., pp. 270-3.

22. 'Intervento di Pietro Secchia' in *Il VII Congresso del PCI Resoconto*, Rome, 1951, pp. 162-3.

23. G. Galli and F. Bellini in their *Storia del PCI*, Milan, 1953, had suggested that Secchia should be considered as the authentic representative of a national (i.e. non-Russian) form of Communism. It seems to me, on the contrary, that Secchia was the authentic voice of the Third International tradition within the PCI.

24. An extended account of this episode can be found in G. Bocca, *Palmiro Togliatti*, Bari, 1973, pp. 543-54. See also Togliatti's own account of this exchange in his report to the Central Committee meeting of 24 June 1956, 'Il "sistema policentrico" e la via italiana al socialismo' in AA.VV. *Il Partito comunista italiano e il movimento operaio internazionale*, Rome, 1968, p. 76.

25. When Togliatti's secretary, Luigi Adamesi, in order to calm him, pointed out that the Cominform was important, Togliatti answered furiously: 'Nonsense! The Cominform is a terrible pain in the neck! "He" would decide everything and then I would have to bully everybody else. If we approved of the dissolution of the Comintern it was because we had our reasons . . . We should do nothing to reinforce the Cominform, quite the contrary. But Stalin does not want to know.' Quoted in G. Bocca, *Palmiro Togliatti*, Bari, 1973, p. 546.

26. Ibid., p. 550.

27. Ibid., p. 551.

28. E. D'Onofrio, 'Il problema della direzione collegiale del PCI', *Rinascita*, No. 11, November 1953.

29. The note of Togliatti to Secchia was eventually published by Marcella Ferrara in *Rinascita*, No. 27, 5 July 1974 ('Dagli appunti di lavoro del direttore di "Rinascita" '). Secchia wrote the article following faithfully Togliatti's indications; it was published at the end of 1954, see P. Secchia, 'L'organizzazione, la voce, il volto del partito comunista nel nostro paese', *Rinascita*, Nos. 11-12, Nov.–Dec. 1954.

30. The Partito Popolare was founded in January 1919. It was the culmination of a process of reconciliation between the Catholics and the Italian state which had begun in 1891 with the Encyclical *Rerum Novarum*. The name 'Christian Democracy', adopted during the war, derived from a left-leaning group within the Catholic political movement early in the century and the adoption of this name symbolized the attempt to emphasize the progressive and non-clerical foundations of the DC. See Gabriele De Rosa, *Il Partito popolare italiano*, Bari, 1972.

31. See the account of Fanfani's fortunes in R. Orfei, *L'occupazione del potere. I democristiani '45/'47*, Milan, 1976, pp. 154-76. See also G. Chiarante, 'La crisi di egemonia riversata sul paese', *Rinascita*, No. 21, 25 May 1973.

32. Fanfani became particularly close with Enrico Mattei, the dynamic boss of ENI. In exchange for a definitive recognition of the role and power of State enterprises, Mattei accepted to link the fortunes of ENI with those of the DC; see Orfei, op. cit., p. 159.

33. G. Amendola, 'Il PCI all'opposizione. La lotta contro lo scelbismo' in AA.VV. *Problemi di storia del partito comunista italiano*, Rome, 1971, p. 124.

34. Ibid., p. 124.

35. The nickname 'Legge truffa' was invented by the Communist leader Gian Carlo Pajetta. This expression encountered such success that it became part of political language. Even today a Christian Democrat, if he wants to refer to that law, will use the expression 'Legge truffa'. This point is made in Amendola, ibid., p. 125.

36. P. Togliatti, *Il Partito comunista italiano*, Rome, 1971, p. 114.

37. Amendola, op. cit., p. 127.

38. Comparisons with the 1948 data are difficult because then the PCI and PSI votes are subsumed in the Fronte Democratico Popolare. The Front had obtained 31 per cent in 1948, the combined PCI and PSI votes in 1953 represented 35.35 per cent. As the PCI obtained 22.6 per cent in 1953 it can be safely assumed that there was an increment of PCI votes; see the data in C. Ghini, *Il voto degli italiani*, Rome, 1975, p. 118.

39. Ibid., p. 119.

40. 'Per un accordo tra comunisti e cattolici per salvare la civiltà umana' in P. Togliatti, *Comunisti Socialisti Cattolici*, Rome, 1974, p. 167.

41. Ibid., p. 169.

42. Ibid., p. 172.

43. Ibid., pp. 175–80.

44. Ibid., p. 179.

45. On the discriminatory policies of the management of FIAT and on their persecution of Communist militants see Renzo Giannotti, *Lotte e organizzazione di classe alla FIAT (1948–1970)*, Bari, 1970 and Aris Accornero, *FIAT confino*, Rome, 1959. The USA intervened by subsidizing the CISL and the UIL, see S. Turone, op. cit., p. 225. Recent evidence of direct US interference has now been confirmed with the publication in the *Rivista di Storia Contemporanea* (No. 2, 1974) of documents relating to a meeting between the US Ambassador, Clare Booth Luce, and the Chairman of FIAT, Vittorio Valletta on 4 February 1954.

46. The CISL obtained 41 per cent and the UIL 23 per cent.

47. Of this Luciano Gruppi writes, with some exaggeration, 'It was, I think, one of the most serious defeats of the Italian Labour Movement after Liberation; in fact, maybe it was the only feat' in *Togliatti e la via italiana al socialismo*, p. 136.

48. D. L. M. Blackmer, *Unity in Diversity: Italian Communism and the Communist World*, Cambridge, Mass., and London, 1968, p. 266.

49. As S. Gavarini wrote: 'Thus while we were winning the battle on the Legge truffa, one of the bastions of the labour movement, that is the class organization in the factories, was crumbling and eventually crashed in 1955 in decisive points such as FIAT' in 'La restaurazione capitalistica (1948–1955)' in *I comunisti a Torino 1919–1972*, Rome, 1973, p. 209.

50. The text of the letter can be found in L. Barca, F. Botta, A. Zevi, op. cit., pp. 188–99. The quote above is on page 190. A frank self-criticism was also made by Di Vittorio: 'For the labour movement a defeat is always the most convincing objective criticism, the real data which impose reflection and change', quoted in S. Gavarini, 'Gli anni '50 alla FIAT: una esperienza storica', *Politica ed economia*, No. 2, Sept.–Oct. 1970.

51. S. Gavarini, 'La restaurazione capitalistica (1948–1955)' in op. cit., pp. 208–9.
52. P. Ingrao, 'Il XX Congresso del PCUS e l'VIII Congresso del PCI' in AA.VV. *Problemi di storia del PCI*, Rome, 1971, pp. 142–3.
53. Ibid., p. 143.

PART II   1956–1964

6.   Polycentrism

Khruschev's report to the Twentieth Congress of the CPSU (14–16 February 1956) was divided into two sections: one 'open' and the other 'secret'. The secret part, which had been circulated beforehand to some Communist leaders, including Togliatti, is remembered as the most remarkable event of the Twentieth Congress by many commentators.[1] The real novelty (from a strategic point of view), however, was contained in the official 'open' section where the CPSU explicitly accepted, for the first time, the possibility of different roads to socialism.

The significance of this statement can hardly be under-estimated. It involved the recognition that, in matters of strategy, there could be no single model. Hence it freed the members of the international Communist movement to pursue independently their best national form of socialism. It was a sign of the existence of some of the conditions for the end of dogmatism in matters of strategy. This 'conquest' could not, of course, be final. On the one hand the leadership group of the CPSU would not always stand by the logical consequences of the Twentieth Congress and, on the other, many Communist Parties were not ideologically and theoretically equipped to take advantage in a new and creative way of the strategic freedom they had gained.

The Italian Communist Party was not in this latter category. In the period we have examined so far it has become apparent that the PCI had always emphasized the peculiarities of the Italian situation, but this had not always been accompanied by an *explicit* recognition of the possibility of an original road to socialism in Italy. The fact that official sanction for this had now come from Moscow shows how far the international Communist movement had not been able to break with the tradition of monolithic internationalism created by the Comintern. This tradition could not be broken by a single speech, but the Congress was the signal for an ideological debate which proved to be the new characteristic of the international Communist movement. The immediate causes of the debate were undoubtedly the new international situation defined by the existence of a strong socialist camp facing a capitalist bloc led by the USA; and by the emergence of new nations which had undergone the experience of decolonization. The old monolithic conception had emerged in a period where the first socialist country was encircled by hostile powers and in which the construction of socialism in one country entailed, rightly or wrongly, the defence of the USSR as the primary task of the international Communist movement. The persistence of this monolithic conception in an entirely different world situation is only another proof that ideological conceptions tend to linger on into changed material circumstances. Togliatti had been aware of this problem and he took advantage of the Twentieth Congress to present the search for an Italian road to socialism as the fundamental task facing Italian Communism. In his speech at the Twentieth Congress he said:

> Naturally we understand very well that the roads the CPSU has followed in order to obtain power and establish a socialist society is not in all its aspects obligatory for all countries but that the road [to socialism] will have and must have its own particularities in the various countries.[2]

Later in March, at the Central Committee meeting convened to discuss the Twentieth Congress, Togliatti, in an attempt to establish some continuity with past policies, insisted that the PCI had not had to wait for the Twentieth Congress to proclaim its own road to socialism.[3] He traced this elaboration to Antonio Gramsci who 'in his entire political activity and particularly in the last period of his life was concerned with the "translation" or rather the "conversion" into Italian of the teachings of the Russian Revolution'. He pointed out that if the Italian constitution had some principles which were of a socialist nature it was because the Italian Communists had rejected in 1946 the illegal road to power and had participated in the workings of the Constituent Assembly. This, added Togliatti, was not understood by all the Communist Parties: he criticized the Greek CP for having boycotted the elections of 1945; 'our line was different and experience proved us right'.[4]

Here we must introduce a distinction between Togliatti's strategic analysis and his tactical pronouncements. At the strategic level, the renunciation of the 1917 model has implications which go well beyond Italian realities. It involves a theoretical distinction between specific forms of State power as well as the thesis that particular strategies must correspond to particular forms of State. An elaboration of Togliatti's reference to Gramsci will illustrate this point. In his prison writings Gramsci, in a famous passage, makes a distinction between the forms of State power in the East and the West using an enlarged concept of the State (as civil society plus political society).[5] The 'East' is a form of State power characterized by the weakness of its civil society, the 'West' is the opposite. To this distinction of State forms correspond specific strategies: a particular articulation of 'war of position' and 'war of movement'.[6] We cannot discuss here Gramsci's profound insight, but we must point out that, in practice, Gramsci is not putting forward an idea of an 'Italian road to socialism', but more an indication for a 'Western' road to socialism as opposed to an 'Eastern' road. Obviously, this distinction is not a geographical one but a theoretical one: between different forms of states, that is, between different articulations of civil society and political society. Togliatti was well aware of this and we shall try to show that his idea of polycentrism reflects this awareness and that, at the theoretico-strategic level, Togliatti's long-term aim is a development of a revolutionary perspective in the West.

We now turn to the 'tactical' level: strictly speaking, the term 'national roads' to socialism does not entail a categorization of different forms of state. The empiricist, however, would hold that every national state is so different from all others as to require a departure from the 1917 model, based not on a different articulation of civil and political society but on the 'fact' of the nation. So, 'national roads', in the *strict* sense, entails that one cannot talk about the specificity of revolution in the West, but only that, say, Italy is as sufficiently different from France as it is from Iraq. I have called this level of analysis of 'national roads' tactical because the adoption of this perspective is determined by tactical needs: in other words, Togliatti could not, for reasons internal to the international Communist movement as well as to his own party, argue systematically for a 'Western' conception of the revolution; rather he had first to argue for a position in which he could demand complete autonomy for all parts of the international Communist movement. In practice, Togliatti's elaboration would contain elements of both this tactical as well as of the strategic approach. In other words, he went as far as he could with his developments at the strategic level. This, of course, meant that an elaboration of his ideas at the theoretical level could not be arrived at, hence the apparent empiricist form which many of his pronouncements took.

What is particularly striking is the way in which there is no theoretical justification of the modifications Togliatti introduced. These were presented in an essentially pragmatic way which simply affirmed that certain points are now historically obsolete while others remain valid. It would be possible to argue that Togliatti is simply carrying out at the political level a historicist framework of analysis where the new realities ('hard facts') are the determinants of the modification of the theory and that therefore the theory does not explain what is an empirically given reality, but must adapt itself to it. This can be a one-sided view, for it can also be argued that Togliatti uses implicitly the Leninist method in order to isolate those principles which are valid and acceptable from those which are not. Which ever way we look at it, and only a careful study of Togliatti's text can solve this problem, it is clear that Togliatti is attacking the 'dogmatist' tendencies within the Communist movement. These attacks will bring forth what can be described as 'reformist' tendencies which will be the centre of subsequent ideological debates within the PCI.

The presence of a strong 'tactical' element is evident in the fact that Togliatti, at the April meeting of the Central Committee, did not touch the most explosive question: the question of Stalin. Again on 3 April during the workings of the National Council of the PCI which had assembled to prepare the campaign for the local elections, there was no mention of Stalin. Togliatti concentrated his report on internal matters. Amendola was less restrained and stated polemically, referring to the USSR, that the PCI was finally free of 'external debts',[7] thus exemplifying the liberating effects which the unfettered search for a national road could have. The question of Stalin was decisively tackled by Togliatti only after the publication in the *New York Times* of 4 June of Khruschev's speech on de-Stalinization.

The question of Stalin was closely related to the problem of national roads because the rejection of the 1917 model could not be separated from a critical analysis of the entire experience of the construction of socialism in the USSR. The debate on Stalin presented the different Communist Parties with the opportunity to establish a new relationship with the CPSU different from the monolithic one which dominated the international movement. Only the Chinese and the Italian Communist Parties took advantage of this opportunity. What Togliatti did was not merely to delve more deeply than the CPSU into the question of Stalin, but also to polemize openly with Khruschev on problems of methodology. The principal locus of this discussion was the famous interview he gave to the journal *Nuovi Argomenti*.[8]

What Togliatti finds unacceptable is the concept of 'personality cult'. This concept cannot be used as the universal key for the explanation of everything which went wrong in the USSR and in the international Communist movement. To use this concept as Khruschev did is simply to reverse the previous position which consisted in attributing every success to the personality of Stalin. Togliatti could not accept this rather naïve inversion:

> . . . as long as one limits oneself to denounce Stalin's personal defects as the cause of everything one remains within the terms of the personality cult. Before, all that was good was due to the superhuman

positive qualities of a man; now all that is evil is attributed to his similarly exceptional and amazing defects. In both cases we are outside the criteria of judgement which are proper to Marxism.[9]

He establishes two areas of investigation: the first was the period during the twenties when, according to Togliatti, all the 'healthy' forces of the party joined Stalin's camp, but accepted such changes in the leading party and State apparatuses that it became impossible to stop the degeneration of Soviet democracy. But the problem could even be more serious: 'Perhaps it would not be wrong to say that the damaging limitations to the democratic regime and the gradual emergence of forms of bureaucratic organization began in the party itself.'[10]

The second area of investigation Togliatti established was the period of the first five-year plan and of collectivization of the agricultural sector. Having recognized the effective success of what he called the creation of a powerful socialist industrial society and the transformation of the countryside, he pointed out the excessive hurry with which this process was carried out and the fact that the inevitable contradictions which emerged were not openly tackled by relying on a mass movement of workers and peasants. The first damaging consequence of these modes of operation was that any 'creative debate' was immediately suppressed and, therefore, the democratic-socialist institutions which had been the produce of the Soviet revolution were weakened or destroyed. The second damaging consequence was a tendency to attribute any delay or difficulty in the realization of the plans to the conspiratorial activities of groups of counter-revolutionaries.

Togliatti faced the question of how much the whole leadership group shared responsibilities, including 'those comrades who have today taken the initiative both in denouncing and in correcting the harm which had previously been done and the consequences stemming from it'.[11] He rejected as a possible explanation of the reason why Stalin was not removed from office the thesis that his power depended entirely on a 'military, terroristic apparatus' and pointed out that Stalin's power relied also on the consensus of the overwhelming majority of the party cadres and of the masses and that he had been able to obtain such a consensus because many of his policies had been correct.

There is little discussion in the 'Interview' of the behaviour of the non-Soviet leaders of the international Communist movement (of which Togliatti himself was one of the leading figures). It is clear, however, that Togliatti was absolutely convinced that there had been no major errors in the policies of the international Communist movement after the 'Third Period'. These policies he had helped to shape and he would stand by them.

The question of Stalin cannot be reduced to a matter of relations between the PCI and the CPSU. It erupted within the Italian Communist Party and constituted an issue around which strategic and ideological problems not directly related to the question of Stalin were fought out.

Although this question was not at the centre of the Eighth Congress of the party held in December 1956, the spirit (or the ghost) of the man who had led the international communist movement for thirty years haunted the assembled delegates. The bewilderment of the rank and file was signalled by V. Bertini, the delegate from Florence, who said: '. . . there are comrades who have lost their faith in the Party and in the Soviet Union and do not know what to believe of what is being said of Stalin's policies.'[12]

Prestipino, the delegate from Messina (Sicily), expressed openly what was in the minds of many when he said that 'no one can deny the fact that in Southern Italy hundreds of thousands of peasants and workers have come to us because of their enthusiastic faith in the infallibility of Stalin's directives',[13] and he added: 'We must explain to them that . . . Stalin was wrong. One fact cannot be forgotten: our Southern peasants are no longer anarchist, thanks to our party, but, ideologically, they still remain on extremist and infantile positions.'[14]

But the Southern peasants were not alone — Concetto Marchesi, an intellectual and a former Rector of the University of Padova, affirmed his loyalty to Stalin, 'the man who symbolized the soul and the strength of the Soviet Union in those long and terrible years', and he added with unmistakable hostility towards de-Stalinization, 'let us by all means shake the enemy's hand, but let us not provide him with the wood so that he may make a hatchet'.[15]

The 'reformist' position was expressed by Giolitti who pointed out that it was necessary to examine the question of shared responsibility particularly over the question of Tito.[16] Giolitti showed the consistency of his political line by focusing on Togliatti's co-responsibility in the Yugoslavian question (rather than, for instance, on the more obvious question of the Moscow trials). This issue in fact not only took place in the crucial years 1948–53, but centred on the all-important question of the relationship between the CPSU and the international Communist movement.

Togliatti tried to overcome the polarization between the so-called 'sectarians' (or 'dogmatists') and the 'reformists' (or 'revisionists') by reiterating his criticisms of the Twentieth Congress for failing to go beyond the category of 'personality cult' into examining the real causes of the deformation of the Soviet political order.[17] When examining Stalinism in Eastern Europe, Togliatti attempted to give some indications for further research into the question. He put forward the view that immediately after the Second World War a series of attempts had begun in Eastern Europe to implement radical reforms in alliance with other political forces. But these were destroyed by the Cold War, which was the principal cause for what Togliatti calls 'the servile imitation of the Soviet model'. He called this a fundamental mistake both in matters of principle and of practice. Instances of this 'servile imitation' were having to give priority to the development of heavy industry and the collectivization of agriculture. Furthermore the newer socialist regimes did not have any rooted form of organized direct democracy which could integrate the activity of parliamentary assemblies; and also the trade unions could not assume their proper role in economic life as the defenders of the immediate interests of the workers.[18] This analysis cannot simply be considered an attempt to place a share of the blame on the Western powers, culpable of having launched the Cold War. It was also a way of proclaiming that the PCI would not, even if it could, impose on the Italians the enormous cost of rapid collectivization, that it would respect the principles of democracy and would maintain the autonomy of the trade union movement.

Few, if any, of the discussions around Stalin tried to develop one of the most fruitful elements of Togliatti's references to Stalin at the Eighth Congress: the question of the relation between the political and the economic level. Togliatti said:

> I remain convinced that our research must be particularly directed to clarify the relations, contrasts and reciprocal influence between economic developments and the political superstructures to which even the highest political leadership belongs. When the economy had reached a point which allowed and demanded an extension of democratic life, this did not take place and instead there occurred new restrictions and artificial impediments.[19]

This would, however, be constrained by the real political movement of international relations and by the real 'relations of forces' existing between the various Communist Parties. It was one thing to declare a right of political autonomy and another to conquer it and maintain it.

The relative and recently acquired freedom of movement of the Italian CP was to be put to the test by the Hungarian and Polish events of 1956. It was in this context that Togliatti's strategic pronouncements were constrained by tactical requirements. It should also be noted that the Twentieth

Congress had sparked off a debate in most other Communist Parties. In Poland, in particular, the large-scale workers' demonstrations which erupted in Poznan on 28 June 1956 found the leadership group of the Polish CP (the Polish United Workers' Party) divided into two factions, one favouring liberalization measures and the other adopting a more intransigent posture. The 'hard-liners' were politically closer to the USSR in a conflict which was increasingly seen as an attempt to assert the independence of the Polish transition to socialism against serious interference from the USSR.

One of the elements of the Polish crisis — and it is the one which is of interest to us here — was that the crisis presented itself as a testing ground for the new tendencies of the international communist movement as they had shown themselves at the Twentieth Congress of the CPSU. The two new tendencies which appeared in the Polish CP were also present in the Italian CP interpretations of the workers' demonstrations as the result of the activities of USA-inspired saboteurs, *agent provocateurs* and counter-revolutionaries co-existed with views which saw the workers' unrest as the manifestation of a deep-seated crisis within Polish Communism and as a demand for greater democracy.

It seems that at this stage the prevailing tendency within the PCI was to interpret the Polish events as a crisis of Polish Communism and as a confirmation of the necessity for autonomy. However, it soon became apparent that the long-standing centripetal tendencies of the USSR could not be eliminated quickly, particularly on an issue so close to home. This was confirmed by a resolution of the Central Committee of the CPSU of 30 June which interpreted the Poznan uprising as being completely master-minded by the USA and rejected completely any other interpretations.[20] The resolution was published in *Pravda* on 2 July and it was too late for Di Vittorio's editorial, offering a completely different view of events, to be withheld from the issue of *L'Unità* of the same day.

Di Vittorio did not discount the presence of provocateurs but insisted that they would have had no chance of success if there was not a deep-seated discontent among the Polish working class. He maintained that the workers in a socialist country have the right to determine the limits of any sacrifice which might be needed for the construction of socialism. He further stated that even in a socialist country the unions 'have the task of defending energetically the just demands of the workers, in relation to the demands of the general development of socialist society'.[21]

In the heat of the events of June–July 1956, Di Vittorio's original stand in *L'Unità* could only be interpreted as hostile to the USSR. A resolution of the Central Committee of the CPSU offered 'hard' interpretation of the

Polish events while explicitly attacking Togliatti and his interpretation of the Stalin question as explained in the interview to *Nuovi Argomenti*.

Togliatti's reaction was to modify the position of the PCI: on the one hand he would assert, at least implicitly, the right of the PCI to take an autonomous position in principle, on the other he would uphold the Soviet interpretation of the Polish crisis. This line, characterized by a tactical duality, is seen at work in two short articles published in *L'Unità* of 3 July and 4 July, the first being in a leading article of 3 July entitled 'La presenza del nemico', clearly Stalinist in tone:

> The enemy does exist. He is strong, he is active, and he is without pity. He is still powerful outside our camp and does not lack strength and points of influence even within our camp. Woe betide us if we forget this. The events that have taken place at Poznan remind us of it particularly strongly . . . The enemy is, therefore, present. He was present at Poznan, in a way which is becoming increasingly clear . . . But he is present elsewhere as well, trying to make us deviate from our path, to sow confusion and defeatism . . .[22]

Significantly *Pravda* reprinted Togliatti's editorial the next day. But in the second article on 4 July Togliatti replied to the accusations of the Soviet Union over his *Nuovi Argomenti* interview and maintained his right to hold different views. Togliatti's balancing act was to be further complicated by the ensuing Hungarian events which were to prove far more serious than the Polish crisis. The success of the 'liberalization' faction within the Polish Communist Party had been crowned by the return of Wladyslaw Gomulka to the leadership. However, when a few days later the Hungarian crisis erupted, the initial reaction of the PCI was to follow the 'hard' line adopted eventually for Poznan. *L'Unità* of 26 October 1956 wrote of American provocation and of counter-revolutionary troops and added:

> Tomorrow we may even discuss our differences . . . Today we must defend the socialist revolution . . . When the guns of the counter-revolutionaries are in operation one must be on one or the other side of the barricades. There is no third camp.

This initial position was slightly modified when further news established that political power was in the hands of the 'liberal' faction in the Hungarian CP led by Kadar and Nägy, that this faction had accepted some of the demands of the rebels and that the Soviet government supported the new government and had withdrawn its troops.

By 3 November, the Executive Committee of the PCI had re-defined the position, stressing all the elements favourable to autonomous roads to socialism while attempting to avoid any rupture, however slight, with the policies of the USSR. The Communiqué of the Executive Committee viewed the Polish and Hungarian events as a confirmation that the criticism at the Twentieth Congress of Stalinist methods and organization was urgent and overdue.[23] The PCI traced the cause of the Soviet intervention to the lack of an established 'Hungarian road to socialism'. The view which seemed to inspire the Italian Communists was essentially simple: the non-development of national roads, the mechanical imitation of the Soviet model inevitably created profound ruptures and discontent in a society on the road to socialism. When these ruptures and discontent manifest themselves openly and violently, they favour the intervention of provocateurs which, whether these be from within or without, open the door for a change in the international ideological (and hence political) position of the society in question. This cannot be tolerated by the most powerful socialist country, the USSR, because (quite apart from questions of *realpolitik*) any such change must inevitably correspond to a weakening of its international position. Thus the intervention of the Soviet Union in these circumstances is not a mere defence of the revolution in one country only (and hence an interference into the class struggle of another country), but an intervention in the international class struggle which contributes both to a strengthening of the international Communist movement and a weakening of imperialism. This is not a definition of the situation, but rather an attempt to define the situation *as seen by the Italian Communist Party* using a contextual analysis of its official pronouncements.

So far we have tried to establish that a strict or narrow conception of national roads to socialism is not compatible with the possibility of formulating a strategy for the West; we have therefore assumed that a defence of the 'narrow' conception of national roads must be due to tactical factors. But there is also the possibility that the fight for national roads was the mechanism which would pave the way for a polycentric view, i.e. one which recognized the possibility of a multiplicity of 'regional' centres.

The possibility that the PCI's 'narrow' conception of national roads was a tactical one is then only one of two hypothetical interpretations. The other rests on the following hypothesis: national roads seen as *de facto* autonomy, that is, the real possibility for each individual party to reconstruct with other parties, from an autonomous position, a new relationship better suited to the new international conditions. It is this second hypothesis which is perfectly compatible with polycentrism.

To demonstrate this we shall have to examine in greater detail the conditions limiting the real autonomy of Communist Parties. Schematically the problem can be thus expressed: how can one reconcile the right of Communist Parties to be free of outside interference with the necessity for each party to express their position on matters of international importance? If any two parties express a different position, it can be construed that one is interfering in the affairs of the others. If a fictitious unanimity is imposed then parties are not autonomous. The Hungarian case was a clear example of this problem: either a Communist Party conformed to the Soviet position (against its own views), thus relinquishing its independence (even if only momentarily), or it opposed the Soviets, thereby 'interfering'. The problem can be re-phrased this way: what new conception of proletarian internationalism was required once the old monolithic conception was discarded? It is for an answer to this problem that one should read the analyses of the Italian Communists on the question of polycentrism.

Togliatti first used the expression 'polycentrism' in his Interview to *Nuovi Argomenti*:

> The whole system is becoming polycentric. Within the Communist movement itself one cannot talk of a single guide, but of progress which is achieved by following roads which are often diverse.[24]

Thus, at this stage, a polycentric system seems to denote the absence of a single guide. In fact, from the context, it is not even clear whether Togliatti is referring only to the Communist movement as becoming polycentric or to the world system as a whole. The reference to the end of a single guide is couched in objective terms: it is the existing situation which rules out monolithism. The fact that 'one cannot talk of a single guide' is determined by material factors and not by ideological considerations alone. Once monolithism is ruled out, there remain two alternatives: full autonomy for every party and bilateralism as the form of co-ordination of the international communist movement on the one hand, on the other a multiplicity of regional centres or polycentrism.

It seems clear that in the period 1956–64 (but also later) the first alternative prevailed in the international movement, while the second prevailed inside the Italian CP; it was this contrast which made it so difficult for the Italians to develop polycentrism. From the outset the very word itself came under attack, and this, eventually, made it impossible for the PCI to include the term polycentrism in their official documents.[25]

In fact a few days after the Interview, at a Central Committee meeting (24 June) Togliatti qualified his remarks on polycentrism:

Thus there appears diverse points or centres of orientation and development. A polycentric system comes to be created and it corresponds to the new situation, to the changes in the structures of the world and the structures of the working class movements, and to this system corresponds also new forms or relations among the Communist parties themselves. The solution which today probably corresponds the most to the new situation can be that of the full autonomy of the single movements and Communist parties and of bilateral relations between them, in order to create a complete reciprocal understanding, a complete reciprocal trust, conditions for collaboration and conditions to give unity to the Communist movement itself and to the entire movement of the working class.[26]

There is also the growing realization that the rigid separation of the world into two blocs is slowly coming to an end and that 'the world has become polycentric' because even in the imperialist camp there are growing differences.[27] Thus whereas the opposition to the spirit of the Atlantic defence system remains a constant element of the PCI, there is now the introduction of a more differentiated position. It is now acknowledged that:

Even within the Atlantic Treaty, Italy can and must have an independent position which must have the tendency to transcend the division of the world in opposing armed blocs and to solve through negotiations those problems which are not yet solved, to press for disarmament, the prohibition of nuclear weapons and a proper consolidation of *détente* and peace.[28]

This could be seen as the beginning of the recognition that not only Italy occupies a delicate and particular position in the international system, but that this position cannot be changed unilaterally, that is, that a withdrawal from NATO could not really be considered outside a general international realignment, particularly in Europe (in practice, however, the slogan 'Italy out of NATO' would survive until the 1970s).

With regard to Europe Togliatti declared that the Italian Communists were 'European too' and that they intended to take part in the existing European organizations in order 'to work within these for a policy of peace as representatives of an important part of the Italian people'.[29] Having stated that there was no contradiction between the policies of the Italian Communists and the interests of the nation, Togliatti re-affirmed the principles of international solidarity and national roads with the slogan 'unity in diversity'.[30]

At the Eighth Congress of the PCI, Togliatti himself would admit that 'polycentrism' had not been accepted:

> As there is no longer a single organization and hence a single directing centre, a system of multiple centres had been thought of, but this organizational form has seemed not compatible with the full autonomy of each party . . . A system of bilateral relations can satisfy the conditions of autonomy.[31]

Polycentrism as such was not mentioned again until the debate of the Central Committee of November 1961 when speaker after speaker talked of polycentrism as a *de facto* reality. But the 1961 debates must be inscribed in a new situation characterized by the beginning of the great Sino-Soviet schism which would split the international movement.

The actual ideological battle of the PCI between 1956 and 1961 was centred on demolishing once and for all any attempt to return to a single centre. It may seem that such a battle could be easily won. After all the necessity for different roads to socialism had been put forward by Khrushchev himself at the Twentieth Congress of the CPUS and only Mao Tse-Tung seems to have disagreed with any attempts to change the monolithic nature of the international movement.

Furthermore the end of the concept of centralized direction was officially sanctioned by the disbandment of the Cominform in April 1956, a development positively underlined by Togliatti at the Eighth Congress of the PCI and confirmed in the Party Theses.[32]

In spite of this apparent unanimity against centralization, Togliatti's insistence in emphasizing that the new international situation required the end of monolithism was a sign that the battle for autonomy was far from being won. In the 'best' Communist tradition he would always attempt to show that his statements were in full conformity with the general line. At the Central Committee meeting of 24 June 1956, he would use the results of the Twentieth Congress to produce a polycentric analysis by characterizing the international conjuncture as dominated by three elements:

1. A system of socialist states.
2. The collapse of colonialism.
3. 'The tendency for the new peoples and states, which are no longer under the dominium of imperialism, not to follow the road to capitalism in their economic, political and social development.'[33]

This conjuncture is seen to be favourable to socialism to such an extent that, not only is war no longer inevitable (i.e. the theses of Zhdanov's report to the founding of the Cominform, and which were the basis of Cominform policies, no longer held any validity) but:

> . . . one can obtain great and specific results in the march towards socialism without abandoning the democratic method following different roads from those which were nearly obligatory in the past, thus avoiding those ruptures and the bitterness which were then necessary.[34]

Clearly here the national roads to socialism are not an immutable principle of a Communist strategy, but an element which is determined by a favourable world conjuncture. This is not to say that the question is a new one, as Togliatti himself pointed out. He stated that this principle had already been treated in the classics of Marxism and that the new situation allows one to deal with this theme with 'greater clarity' than before.[35] When he mentions Lenin again it is only to suggest a departure from what may have been thought to be an established principle. Togliatti explains that Marx had put forward the thesis that socialism could only be established in those countries which had reached the highest level of capitalist development. Lenin had revised this thesis in his writings on Imperialism and in his concept of the 'weakest link', and the time had come to elaborate further Lenin's 'correction'. The presence of ex-colonial countries attempting to by-pass capitalism made this imperative.[36]

This constitutes the Togliattian starting-point for a general re-examination of doctrinal points which had become part of the ideological armoury of the international communist movement. He used as his key analytical element a method of differentiated analysis which laid great emphasis on the concept of uneven development, a concept of impeccable Leninist origin and one which had been at the centre of Togliatti's thinking even during the Third Period policies.[37] His argument implies the recognition of a disjunction (or lack of correspondence) between the rapid structural developments which have occurred in the world system and the political strategy of the various Communist Parties.

The causes of this disjuncture were to be found in the actions of the ruling classes as well as in the mistaken political positions adopted by the Communist Parties; these were the elements which 'have slowed down — or even impeded — the development of Communist Parties'.[38] There are, he added, great differences in the forms of organization, economic structure, and political traditions among the other socialist countries. And outside the 'socialist camp' the diversities are even more pronounced:

for example, there are ex-colonial countries trying to move towards socialism without Communist Parties in power or even present in great force.

Clearly implied in this 'revision' is the total break with all dogmatic conceptions of vanguard states and vanguard parties whether nationally or internationally.

This position encountered a certain resistance in the international movement. Garaudy, then one of the 'official' philosophers of the French CP wrote in January 1957 a harsh attack against the Italian road to socialism.[39] More importantly the international conference of the Communist Parties which assembled in Moscow in 1957, though paying lip service to the principle of different roads to socialism clearly stated that there are a number of 'basic laws applicable in all countries embarking on a socialist course'.[40] This statement would seem unexceptional if it were not for the fact that these basic laws could only be 'strategic laws'. Furthermore the very fact of an international conference with a final resolution 'unanimously' accepted by all parties implied that, in place of a centralized direction there would be periodic conferences of all Communist Parties, and that these conferences would attempt to lay down general principles. Togliatti's speech at the conference, which was not published until 1959, not only did not mention 'basic laws' but implicitly criticized the formalism of the final resolution:

> It is not difficult to give the impression of unity in general formulations, but this is not the sort of unity we need . . . We must not be in a hurry in trying to create new international organisms.[41]

There was obviously a real fear within the PCI that there would be attempts to re-create a new international centre. The PCI's fear had real roots: bilateralism as an organizational form for the international movement could not really be a satisfactory solution. Those parties which supported it (such as the Polish and the Yugoslav) did so because they were even more opposed to any new international organizations.

The discussion on 'polycentrism' started again in 1961 during the Central Committee meeting of 10–11 November. For many speakers 'polycentrism' was a *de facto* situation to which the international communist movement had to adapt itself.[42] The Moscow Conference of 1957 came under attack by many speakers. Amendola described the 1957 Moscow Conference as resulting in a 'fictitious unanimity' and added: '. . . the system of bilateral contacts, internal polemics, summit contacts and conferences is no longer adequate and is even something of a hindrance to us.'[43] This dissatisfaction with international conferences resulted also from the 1960 Moscow Conference which ended with a compromise resolution in an attempt to smooth over the differences between the Chinese CP and the CPSU. The general view emerging from the discussion at the Central Committee meeting was a revaluation of polycentrism and in particular of the need for a new approach to the question of revolution in the West. Polycentrism was seen as determining the specificity of Western Europe.

The international reactions to these debates were remarkable. The central committees of the Czech, Polish, East German and French Communist Parties all condemned polycentrism in no uncertain terms.[44]

L'Unità was forced into a tactical retreat and an editorial on 26 November 1961 declared:

> . . . the resolution which we published today leaves no doubt as to the decisive importance we give to the unity of the movement, and leaves no room for any interpretation of polycentrism as a multiplicity of centres of regional directions.[45]

The total inconsistency of *L'Unità*'s declaration is demonstrated by the fact that Togliatti himself in his report had mentioned 'a multiplicity of leadership centres', although he had not used the term 'polycentrism'.[46]

There is clearly a difficulty in attempting to disentangle the tactical level from the strategic level. If, as the PCI claimed, there was no difference between an 'absence of a single centre' and 'polycentrism', in the sense that one was a necessary though not a sufficient condition for the other, it could not be claimed that 'polycentrism' and 'full autonomy' were the same thing except in one sense: the formation of regional centres could not take the form of a new regional organization, that is, there could not be the creation even at the regional level of a monolithic type of organization. The full autonomy of each party was a necessary pre-condition for the organization of 'regional' centres according to a new form of co-ordination based on the common recognition by the 'regional' members of an objective necessity to co-ordinate action. It was not clear in the period 1956–64 what these common elements could be, nor how the new 'centre' could come into being.

The dominance of the tactical element meant that, in so far as the PCI was concerned, the general priority was to obtain full autonomy for itself. As we have stated the theme 'polycentrism' (in both its explicit and implicit form) was held in abeyance from the Eighth Congress of the PCI to the end of 1961. The post-1961 formulations were due principally to three factors: the beginning of the schism between the CPSU and the Chinese CP, the initial re-thinking on the part of the PCI on the whole

question of the Common Market and, internally, the attempt on the part
of the Italian ruling class to rationalize the problems of Italian capitalism
by an 'opening to the left' and the subsequent incorporation of the Italian
Socialist Party into the area of government.

The schism between the CPSU and the CCP (which we cannot discuss
here) was the practical demonstration that monolithism was truly dead.

As for the Common Market, the initially hostile attitude of the PCI
underwent gradual modification, but it was only in 1962 that there
occurred a real shift in position. The first stage of this shift took place at
the Conference on the tendencies of Italian capitalism held in Rome in
March 1962. Giorgio Amendola, who gave the main paper, declared:

> Our position, a politically responsible one, in criticizing the EEC, was
> accompanied, however, by an erroneous overestimation of the economic
> difficulties which would have followed the application of the Com-
> munity regulations and by an underestimation of the new possibilities
> for the expansion of the Italian economy which arose out of the initial
> formation of a European market. In fact it is in the interest of the
> working class to favour an economic development which would allow
> the Italian economy to acquire competitive capabilities in the inter-
> national market. Technical progress and the modernization of the
> Italian economy are exigencies which must be supported in a context
> of a policy of democratic development and not of conservation of the
> backward positions of minor groups of the Italian bourgeoisie. Inevit-
> ably the EEC contributes to the processes of capitalist centralization
> and concentration, causes the crisis of re-adjustment, sweeps away
> positions which are working on excessively high unit costs. But all
> this necessitates the development, on the part of the working class,
> of a 'European' struggle, in full agreement with the working forces of
> the other EEC countries against the monopolistic forces which control
> the executive organs of the EEC.[47]

The new tendencies of the PCI towards Europe were formalized at the
Tenth Congress of the PCI (December 1962) albeit in a qualified form.[48]

The strategy which would guide the activities of the left in Europe
was based on a fundamental principle: peaceful coexistence. The strategy
of peaceful coexistence would create a zone of disengagement in Europe
and this would be 'an important step on the road to international
detente'.[49] The creation of this zone entailed the phasing-out of the two
power blocs and a process of *détente* which would facilitate the re-
acquisition of autonomy on the part of Italy. It was in fact the question

of *détente* which was the foremost element in Togliatti's report to the Tenth Congress.

By implication international *détente* could be a process which allowed the European countries to withdraw from the American sphere of influence, a sphere which had resulted from the Cold War, the division of Europe into two counterposed sides and the expulsion of the Communists from the governments of France and Italy. But in Togliatti's report detente is still mainly seen as providing a terrain for an autonomous political development at the national level and the question of 'regional' autonomy (of, for instance, the 'Western European sector') does not receive much support: autonomy still means purely national autonomy. This is in evidence in the call for a unilateral withdrawal from NATO (within which the stark choice is said to be only between the subjection to the USA or to the German–French axis).[50] This call, we must assume, entails the possibility and the assumption that such withdrawal will facilitate this process. This assumption would be rejected only at the Fourteenth Congress of the PCI (1975).

Togliatti's political 'operation' was rendered more difficult by the schism with the CCP because, if on the one hand the schism itself had more or less destroyed monolithism, on the other the Chinese position was totally hostile to peaceful coexistence and the Chinese themselves seemed to favour a new international organization. Togliatti, however, opposed any Soviet attempt to convene an international Communist conference which would have the explicit aim of condemning the CCP. Clearly the rejection of the international conference was not motivated by any great commonalty of ideas with the CCP but by objections to the very idea of international excommunications. It was not merely a question of principles (Togliatti had admitted that the exclusion of the Yugoslav CP in 1948 was a grave mistake), but one which was also based on the view that the activity of individual Communist Parties should not be subject to the approval of any international organization even an *ad hoc* one such as an international conference.

These objections to any return to monolithism in any form were reiterated in a confidential document addressed to the leadership of the CPSU a few days before Togliatti's death in Yalta. This document, the 'Yalta Memorandum', was published in *Rinascita* shortly afterwards and represents the most complete pronouncement of the Communist leader on questions of general interest to the international Communist movement.[51]

In the memorandum the link between the 'unitary' aspect of the international Communist movement and the necessity for autonomy is stressed with great lucidity. The search for unity cannot be based on expulsions, administrative measures or a return to outdated conceptions of internationalism. The international situation is seen as unfavourable, the political debate in the USA is assuming right-wing tones (the threat of the election of Goldwater was then considered very real), and in Europe many Communist Parties do not have a mass base.[52]

There is therefore an urgent need for a fundamental rethinking on major questions: the possibility of democratic planning to counterpose capitalist planning in the struggle for socialism, the fact that in most socialist countries there does not seem to have been rapid progress towards greater liberties. All these questions cannot be detached from the need to solve the 'Chinese question'. One of the steps suggested to solve it is a beginning of a round of meetings and talks *per groups of parties* for a better definition of the tasks facing the 'different sectors of our movement, *Western Europe*, Latin America, other third world countries, people's democracies, etc.' (my emphasis). The 'Western European' sector presented in Togliatti's view a common element in a situation which is otherwise very differentiated, a result of the process of further monopolistic concentration of which the EEC is the political expression.[53] Clearly, great importance is given by Togliatti to the EEC; it becomes the chief instrument of a common process, a process of European unification of such proportion that it becomes a particular sector presenting particular tasks for a group of Communist Parties and thus necessitating a particular relationship. Here the case for a definition of Europe as a 'centre' of a polycentric world receives its first truly authoritative formulation.

Togliatti died a few days later. His funeral in Rome was attended by one million people. The last major European Comintern figure had left a sufficiently weighty political heritage that the importance of international processes and international considerations would not escape his successors.

Notes

1. In March rumours about Khruschev's secret speech began to appear in the press. *L'Unità* admitted its existence on 18 March, the first Communist newspaper to do so although it did it with obvious embarrassment. See P. Ingrao, 'Il XX Congresso del PCUS e l'VIII Congresso del PCI' in AA.VV. *Problemi di storia del PCI*, Rome, 1971, p. 154.
2. P. Togliatti, 'La via italiana al socialismo' in *Rinascita*, No. 2, February 1956. It was the first time that Togliatti mentioned the 'Italian road' since his Florence speech of 1947 ('La nostra lotta per la democrazia e il socialismo').

3. P. Togliatti, 'Le diverse vie verso il socialismo' in AA.VV. *Il Partito comunista italiano e il movimento operaio internazionale*, Rome, 1968, p. 11.
4. Ibid., p. 12.
5. The passage is the following: 'In Russia the State was everything, civil society was primordial and gelatinous; in the West there was a proper relationship between State and civil society and when the State trembled a sturdy structure of civil society was at once revealed. The State was only an outer ditch, behind which there stood a powerful system of fortresses and earthworks: more or less numerous from one State to the next, it goes without saying − but this precisely necessitated an accurate reconnaissance of each individual country', in A. Gramsci, *Selections from the Prison Notebooks*, London, 1971, p. 238.
6. Gramsci, op. cit., pp. 238–9.
7. Quoted by P. Ingrao, op. cit., p. 154.
8. P. Togliatti, 'L'Intervista a *Nuovi argomenti*', originally in *Nuovi argomenti*, No. 20, May–June 1956, now reprinted in P. Togliatti, *Problemi del movimento operaio internazionale 1956–1961*, Rome, 1962, p. 85.
9. Ibid., p. 102.
10. Ibid., p. 104.
11. Ibid., pp. 99–101.
12. 'Intervento di Eligio Bertini' in *VIII Congresso del Partito comunista italiano*. Atti e risoluzioni, Rome, 1957 (henceforth cited as *VIII Congresso*), p. 132.
13. 'Intervento di Giuseppe Prestipinio', ibid., p. 96.
14. Ibid., p. 101.
15. Quoted in 'Panorama dell'VIII Congresso' in *Rinascita*, No. 12, December 1956.
16. 'Intervento di Antonio Giolitti' in *VIII Congresso*, p. 233.
17. P. Togliatti, 'Rapporto all'VIII Congresso' reprinted in *Nella democrazia e nella pace verso il socialismo*, Rome, 1963 (henceforth cited as 'Rapporto VIII'), pp. 24–5.
18. Ibid., pp. 26–7.
19. Ibid., p. 37.
20. The original resolution was to be entirely devoted to an explanation of the new line against the 'personality cult' and to the demands for clarification of the Twentieth Congress. The intervening Polish events caused the adoption of a paragraph which, among other things, stated that the recent US Senate appropriation of 25 million dollars for 'encouraging freedom behind the Iron Curtain' had been partially used to finance the 'anti-popular' demonstrations in Poznan, see D. L. M. Blackmer, *Unity in Diversity. Italian Communism and the Communist World*, Cambridge, Mass., 1968, p. 70.
21. Ibid.
22. Quoted in ibid., p. 73.
23. 'Il giudizio della Direzione del PCI sui fatti di Ungheria e di Polonia. Comunicato della Direzione del PCI del 3 Novembre 1956' in AA.VV. *Il PCI e il movimento operaio internazionale*, Rome, 1968, p. 87.
24. Togliatti, 'Intervista a Nuovi argomenti', op. cit., p. 116.
25. As Luciano Gruppi wrote: 'It was decided not to use the concept of polycentrism in the documents of the PCI. The concept could give rise to misunderstanding', in his *Togliatti e la via italiana al socialismo*, Rome, 1974, p. 181.
26. Togliatti, 'Il "sistema policentrico" e la via italiana al socialismo' in AA.VV. *Il Pci e il movimento operaio internazionale*, op. cit., pp. 68–9.
27. Togliatti, 'Rapporto VIII', p. 23. Here 'polycentric', applied to the world system, seems to have maintained its original meaning of 'multi-centres'. The rigid East–West dichotomy will eventually be rejected by the Italian Communists and the international conjuncture will be characterized by three elements (all internally differentiated), namely, the socialist camp, the capitalist camp and

the new nations emerging out of the collapse of colonialism. This three-dimensional characteristic is underlined by Togliatti in his reports to the Eighth, Ninth and Tenth Congress of the PCI.

28. See the Theses of the Eighth Congress in *VIII Congresso*, p. 929.
29. Togliatti, 'Rapporto VIII', p. 22.
30. Ibid., p. 34.
31. Ibid., p. 32.
32. Togliatti 'Rapporto VIII', p. 32 and 'Theses' in *VIII Congresso*, p. 927. Togliatti's judgement on the Cominform was totally negative. See his report to the Central Committee of the PCI held on 21–3 April 1964, reprinted in Togliatti, *Sul movimento operaio internazionale*, Rome, 1964, p. 327 with the title 'Per l'Unità del movimento operaio e comunists internazionale'.
33. Togliatti, 'Il "sistema policentrico" e la via italiana al socialismo', op. cit., pp. 62–3.
34. Ibid., p. 64.
35. Ibid., p. 65.
36. Ibid., p. 66.
37. The most important early instance of the application of a differentiated analysis is contained in Togliatti's intervention at the Twelfth Plenum of the Comintern (2 September 1932), see P. Togliatti, *Opere*, Vol. 2, tome 3, Rome, 1973, pp. 104–28. Extracts were published in *Stato operaio* of September 1932 with the title 'Against the false analogies between the Italian and the German situation'.
38. Togliatti, 'Il "sistema policentrico" e la via italiana al socialsmo' in op. cit., p. 66.
39. Blackmer, op. cit., p. 126.
40. Ibid., p. 135.
41. P. Togliatti, 'Suigli orientamenti politici del nostro partito (Intervento alla riunione dei 64 partito comunisti e operai. novembre 1957)' in *Rinascita*, No. 11, November 1959.
42. A translation of the debate appeared in *New Left Review*, No. 13–14, Jan.–Apr. 1962 under the title 'Debate of the Central Committee of the Italian Communist Party on the 22nd Congress of the CPSU', The *de facto* nature of polycentrism was explicitly stressed by E. Santarelli (p. 162), A. Occhetto (p. 168), G. Amendola (p. 169), A. Cossutta (p. 172) and C. Luporini (p. 189).
43. Ibid., pp. 169–70.
44. Blackmer, op. cit., p. 196. Thorez had declared: 'In certain quarters the thesis of polycentrism is still being advanced. This formula covers, we fear, a tendency to fractionalism . . .There is no longer a single centre of direction: why speak of establishing several different ones?' The resolution of the Central Committee of the French CP stated: 'The view that it would be useful to create several "centres" of Communism in different parts of the world, can only undermine Communist unity of thought and action . . . .' (Both quotes appear in Perry Anderson's introduction to the translation of the debate of the Central Committee of the PCI in op. cit., pp. 154–5.)
45. Quoted in ibid., p. 115.
46. See Blackmer, op. cit., p. 196. Longo later recommended that the term 'polycentrism' be dropped.
47. G. Amendola, *Lotta di classe e sviluppo economico dopo la Liberazione*, Rome, 1962, p. 86.
48. P. Togliatti, report to the Tenth Congress of the PCI in *Opere scelte*, Rome, 1974, pp. 1080, 1084, 1089 and 1098-9.
49. See the declaration of the Communist Parties of the EEC countries which met in Brussels (2 April 1959) in *La politica economica italiana 1945–74*, Rome n.d., p. 185.
50. Togliatti, report to the Tenth Congress, in *Opere scelte*, p. 1090.

51. Now in *Opere scelte*, pp. 1170–81.
52. Ibid., pp. 1172–3.
53. Ibid., pp. 1171 and 1173.

7.   Socialism and Democracy

The conquest of an autonomous space for Italian Communism within the international Communist movement could not be done through declarations of independence alone. The effects of the Twentieth Congress of the CPSU provided a new terrain for an original strategy. This terrain was to be dominated by the themes of the relation between socialism and democracy and the organically-linked strategy of structural reforms.

The Soviet denunciation of Stalinism was reduced to a condemnation of the 'personality cult'. In so doing, it removed from criticism all other 'superstructural' components of Soviet society. When Togliatti formulated his objections to the thesis of the 'cult', he opened, politically, a major terrain of investigation: the relation between socialism and democracy. This is not a problem which could in any way be separated from the search of a national road because the rejection of the Soviet model entailed a rejection of the Soviet 'solution' to the question of socialism and democracy. This (rejected) solution had collapsed the principle of democratic centralism in the vanguard party with the organization of society: that is, society was to be organized like a political party. A monolithic principle was applied to the State. A method of direction which was, fundamentally, based on administrative coercion became the Soviet State's principal method of direction.

This is not to say that this 'solution' was definitively eliminated by the liberatory force of the Twentieth Congress leaving the field empty, or that the Italian Communists were provided with an open ideological space ready to be 'filled' with a new conception of the relationship between socialism and democracy. Ideological spaces are never 'empty': the Italian one contained both the remnants of the Soviet conception and the germs of its own historical solution. This was represented principally by Togliatti's considerations on the 'progressive democracy' the PCI had wanted to create but had been unable to because of the impact, in Italy, of the separation of Europe into two spheres of influence. What 1956 did was to provide the conditions for the growth and development of the Togliattian conception.

Thus the theme of socialism and democracy as it was to develop after

1956 is not new, but acquired a position of dominance in the ideological field after the official recognition of the necessity of national roads.

We shall examine this debate in the period up to 1964, but it will be preferable at the outset to offer a conclusion: during the eight years in question the theoretical treatment of the nexus between socialism and democracy was practically non-existent. Its political treatment was consistently conditioned by immediate tactical factors and, in particular, by the end of left unity in Italy with the inclusion of the Italian Socialist Party in the ruling coalition in 1963.

After the death of Togliatti and mainly after the great events of 1968–9, which would see the development of a mass movement with a cohesion, consistency and radicalism unrivalled in Europe, the relation between socialism and democracy would receive a qualitatively different treatment. Nevertheless the basis for this operation was laid down in the period we are examining.

Writing in March 1956, Luigi Longo explained that:

> When we say that we intend to follow in Italy the democratic road to socialism, we mean that we act on the basis of the democratic road indicated by the Constitution, where majority and minority coexist and where the minority must always have the possibility of becoming the majority.[1]

This is the acceptance of a principle which had been considered by the majority of Communist activists as specific only to bourgeois democracy. It is impossible to derive from this simple statement a comprehensive view of Longo's vision of a 'pluralist' system on the road to socialism. Nevertheless, the explicit acceptance of the interplay between majority and minority must entail the acceptance of a plurality of parties, hence the acceptance of Parliament as a body which in some way or other 'reflects' the political and ideological division of forces in the nation and determines in some way or other the policies to be adopted by the government.

In a sense the principles of party pluralism were already implicit in the slogan of 'progressive democracy' which had been adopted during the Resistance. But as we have seen, the slogan itself had not been particularly developed and analysed and hence it is unlikely that its full implications had sunk in the minds of the PCI cadres and membership even as late as 1956.

Obviously Longo does not accept 'Parliamentarism', that is the view that Parliament alone is the proper locus for the debating of all political choices, but looks forward to a transcendence of formal bourgeois democracy, at the same time demanding an extension of democratic control.

This is articulated in the following way: the demand for the creation of various political centres becomes a specific indication of struggle, the struggle for a regional and local devolution of power.

In the years to come this would be one of the major fields of political activity for the Italian Communist Party, which would become the strongest defender of local autonomy and the foremost exponent of those forces which demanded the implementation of the Constitution in the area of regional autonomy.

Longo's article represented an attempt to develop the Italian road to socialism, but it was also trying to do so from a tactical standpoint which was as close as possible to the USSR. It was an attempt to make sure that the inevitable debates and discussions which were to take place would seek to remain within the relatively 'safe' arena of internal affairs without examining too much the whole question of Stalinism and without questioning too deeply the past policies of the CPSU or of the PCI.

However, Longo's article, written before the publication of Khruschev's secret speech, rejected a dogmatic counterposing of bourgeois to socialist democracy. This rejection contributed towards the acceptance of political pluralism from the domain of tactical consideration in order to inscribe it in a broad strategic design. This operation, that is, the transference of elements which belonged — in the minds of some Communist supporters and their opponents — to the tactical domain on to the strategic domain, would be carried out repeatedly. It is by bearing in mind this characteristic that we can explain the confusion of two separate interpretations of the PCI's evolution. One interpretation ('internal', so to speak, to the PCI) was the inability to recognize the turning-point of 1956 because it was blinded by the continuity of thought exhibited by Togliatti and the leadership group around him since the Resistance.

The concept of progressive democracy was, after all, part of a general strategic design and not a mere tactical directive. What one must bear in mind is that the difference between 1943–56 and 1956–64 is that throughout the first period the defence of democracy was considered by the rank and file mainly as a necessity determined by specific circumstances.

This was, in part, due to an ambiguity in the directives emanating from the top, which in turn derived from a certain reluctance to challenge dogmatic conceptions which had become entrenched in the party.

After 1956 there was a new direction towards explicitness in specifying the Communist position on all matters concerning democracy.

The second misconception, the mirror image of the first, also ignores the significance of 1956, but does so in order to reduce all Communist pronouncements to purely tactical considerations.

The 'tactical' view saw democracy in an essentially instrumental way. It considered democracy and democratic institutions as the best terrain of struggle for the Communist Party. It maintained that civil liberties were to be defended because they were necessary for the unimpeded activity of the Communists. In so doing the tactical view was not — at least initially — in total conflict with Togliatti's elaboration in the sense that they could coexist because, concretely, they entailed the same thing: a struggle for democracy undifferentiated from a struggle for socialism.

That a discussion on pluralism was in order had been proclaimed by Togliatti at the Central Committee meeting of June 1956.

> The question of the existence of different parties in a socialist society and the question of the contribution that different parties can give to the march of socialism present themselves to us.[2]

Party pluralism as such was in principle accepted in the international communist movement as a possibility even during the transition to socialism. Different political parties did exist in various Eastern European regimes and different parties were (and still are) legal and recognized in China. At the same time it cannot be maintained that these parties have any autonomy whatsoever, or that they represent significant political forces. It is well known that some of these parties were and are little more than Communist fronts created by the Communist Parties in order to give some semblance of truth to their original declaration that their 'people's democracies' were an intermediate form between a bourgeois regime and a socialist one. It is obvious that Togliatti is not talking about this form of pluralism although, for tactical reasons, he mentions the Eastern European experience.[3]

He presents the question cautiously as 'material for discussion' and it is evident that when he offers the possibility of several parties coexisting in the transition to socialism he also rejects the Soviet model of the one party State as applicable to Italy.

This 'caution' is completely abandoned by the 1960s:

> We agree, nay more, we insist on maintaining and underlining that the existence of the political party — in fact, to be precise, the existence of political parties — is indispensable for the very existence and for the development of a democratic system . . .[4]

Nevertheless, it would be true to say that no serious discussion on political pluralism takes place in the period under examination. On the contrary Longo, in his *Revisionismo nuovo e antico* (1957), seems to contradict Togliatti's and his own position of 1956 on the question of the right of the minority to become the majority:

> The direction of the working class is necessary for the socialist transformation of society. This transformation cannot but imply a reduction, and eventually the complete abolition, of the rights and powers of the opposing forces who are hostile to this transformation, that is, it cannot but imply forms of dictatorship, because politically, substantially and juridically the concept of proletarian dictatorship must be reduced to this: the negation of certain rights to those social forces who are opposed to a socialist transformation.
>
> That this negation is decided by a 'majority' or a 'minority' has no great importance. What counts in so far as the concept of formal democracy is concerned is precisely the right of the minority to annul the decisions of the previous majority, independently of any class consideration.
>
> . . . What counts above all for the concept of class dictatorship is something else: to stop the classes hostile to socialism from regaining the possibility of impeding the march to socialism. But this is violence, some people will say! No. Only in acting in this way does one not violate history, because it is history and social forces which, at a determinate level of development, make necessary the socialist transformation.[5]

The rhetoric and the theoretical underpinning of this declaration are clearly Stalinist. The appeal to history and its march are clearly teleological. The emphasis is not on hegemony, but on force. The contradiction with the tradition of Italian Communism could not be clearer. Strictly speaking, of course, the plurality of parties is not denied, provided that the political parties are all on the side of 'the march to socialism'. But there is no substantial difference between this declaration and the logic of development of the experience of the People's Republics of Eastern Europe. Longo was then the number two in the party and his statement must be given the utmost importance. It should, of course, be seen in its context: a polemic against the 'arch-revisionist' Giolitti at a time when thousands of intellectuals were leaving the party and where the tendencies orientated towards a complete break with the USSR were multiplying.

In elaborating, though, as we have seen, in a fragmented and unsystematic form, the relation between socialism and democracy, it was necessary for the PCI to deal with the concept of the dictatorship of the proletariat. It is here in particular that the Italian Communists would attempt to instil a new and richer content in a classical terminology. This, of course, would be a long and painful process which, however, would eventually leave the post-Togliattian leadership group with a wider room for manœuvre.

The length of the process had the positive side of providing an ideological framework which would be deeply rooted in the party as a whole and avoided the abruptness of the French Communist Party's official 'abolition' of the dictatorship of the proletariat in 1976.

Characteristically, Togliatti, in tackling the question, stressed the continuing validity of the classical Marxist thesis, underlined by Gramsci, that 'every state is a dictatorship':

> This is true and it is still valid. The construction of a socialist society constitutes a transitional period between the revolution which destroys capitalism and the triumph of socialism and the transition to Communism. In this transitional period the direction of society belongs to the working class and its allies; the democratic character of the proletarian dictatorship derives from the fact that this direction is realized in the interests of the overwhelming majority of the people against the remnants of the old exploiting classes.[6]

Thus what is still valid is the view that dictatorship is equivalent to *political* direction exercised by the proletariat and its allies *against* the remnants of the exploiting classes.

This equivalence between dictatorship and political direction was taken up again by Longo in his report to the Central Committee meeting of October 1956. However, instead of 'political direction' Longo used the expression 'proletarian direction', a concept, he said, which is always accompanied by the concept of alliance with other social groups.[7]

Proletarian direction is the direction of the proletariat within a coalition of classes which in turn exercises a political direction over the rest of society. This system of power is, for Longo, the dictatorship of the proletariat. Clearly other questions come to mind and one in particular: how are these different 'directions' exercised? For Longo hegemony refers to the relations existing within a given historical bloc while 'dictatorship' defines the relations between a historical bloc and its opponents.[8] Thus the working class exercises (or attempts to exercise) hegemony over all its allies and dictatorship over its oponents.

Togliatti, less schematically, in a paper he gave at the Gramsci conference of 1958, wrote:

> Is there in Gramsci a difference . . . between the concept of hegemony and that of dictatorship? There is a difference but not one of substance. The first concept refers prevalently to the relations established in civil society and it is hence wider than the second. But we should bear in mind that for Gramsci the difference between civil and political society is only methodological not organic. Every state is a dictatorship, and every dictatorship presupposes not only the power of a class, but a system of alliances and mediations . . .[9]

Behind these formulations there is a clear political project: the rejection by the establishment of any real opposition between hegemony and dictatorship. What is constantly underlined is their complementary character while for 'revisionists' such as Giolitti, hegemony was a type of working class power which would be different in kind from that of the dictatorship.[10]

It is also clear that this complementary quality of the two terms — stressed by both Longo and Togliatti — does not only have a theoretical basis, but it is also part of an attempt to establish the principle of change in continuity against the demands of the 'revisionists' who would have liked a much faster break with tradition.

Togliatti always insisted on reaffirming the continuity of the present line not only with the national tradition of the party, but also with that of the international movement. The acceptance of the 'democratic method' coupled with a political practice based on a vast framework of political alliance 'did not constitute', according to the PCI leader, 'a revision of our principles. The dictatorship of the proletariat, that is, the political direction of the working class in the construction of a socialist society, is a historical necessity.'[11]

The Leninist language of the 'dictatorship of the proletariat' would soon disappear and a more overt use of classical Gramscian concepts would be adopted. Gramsci had made a methodological distinction between 'domination' and 'direction'. The oppositional couple domination–direction corresponds to the couples 'political society/civil society' and 'dictatorship/hegemony'. The fundamental Gramscian passage on this point is the following:

> The methodological criterion on which our study must be based is the following: that the supremacy of a social group manifests itself in two ways, as 'domination' and as 'intellectual and moral direction'. A social group dominates an antagonistic group which it tends to 'liquidate' or to subjugate perhaps even with armed force; it directs kindred and allied groups. A social group can, and indeed must, already exercise

'direction' before winning governmental power (this indeed is one of the principal conditions for the winning of such power); it subsequently becomes dominant when it exercises power, but even if it holds it firmly in its grasp, it must continue to 'direct' as well.[12]

On the whole the renewed influence of Gramscian concepts fits in with the general tendency (in this period) to give less import to the originality of the Italian development of Communist strategy in order to emphasize 'exceptionalism' as a reason for departing from establishing classical directives. This political caution had a price: ambiguity.

The exceptionalism attributed by Togliatti to some aspects of the Leninist concept of the dictatorship of the proletariat could not but invest also another fundamental aspect of the classical Marxist theory of the State: the view that the apparatuses of the bourgeois State must be destroyed and that a new (proletarian) state machinery must be built. This position, explains Togliatti, was not always that of Marx and Engels:

> . . . they came to this position after the experience of the Paris Commune and it was particularly developed by Lenin. Is this position still valid today? This is a point to be discussed. When we maintain that today it is possible to advance towards socialism not only on the democratic terrain, but also by using parliamentary forms, it is evident that we are correcting something of this position, bearing in mind the transformations which have taken place and which are still taking place in the world.[13]

A few months before in his March speech to the Central Committee, Togliatti had explained the conditions for the possibility of using parliamentary forms:

> Our fundamental thesis must be that the utilization of Parliament for a politics of positive transformation of society is possible where there exists a large socialist and labour movement which is directed by large parties which have a clear perspective and programme for an advance in the direction of socialism.[14]

Thus the conditions for the 'rectification' of accepted principles are determined by historical conditions. Strictly speaking this 'rectification' has theoretical consequences. When Togliatti, as we have pointed out, underlines Gramsci's thesis that the distinction between civil society and political society is a methodological rather than an organic one he produces a new terrain of analysis: the concrete intertwining between political society and civil society. This will vary according to the historical conditions and determine the forms which the class dictatorship (of the bourgeoisie *or* the proletariat) assumes. Thus there can be more forms of the dictatorship of the proletariat just as the class dictatorship of the bourgeoisie has given rise to the most diverse political systems: parliamentary republics, fascist dictatorships, constitutional monarchies, presidential systems, etc. Thus, even when the Italian Communists used the expression 'the dictatorship of the proletariat' (in practice no longer used in official documents), they would not give it the meaning which was given to it in 1917 in the Soviet Union:

> . . . in this light must be seen the problem of parliamentarism. It is absurd to demand that the proletarian revolution would give rise to a parliamentary regime in a country where parliamentarism had never existed. But in other countries, where Parliament has achieved a democratic content . . . one can solve through parliament the problem of enabling the working class not only to express their will but also to participate in the direction of political and economic activities, while maintaining firmly that the coming to power of the workers must inevitably entail an extension of the forms of direct democracy.[15]

While, as we have written, many of the 'rectifications' of the Italian Communists have theoretical consequences and while we find quite often (particularly in Togliatti) elements for a theoretical analysis, it remains true to say that the element which is missing in the Communist debates in the years following the Twentieth Congress is precisely the theoretical mediation between the redefinition of the political strategy and what can be described as 'classical' Marxist indications on the political struggle. Here our concern will not be an attempt to analyse the relation between 'classical' Marxism and the Italian road to socialism, but rather how this relation was ideologically expressed by the Italian Communists.

We have already pointed out that the initial Togliattian definitions of the elements for an Italian road to socialism, as put forward during and after the Resistance, contained no theoretical justifications. There was a conspicuous silence on questions of political theory. A theoretical presupposition of the Italian road had not been given. It is striking that even during the stormy debates of 1956 there were few attempts to justify the apparent 'revisionism' of the Italian Communists in terms of the writings of Marx and Lenin. As we have noted, when Togliatti intervened to indicate the elements where a 'revision' of existing principles was acceptable, he always seemed to justify these 'revisions' by referring to the 'present situation'. This attitude, of course, is profoundly empiricist in that it implies that all the elements of Marxism must constantly be tested against the concrete situation and rejected if they do not 'fit'. The obvious advantage of this method is that it rejects the schlerotic attitude which put many Communists in the position of interpreting facts so that they would fit the 'theory'. Yet Togliatti's position, because it was the simple inversion of the traditional dogmatic one, maintained intact the same empiricist form. If the theory must be changed according to new developments of the situation, then it is a theory which cannot explain the situation because it does not answer the question of how we arrive at the knowledge of the new situation. It seems that the Italian Communists could not escape from the trap of empiricism.

The practical ideological consequences of these debates, however, were to open up for 'revision' or 'adaptation' particular established principles such as those which could be said to form the elements for a Marxist theory of the State.

Such 'rectification' had the purpose of defining in a non-instrumental way the use of parliamentary forms of struggles. The utilization of Parliament *per se* was not a particularly controversial question for the Italian Communists. What was not clear in the mind of many was the specific role that Parliament could play and the political status which would be attributed to Parliament. Togliatti, at the June meeting of the Central Committee (1956), had declared:

> The utilization of Parliament is one of the possibilities open for the development of democratic activities in order to obtain structural reforms. For this possibility to be realized particular conditions are needed: *Parliament must be the mirror of the nation*, it must function and there must be a great mass movement which would voice those demands which would then be satisfied by a Parliament where the popular masses had obtained a sufficiently strong representation.[16]

The crucial phrase is 'Parliament must be the mirror of the nation'. This means that there must be an adequate reflection in Parliament of the actual balance of forces in the country; thus Parliament cannot be, in the Togliattian analysis, identified as the instrument of one class or faction of classes once and for all. The class (political) status of Parliament would change with the changing balance of forces (but only if it fulfils properly its function of being 'the mirror of the country'). In a sense it can be a neutral instrument (as in the Kautskyist analysis), but for Parliament to become a 'mirror', a struggle, that is a class struggle which would reform the State, is necessary. Thus the transformation of Parliament into the 'mirror of the nation' is itself a conquest of the working class and its allies, it is a gain which is represented by the wrestling away from the ruling class of a 'piece' of the State machinery and its consequent transformation. This is not, as many leftist opponents of the PCI have maintained, an example of parliamentarism, unless that term is simply used to describe any political force which puts up candidates for elections (according to such a naïve definition, both the Bolsheviks and the German National Socialist Party were 'parliamentarist' parties). It is clear, in fact, that for the Italian Communists, the political struggle is never reduced to the parliamentary struggle, but rather that the parliamentary struggle is one of the forms of political practice and that its rank in a hierarchy of priorities is wholly determined, *like all forms of political practice*, by the prevailing conjuncture.

What remained evident for the Italian Communists was the principle that 'true' democracy depends, for its effective existence, on political power being in the hands of the working classes. The question of who controlled political power was seen as the decisive element for the solution of all other problems. The primacy of *the political* is clearly established in the following statement from the 'Elements for a Programmatic Declaration':

> The solution of the question of political power is the indispensible condition for the thorough transformation of social and economic relations and for the passage from capitalism to socialism . . . Democracy becomes truly effective only when the working class conquers political power and it uses it for the transformation of the economic structure of society, just as the bourgeoisie, in the past used democratic institutions in order to destroy the feudal order; but the bourgeoisie today is an obstacle to the full development [of democracy] and is even ready to suppress it in order to defend and maintain the economic relations upon which it has established its rule.[17]

The overt refusal to identify the parliamentary road with the Italian road to socialism was necessitated, at least in part, by a confusion among party activists.[18]

Togliatti, in a polemical article against the 'revisionist' Onofri, wrote:

> It is . . . erroneous to say that the 'Italian' road and the 'parliamentary' road are equivalent terms . . . how will we be able to use Parliament for an advance towards socialism? The problem can be posed and solved in every situation by taking into account the concrete data.[19]

The same holds true for any identification of the Italian road with a peaceful road.[20] The Italian road is not necessarily peaceful because the degree of violence required for the transition to socialism does not depend solely on the will or the intention of the revolutionary party.

> The peaceful painless development will depend on a complex inter-twining of conditions, some of these depend on us, others on the objective course of events, others on the action of the enemy.[21]

It is again evident that the Italian road as a formulation gives no concrete indications: it is not necessarily violent nor necessarily peaceful, it is not only parliamentary but also extra-parliamentary, it is not necessarily defensive or offensive. At this stage it is but the name for the strategy of the Italian Communist Party. To analyse the Italian road requires an analysis of the party's strategy, the sort of analysis which we have been conducting so far.

There is little doubt that the PCI's recognition of the value of parliamentary institutions depended, at least in part, on the historical formation of the Italian Parliament. Unlike Britain, where Parliament had represented for many centuries the principal focus of activities well before the entry of the labouring masses in the realm of politics, Italy could not point to a 'Parliamentary tradition'. The Parliament which Togliatti wanted to transform into the 'mirror of the nation' had been the result of a specific anti-fascist struggle and all the links of continuity between the pre- and post-fascist Parliament cannot obliterate the all-important fact that the first Parliament of the Italian Republic owed its existence at least in part to what quickly became the principal party of the working class.

There is also the view, not entirely free from teleological assumptions, that the development of capitalism in Italy no longer promotes democracy, but that, on the contrary, once capitalism has entered its monopolistic phase it begins to threaten even traditional bourgeois democratic institutions.[22] As Togliatti put it at the Ninth Congress (1960):

> Monopoly capital tends towards a particular objective: the end of the democratic regime or its reduction to a wilted and dead form. It had already tried to do that in our parliament.[23]

What is being attacked here is the view, held in Italy by various leftist tendencies, that the bourgeoisie is permanently able to absorb and control the entire system of democratic relations.[24]

In this context the Italian Communists are claiming that the struggle for democracy in Italy inevitably acquires an anti-monopolistic character. As Rossana Rossandra explained in a theoretical–political article in *Critica Marxista*,[25] the development of capitalism destroys the 'social contract' models on which it had attempted originally to base its ideological hegemony. There is a constant tension between the productive structure and the formal nature of its ideology. This opens a space for an antagonistic system of ideas: Marxism. At the same time a rapid expansion of productive forces constantly poses the problem of a reorganization of the institutional forms of capitalist society. The crisis is particularly strong in Italy where the ruling class is subject both to a rapidly changing productive system (the results of the 'economic miracle') and to the pressure of subordinate classes organically organized by a powerful Communist Party.

It is for these and other reasons that the Italian Communists could not be — like some other Communist Parties — 'anti-constitutionalists': on the contrary the Constitution was seen as one of the great (and few) achievements of the short period in which the PCI took part in the affairs of government. The Constitution was the product of a particular set of class relationships. It was drafted in a period when the old ruling classes had been politically defeated. What the Constitution did was to enshrine the new relation of forces which had been the result of the anti-fascist struggle. In so doing the Constitution also guaranteed the conditions for a real change in the relations of forces.

The so-called 'restoration of capitalism' by De Gasperi could not automatically entail a new Constitution. What changed after the end of the anti-fascist unity was the ideological interpretation of the Constitution.

As Togliatti pointed out in a speech in Modena on 15 September 1957:

> It is not sufficient to enshrine certain rights, certain constitutional principles, the norms of democracy in a law, to approve it and then to put it away; it is necessary to apply it; unless it is applied a law is worth nothing . . . If we examine the question in this way we can immediately understand that democracy is not only something to do with the laws, but is also to do with the relations which are established among the classes, with the relation of forces . . . This is the relation which must be changed; here we must intervene with the action of the advanced forces of the workers if we want to defend democracy, if we want to advance it.[26]

This view entails the acceptance of the idea of a disjuncture between the prevailing mode of production and some element of the legal–political superstructure, and not only that, but also the appreciation of the fact that the governments of the period 1945–7 constituted the basis for a 'democracy of a new type'. Furthermore, this view confirmed that the principal immediate objective of the Italian Communist Party was not a socialist revolution but an advanced democracy which would pave the way for socialism; in this context the party's strategy in 1956 logically involved a return to the tripartite formula, that is a government with the Christian Democrats. This, of course, was neither spelt out nor indicated in 1956. There could have been tactical–political reasons for this, or even an element of *'doppiezza'*, or it could have been Togliatti's realization that the time had not come to launch what in 1973 would become known as the 'historical compromise'. The most likely possibility, however, is that the logical consequences of the strategy of the PCI had not been completely worked out in 1956.

The Eighth Congress confirmed the general trends of the pre-congressional debates on the question of the Constitution. On the whole the changes that occurred were more in emphasis than in content. After all, the upholding of the Constitution had always been a key element of the Communist strategy. Now the exact role of the Constitution was spelt out clearly with the 'thesis of the possibility of an advance towards socialism within the forms of democracy and parliamentary legality',[27] with the declaration that 'The greatest conquest of the working class and of the people has been the Republican Constitution',[28] and with the affirmation that the Constitution was an important conquest of the Italian road to socialism.[29] As Togliatti explained at the Eighth Congress:

> The working class has not yet succeeded in conquering the political direction of the State. However, it has had the leadership of the popular movement which has given rise to this State, and this State has a Constitution which proclaims itself 'based on labour' and which affirms the need for those economic and political transformations which are necessary for the renewal of the nation and for its transition to socialism.
>
> This is the original result of the class struggle as it has occurred in this country. The respect and the application of the Constitution thus becomes the terrain where the forces of socialist renewal and the forces of conservatism and reaction confront each other.[30]

What is lacking in the analysis of the Italian Communists is a specification of the socialist basis of the Constitution. As we shall explain in the section dealing with the Constituent Assembly (in Part II), the Constitution must be considered the result of a compromise between the Communists, the Socialists and the Christian Democrats, that is between the principal forces of Italian political life. Thus the Constitution was the tangible result of a tripartite coalition which broke up soon after. When we examine, as we are doing, the various pronouncements of the

Italian Communists in the thirty years which precede the proposal of a 'historic compromise' one cannot but be struck by the relative continuity which exists in the strategy of Italian Communists.

The relative absence of a theoretical treatment of the strategy of the party, particularly where the Italian Constitution was concerned, gave rise to several 'deviations'. The most frequent was probably a position which sought to identify the struggle for the implementation of the Constitution as part of that bourgeois–democratic stage which was, according to a particular reading of Marx and Lenin, the necessary prerequisite for the second socialist stage.

Against these 'deviations', Emilio Sereni, in an undoubtedly authoritative article which reflects the position of Togliatti and the results of the Eighth Congress, argued that when the Party Theses defined the actual stage of the revolution in Italy as a 'democratic and socialist revolution', the intention was not to differentiate between the two concepts, but on the contrary to affirm the democratic content of any advance towards socialism and the socialist content of any expansion of democracy.

> Our revolution is correctly defined as democratic, not only to underline the method which we propose to follow, but in order to clarify the importance of the democratic tasks which our bourgeois–democratic revolution has left unsolved in our country and which only a democratic and *socialist* revolution can by now tackle and solve; the socialist character of the revolution which is before us arises from the fact that the form of power and the crucial relations of production which must be destroyed or transformed (in our country) in order to pave the way for the development of the productive forces and of the entire society are capitalist and not feudal.[31]

Accordingly Sereni rejected any interpretation of the Constitution as a purely democratic–bourgeois one and maintained that the republican Constitution, or at least some of its principles cut across the framework and the limitations of bourgeois democracy, while not being a purely socialist document.

From this it followed that in the course of their struggles the Italian Communists would gain from some specific elements of the Constitution. Those attracting particular attention and which were designated as being of fundamental importance were the (still unimplemented) articles concerning the creation of regions with a certain degree of autonomy. It was proclaimed (in the 'Political Motion') that there was no contradiction between local autonomy and devolution of power on the one hand and the unitary structure of the Italian State on the other. Furthermore, 'the struggle for local autonomy is in the first place a struggle for the thorough transformation of the administrative and political order and for the implementation of the Constitution'.[32] Decentralization was obviously seen as offering the possibility for large-scale action around semi-autonomous centres of power in the villages, towns and regions and the possibility for experimenting with new forms of democracy.[33] The republican Constitution is seen as an attempt to modify the centralism '. . . which has been typical of the Italian State throughout its development', and this attempt highlights the strongly-felt need to 'bring closer the people to the exercise of power by creating a democratic system territorially articulated in three instances: the municipality, the province and the region'.[34]

It was not until after the institution of the regions in 1970 that the question of decentralization was increasingly seen as a possible solution to the limited democratic content of a purely representative democracy. This development was mainly due to the growth of a mass movement which was able to maintain its impetus well after the 'rupture' represented by the 1968–9 student and trade union battles. It was through the formation of decentralized instances of popular power in the factories, in the schools, around neighbourhood councils, and, at a more formal level, around the regions that the classical Marxist thesis of the withering away of the State began to lose its Utopian flavour and acquired a concrete political content. In the years after the Eighth Congress the theme of regional autonomy, and more generally the theme of local autonomies at various levels, was particularly intertwined with that of central planning. It was thought that the only guarantee against the bureaucratic tendencies incipient in any central plan could only be a form of popular control which would be able to have a considerable degree of autonomy in the actual local application of a central directive. It must be emphasized that the entire question of regionalism was never seen as a substitute for a representative parliament, but rather as a complement to it. The creation of decentralized instances of power would enrich the democratic content of representation. At both the Ninth and Tenth Congresses Togliatti would stress the close links between a new democratic economic policy and an actual reform of the State.[35]

Although the link was never made (in 1956–64), it seems to me that the 'rectification' of the Leninist thesis on the destruction of the State machinery must be seen as being closely related to the new problematic question of devolution of power and local autonomy. The 'progressive democracy' envisaged by the Italian Communists, the new social order, which is not yet socialist but no longer purely capitalist, is no longer the same old State, but a profoundly modified one which escapes the logic of a purely representative system. The construction of this State need not even wait for the actual formation of a government with Communist participation, but the reforms which change gradually the nature of the State can be achieved not just before 'the revolution', but even under capitalism.

This sort of battle does not of course depend on the will of a single party. It was unlikely that it could develop sufficiently in the period we are examining and this partly explains the relative absence of elaborate analyses. What, however, existed was a profound institutional crisis which superimposed itself on the secular crisis of the Italian political system. This crisis, as Pietro Ingrao pointed out in an article in 1963, was determined by the coexistence, at the legal–political level, of institutions inherited from the old pre-fascist State and new institutions created by the republican Constitution.[36]

According to Ingrao this crisis engenders three types of answers. There is the 'liberal' answer which advocates the supremacy of the executive over Parliament and seeks to reduce the influence of political parties by conceiving of the parliamentary assembly as a sum of individuals and not as the expression of political wills. Behind the liberal answer there is an attack against the party system (the 'partitocrazia') and the defence of a nineteenth-century model of Parliament entirely separated from the people except at election time.[37]

The second answer is the 'technocratic' one based on 'neo-capitalist' ideologies arising out of the economic 'miracle' of the late 1950s. The supporters of this position put forward a model of society strongly influenced by American political science in which decision-making would take place in a new centre constituted by big business, the State (i.e. the State technocrats) and the trade unions transformed into pressure groups.[38] These theses were put forward by the left of the DC, the PSDI, and the Republican Party, as well as by some leaders of the Socialist Party.

In this context, the activities of the labour movement should be, according to Ingrao, directed towards providing a solution in which the necessary starting-point would be the recognition that the institutional crisis is not something which regards 'only' the institutions but also democratic life and the principle of popular sovereignty.[39] What is proposed is not only a reform of Parliament (in order to increase its control over the executive). A renewed Parliament would be connected to a 'vast articulation of the representative system, as it is demanded by the Constitution, and hence a diffusion of elected political assemblies horizontally and at different levels: Region, Province, Municipality'.[40]

Ingrao, who remains to this day the leading advocate of local autonomy, concluded thus:

> One can see how far we are from the ridiculous instrumentalism of which we are accused and how far we are from a conception of [national] unity as a 'totalitarian bloc' prefabricated once and for all. We have proposed a path for an advance of socialism which would implement the radical transformation of the structures of our society not through the political monopoly of a single party, but through the co-operation of a plurality of political forces in the context of an organized democracy which would exalt and articulate the intervention of the masses at all levels. Anyone who really wants to vie with our positions will have to debate with these perspectives.[41]

What is equally clear is that the Italian Communists' thinking on the political and legal arrangement of a social order was not in any way divorced from their proposals for economic restructuring. A mere re-arrangement of the State machinery which would leave untouched the fundamental levers of economic decision-making can be only a formal rearrangement.

The link between the political level and the economic level is expressed in the PCI through the relation between the problematic question of socialism and democracy and the strategy of structural reforms and democratic planning. As Togliatti indicated in his political testament:

> There arises in some major countries the question of the centralization of economic life with planning from above in the interests of the larger monopolies and through the intervention of the State . . . This question necessitates the development and co-ordination of the immediate demands of the working class and of proposals for structural reforms of the economy in a general plan of economic development to counter-pose to capitalist planning . . .
>
> The struggle for democracy assumes, in this context, a new content which is more concrete and more closely linked to the reality of social and economic life.[42]

We can now turn to what is one of the most interesting contributions of the Italian Communists: the strategy of structural reforms.

Notes

1. L. Longo, 'Costruendo il socialismo si son fatti degli errori, ma la vostra non é democrazia', *Rinascita*, No. 3, March 1956.

2. P. Togliatti, 'Il "sistema policentrico" e la via italiana al socialismo' in AA.VV. *Il PCI e il movimento operaio internazionale*, Rome, 1968, p. 80; but see also the interview to *Nuovi argomenti* in P. Togliatti, *Problemi del movimento operaio internazionale (1956–61)*, Rome, 1962, p. 93: 'The plurality or singularity of parties is not *per se* a distinctive element of bourgeois or socialist societies and it certainly does not represent the demarcation line between a democratic society and an undemocratic one.'

3. Ibid., p. 93.

4. P. Togliatti, speech to the Central Committee meeting of 4–7 December 1963 ('La concezione marxista del partito politico della classe operaia'), in *Opere scelte*, p. 1148.

5. P. Longo, *Revisionismo, nuovo e antico*, Turin, 1957, p. 39.

6. P. Togliatti, 'Il "sistema policentrico" e la via italiana al socialismo' in op. cit., p. 79.

7. P. Longo, *Documenti per l'VIII Congresso del PCI — Un partito più forte e rinnovato*. Supplement to *Voce Comunista*, No. 38, 4 October 1956, p. 7.

8. P. Longo, *Revisionismo nuovo e antico*, Turin, 1957, p. 36.

9. P. Togliatti, 'Il leninismo nel pensiero e nell'azione di A. Gramsci' in *Gramsci* (Rome, 1967), p. 154, see also p. 179 where the same view is put forward.

10. A Giolitti, *Riforme e rivoluzione*, Turin, 1957, p. 29.

11. P. Togliatti, 'Rapporto all'VIII Congresso', reprinted in *Nella democrazia e nella pace verso il socialismo*, Rome, 1963 (henceforth cited as 'Rapporto VIII'), p. 52.

12. A. Gramsci, *Selections from the Prison Notebooks*, London, 1971, pp. 57–8. I have slightly altered this translation which uses the world 'leadership' for 'direzione'. I have preferred to use the more literal 'direction'.

13. P. Togliatti, 'Il "sistema policentrico" e la via italiana al socilismo', in op. cit., p. 80.

14. P. Togliatti, 'Le diverse vie verso il socialismo' in AA.VV. *Il partito communista italiano e il movimento operaio internazionale*, Rome, 1968, p. 13.

15. P. Togliatti, 'Gramsci e il leninismo' (1958), now in *Gramsci*, Rome, 1967, p. 181.

16. Togliatti, 'La via italiana al socialismo' in *Opere scelte*, p. 759. The 'Political Motion' of the Eighth Congress sanctioned the need for Parliament both in the transformation of society and in the new society, see *VIII Congresso*, p. 882.

17. 'Elementi per una dichiarazione programmatica' in *VIII Congresso*, p. 899.

18. A. Natoli, in an account of the debates within the Roman Federation of the PCI which took place shortly after the Twentieth Congress of the CPSU, pointed out that the confusion was such that many activists were under the impression that the Italian road to socialism and the parliamentary road were one and the same thing; see 'Il dibattito sul XX Congresso nella Federazione di Rome' in *Rinascita*, No. 5–6, May–June 1956.

19. P. Togliatti, 'La realtà dei fatti e della nostra azione rintuzza l'irresponsabile disfattismo', *Rinascita*, No. 7, July 1956.

20. A purely 'electoralist' solution is similarly rejected while advancing the idea of revolution as a process: 'It is obvious that when we accept the perspective of an advance towards socialism through democracy and peace, we introduce the concept of a gradual development in which it is rather difficult to establish precisely when the qualitative change will occur. What we foresee for advanced capitalist countries with a rooted democratic organization is a struggle which may be a very protracted one during which the working class fight in order to become the directing class and hence pave the way for the renewal of the entire social structure. To reduce this struggle to electoral competition for parliament and to wait for the conquest of 51 per cent of the votes would be not only naïve but also an illusion' in Togliatti's report to the Tenth Congress (1962) in *Opere scelte*, pp. 1111–12.

21. P. Togliatti, 'La realtà dei fatti e della nostra azione rintuzza l'irresponsabile disfattismo', *Rinascita*, No. 7, July 1956.
22. This view is later maintained also by Luciano Gruppi, *Togliatti e la via italiana al socialismo*, Rome, 1974, p. 195.
23. P. Togliatti, in *Nella pace e nella democrazia verso il socialismo*, Rome, 1963, p. 135. The reference here is to the *'legge truffa'* of 1953.
24. As Togliatti put it to the Central Committee meeting of 12–14 February 1962 ('Passare dai programmi all'azione per una effettiva svolta a sinistra'): 'Without any doubt we must reject the view that, whatever we do the situation will not change because the fundamental nature and structure of our society will not change, neither will the ruling class change and that it will always be the interests of this ruling class which will prevail over everything. This is the traditional do-nothing maximalist view . . .', in *Opere scelte*, pp. 1047–8.
25. Rossana Rossanda, 'Note sul rapporto riforme–rivoluzione nella elaborazione del PCI' in *Critica Marxista*, No. 2, Mar.–Apr. 1963, p. 28. Rossanda was then defending the 'orthodox' position. Later she would become one of the founders of the 'Manifesto' group and was expelled in 1969.
26. In 'Attuare la Costituzione', in P. Togliatti, *Politica nazionale e Emilia rossa*, Rome, 1974, pp. 487–8.
27. Togliatti, 'Rapporto VIII', p. 48.
28. Ibid., p. 47.
29. 'Elementi per una dichiarazione programmatica del PCI' in *VIII Congresso*, p. 911.
30. Togliatti, 'Rapporto VIII', pp. 49–50.
31. E. Sereni, 'Democrazia e socialismo nella Rivoluzione italiana', *Rinascita*, No. 3, March 1957. See also, for a confirmation of Sereni's consistency with the party's official line, the 'Elementi per una dichiarazione programmatica del PCI', in *VIII Congresso*, p. 911.
32. 'Mozione politica', in *VIII Congresso*, p. 883. See also the defence of regional autonomy put forward by Luigi Longo in his article in the March 1956 issue of *Rinascita* ('Costruendo il socialismo si son fatti degli errori ma la vostra non é democrazia').
33. Togliatti, 'Conclusioni' in *Nella pace e nella democrazia verso il socialismo*, p. 97.
34. 'Elementi per una dichiarazione . . .' in *VIII Congresso*, p. 911.
35. Togliatti, 'Rapporto al IX Congresso' in *Nella pace e nella democrazia verso il socialismo*, pp. 138–9 and 'Rapporto al X Congresso' in *Opere scelte*, pp. 1107–8.
36. P. Ingrao, 'La crisi degli istituti rappresentativi e la lotta per una nuova democrazia' in *Critica Marxista*, No. 3, May–June 1963, p. 12.
37. Ibid., pp. 20–1.
38. Ibid., pp. 21–2.
39. Ibid., p. 25.
40. Ibid., p. 29.
41. Ibid., p. 34.
42. *Opere scelte*, pp. 1175–6.

8. Structural Reforms

Our examination of the Italian Communists' investigation of the relation between socialism and democracy has highlighted their conception of *revolution as a process*. Such definition of the principal feature of the 'Italian road' is not unproblematic. In fact, by itself it does not pose the problem of the political (state) forms of transition. We shall come back to this point in our conclusions. Here we shall point out that the concept of 'revolution as a process', which clearly departs from the violent rupture model of 1917, is part of a strategy of structural reforms which is seen as the particular road of access to socialism in advanced capitalist countries. Here we are fundamentally in agreement with Giuseppe Vacca's thesis that the strategy of structural reforms 'delineates an original process of democratic and socialist transformation in Italy and that this constitutes the framework of the Italian road to socialism'.[1]

As with the question of the relation between socialism and democracy, the concept of structural reforms comes to be fully developed only after the Twentieth Congress of the CPSU and particularly in the period of inception of the centre-left government (1962–4). The basis of such development was laid down in the immediate post-war period when the forces which had participated in the Resistance were still apparently engaged in a common project of economic reorganization.

Togliatti constantly attempts to remind his audience of the origins of certain strategic directives as if a historical origin could be a political justification. This is — at least in part — a tactical procedure for it is precisely when the party line shifts more or less dramatically that there is a need to reassure the rank and file by showing them in the distant past the embryonic element of the 'new' political line.

There is no doubt that this was the prevailing Togliattian tendency and that it was shared by a majority of the leadership group around him. This, however, should not exempt us from actually examining Togliatti's, at times unsatisfactory, delineation of the specificity of structural reforms.

As we have documented in the first part of this study, structural reforms were indeed proposed and fought for by the Communists particularly in the period 1944–6. However, in that period, they were mainly seen as a strategy for the dismantling of the socio-economic roots of fascism. After 1956 they acquired a more general conceptual meaning. In his report to the Eighth Congress, Togliatti offered some elements for a definition of structural reforms:

> . . . our struggle . . . for structural reforms is one of the principal fruits of the research for our own road of development towards social-ism in the present conditions. It would be a mistake to confuse the demand for these reforms with what used to be called transitional demands. These were slogans to be promulgated at a moment of acute revolutionary crisis and destined solely to direct the masses in the struggle for power and hence destined to be quickly consumed in the course of the struggle. Structural reforms are a positive objective which we want to realize and which can be realized in the present conditions of political struggle.[2]

In the course of his report Togliatti specified that the test of structural reforms is that they must operate a transformation of the economic structures and open the road to socialism but, at the same time, 'structural reforms are not socialism'.

Though not 'transitional demands' in the classical sense, structural reforms have nevertheless a transitional element: they represent the demands around which the working class can fight at the present time, their successful implementation depending on the existing relations of force. To quote from the 'Elements for a Programmatic Declaration' of 1956:

> The Communists know that a complete socialist structural transforma-tion — and with it the solution of the fundamental contradictions internal to our society — can only take place with the conquest of political power by the working class and its allies. But considering the relations of forces existing between the forces of the proletariat, of the people and of progress on the one hand and the forces of exploita-tion and reaction on the other, considering the urgency of the problems of labour, land and poverty, the Communists declare openly that the demolition of the most backward and burdensome structures of Italian society and the beginning of their transformation in a democratic and socialist direction cannot and must not be delayed until the moment of the conquest of power by the working class and its allies; but that they can and must be considered as concrete and realizable objectives which can be reached with the economic and political struggles of the workers.[3]

Togliatti lists two typical objections to structural reforms: the 'dogmatist' objection which says that the point is not to reform but to destroy capitalism, and the 'revisionist' one which says that many of these structural reforms seem to have been implemented in other countries without these having gone any nearer to socialism. The first objection is dismissed as absurd because it could be used against any demand (whether 'structural' or not). Togliatti attributes great value to the second objection because it has the merit of posing the question of the politics of the struggle for the attainment of structural reforms and he added:

> On its own a nationalization may not mean very much. If achieved in a certain way it may even give some advantage to certain capitalist groupings or to non-progressive political groupings. But things change when this or other measures taken against monopoly capital are an integral part of a continuous action, of a constant struggle which is conducted with great decision by big political mass organizations with the support of a large section of public opinion in order to impose even in the present conditions, an economic policy which would be to the advantage of the workers and of the middle strata and which would involve even the government through Parliament in the anti-monopolistic struggle.[4]

We can read this statement in terms of the conditions which determine the 'structural' content of reforms. The chief condition is that a 'structural' reform cannot exist on its own; it must be part of a continuous action and it must have a mass basis. There is a further consideration: structural reforms cannot be seen in purely economic terms, that is as an intervention at the economic level unconnected to a political intervention. They involve the structure of society as such. This consideration depends on the following passage from Togliatti's report to the Tenth Congress (1962):

> Reforms of the economic structure must be introduced in order to make possible a democratic economic development, that is, one which would arrive as quickly as possible at the solution of those problems which today are so pressing and at overcoming the existing disequilibria. It is for this reason that we must fight against the dominium of existing large monopolistic groupings.
>
> We have always maintained that the work of renewal cannot be undertaken without the intervention of the State and under its direction.[5]

This should not be read as delaying any structural reform to the period after the representatives of the working class capture State power, but rather that no policy of structural reforms can possibly avoid taking into consideration the question of the State and the possibility of forcing the existing State to take actions which do not conform to the interests of the monopolies. In other words, Togliatti refused to consider the government as simply 'the executive committee of the monopolies'.

Thus structural reforms are defined in terms of a specific field, characterized by the relations between classes, relations which are not purely economic but also ideological and political.

It follows that structural reforms are distinguishable from the reformists' reforms because of their organic quality. They entail the refusal to conceive of capitalism as a divisible entity which can be eroded by partial reforms and, at the same time, they entail the reorganization of relations between classes, not their abolition. They are hence to be seen as a strategy for a *transition* to socialism and not as a strategy for socialism. The organic quality we have stressed is also part of a recognition that structural reforms involve not only the political relations of forces but also a reorganization of the productive structures of society. In other words, there is a refusal to identify the 'structure' with the economic level understood in a technical sense. The 'structure' involves the *social* relations of production. As Rossana Rossanda put it: '. . . structural reforms are reforms of the socio-political relations inherent in the productive system not reforms of the technical–productive material organization . . .'.[6]

The reformists' reforms are hence characterized by their sectorial nature, structural reform by the organic quality. But we should add another concept, the concept of political leadership or 'direction'. Structural reforms are in fact to be presented 'as a programme of government' as Togliatti explained in the course of his polemic with Garaudy, the French Communist, whose article (critical of the 'Italian road') had been published in *Rinascita*.[7] Such a programme could be neither that of a government engaged in the building of socialism nor that of a government 'whose task is only the negative one of blocking reactionary developments', added Togliatti, with an evident reference to the popular front governments. The government in question would be one which would direct its activities against the big monopolies. The crux of the matter could be only that of transitional forms of the government of society and of the programme corresponding to these forms. Thus for Togliatti 'structural reforms and changes in political leadership are two aspects of the same struggle'. Underlining the organic composition of structural reforms, he added: '. . . we do not separate the economic struggle from the political one, the utilization of Parliament from the activities of the masses, structural reforms from economic demands'.

The distinction between the organic and the sectorial is important because, as we shall see, it is at the centre of the entire polemic which would counterpose the Italian Communists to the experiment of the centre-left government.

According to Togliatti, the chief component of reformism is its tendency to obliterate from its strategic vision the final goal of the destruction of capitalism and the construction of socialism.[8] This is, of course, the traditional Marxist definition of reformism, but Togliatti proceeds to explain that in the actual conditions of Italian society it is not possible to follow reformist policies without sooner or later affecting the structure of capitalism.[9] Togliatti does not explain in this text why this should be so, but from other sources one can assume that he is referring to the frequently stated thesis of the impossibility of 'rationalizing' Italian capitalism. In any case what follows from his statement is that it is necessary to to support even the reformists' reforms, for the reformists may be pushed further along than they would have liked, provided there is a powerful mass movement. In this situation the task of the revolutionary party is not to lose contact with the masses, not to be isolated from the masses and to be able, while challenging the reformists to be truly reformist, to pose constantly the question of the relation between partial reforms and the long-term goals of the labour movement.

It is clear that Togliatti is moved by the fear that the political project behind the centre-left, the isolation of the PCI, would achieve some success, a success all the more likely if the PCI were to oppose all the measures of the government and were to adopt an intransigent attitude towards all projects of reforms, entrenching itself into a position of pure propaganda and agitation. Togliatti's injunction to challenge the DC to follow a reformist path seriously, even if it is unlikely that he expected the centre-left to achieve any significant reforms, was tantamount to putting the party, if not on a reformist road at least not against it. What he was saying was not just that a reformist strategy did not lead to socialism and that therefore it objectively sought to maintain existing capitalist relations. He was actually forming the conclusion that a reformist strategy could not be conducted without, at a certain stage, being forced to pose fundamental considerations on the class nature of political power.

Here Togliatti must have had in mind a *specific* brand of reformism: that of the Italian Socialist Party and of the left-wing of the DC. It should not in fact require much effort to list a number of reforms under capitalism which do not have the effect described by Togliatti, i.e. that of confronting sooner or later the very foundation of the capitalist structure.

Togliatti was well aware that the history of the development of capitalism in Italy as anywhere else presented itself as a constant reorganization of society. He was also too steeped in Marxism to accept the view that this constant reorganization brings one step nearer the socialist dawn. Thus when he argued against non-structural reforms he referred specifically to reforms which are aimed politically against some aspects of capitalism as were indeed some of the PSI proposals incorporated in the various programmes of the centre-left government. Togliatti did not make the political mistake of reducing the Socialists' plans to plans of pure capitalist conservation. The Socialists remain comrades even though misguided and naïve ones.

This extreme caution is present not only in the Communist judgements towards the PSI, but is extended to the centre-left experiment as a whole. In his report to the Tenth Congress Togliatti would stress that there were positive and negative elements in the political programme of the centre-left government. To ignore the positive aspects — he said — would be a serious mistake.[10]

Togliatti also recognized that the Naples Congress of the DC had been a step forward in the general orientation of the Christian Democrats in so far as it recognized the need for further State intervention.[11] But for Togliatti this was not enough. Insistent as he always was on the politics of things rather than in the things themselves, he proceeded to ask whether such State intervention would be activated in order to rationalize capitalism or in order to break up the large monopolies. For Togliatti it was evident that the DC Congress had opted for the 'rationalization thesis'. The point is that it was the *politics* of State intervention and not the need for it which divided Communists and Christian Democrats.

A powerful element in the DC decision to form a centre-left government had been the realization that it was not possible to continue to manage the social and economic contrasts which were dividing Italy without the elaboration of new policies.

When in 1960 a government was formed under Tambroni with the external support of the neo-Fascists, the popular unrest which followed signalled that there was at least one road which was closed to the Christian Democrats: an alliance with the 'right'. The DC then chose what seemed a daring new project: a political strategy of reforms which did not necessitate the contribution of the Italian Communists. The new centre-left government, which claimed that its reforms were 'structural' too, had, at the strategic level, the effect of forcing the Italian Communists to accelerate their research on the whole thematic of structural reforms. This is the chief reason why our analysis will have to rely principally on contributions of the period 1962-4. In the period 1956-62 the material is fairly scarce and one cannot find extensive pronouncements on the matter.

It is true that the Theses of the Eighth Congress of 1956 attempted to analyse the new emerging features of the Italian political economy. This was a necessary operation because the Italian Communists, as they themselves had admitted, had been taken by surprise by what came to be known as the 'economic miracle' and had not been able to explain the massive changes which had occurred in Italy. Now it was clearly stated that, whereas in the first post-war years the politics of the dominant classes had been entirely directed towards the simple reconstruction of the old infrastructures with the old methods of organizations,[12] now the dominant capitalist groupings had entered a more dynamic phase of struggle. The number of strike hours, which in the year 1956-7 were around thirty-three to thirty-six million, reached eighty million in 1962, and had thus tended to intensify the lopsidedness of the Italian economy, that is, on the one hand modern and relatively efficient large enterprises, on the other various forms of 'paleo-capitalism'.

Another factor noted was the important change in the countryside, a change which is described as having occurred in spite of the resistance of the dominant groups and as a consequence of the agrarian reform (which had been promulgated by the Christian Democratic Party).[13] This change was characterized by the growth of small farms, a process seen as a blow to the dominance of large landed estates whose remaining monopoly powers were an obstacle to the proper development of the national agriculture. However, whereas a relative success was registered in the countryside in the direction of the struggle against the remnants of landlordism, the same cannot be said for the anti-monopolistic struggle, a fundamental point of the Italian road to socialism. The accelerated process of capitalist development had determined, according to the Theses of 1956, the subordination of agriculture to the power of banking capital. In the industrial sector, the major monopolistic groupings had been able to obtain the quasi-totality of new investments and had thus been able to structure around their requirements the location and development of medium and small enterprises.

While no one would deny that the Italian 'economic miracle' had improved the standard of living for a large part of the population, it is also undeniable that it left unresolved most of the fundamental problems of Italian society. Moreover, the end of the period of accelerated growth coincided with a powerful increase in the intensity of the economic class struggle. The number of strike hours, which in the year 1956-8 were around thirty three to thirty six million, reached eighty million in 1962 more than doubling in 1963 to eighteen million and stabilizing itself in 1964 at ninety-one million.

In these circumstances the centre-left government's main claim was that its policy of reforms would solve the imbalances of Italian society. It was hence the task of the Italian Communists to show that this claim was unfounded, and, as it can now safely be said with the strength of hindsight, they were proved right. This is the political context within which PCI leaders would examine and define their strategy. Pietro Ingrao, in a polemic with one of the socialist leaders, Riccardo Lombardi, wrote:

> . . . the absurdity, the abstractness, the demagogic impotence of an action of structural renewal of Italian society which conceives reforms as so many 'bits' separate or separable each from the other is emerging or has emerged. An action which remains sectorial, a single reform, even the most daring is condemned to failure. What is necessary is a *policy of reforms*, gradual but organic.[14]

Ingrao stressed that the impossibility of conceiving sectorial reforms as 'structural' is not merely an ideological question but resides in the fact that even apparently sectorial reforms, if they are proposed within a general anti-monopolistic policy, cannot but lead eventually to fundamental choices involving not only questions of distribution and circulation but also the fundamental question of accumulation:

> . . . determinate structural developments of Italian society, can be overcome only by intervening in the phase of accumulation, that is, at the origin of the problems of income distribution and of direction of consumption.[15]

and he adds:

> It is a fact that starting from generically democratic demands (by that I mean: demands which do not directly question the capitalist system) such as the Southern question, the imbalance between industry and agriculture, etc., one is led today to tackle not something which is at the margin of the system but something which is essential to it.[16]

The basis for Ingrao's remark is the view that the development of Italian capitalism did not occur in spite of the so-called backward sectors of Italian society, but thanks to them; that capitalism has not rationalized Italian society, but on the contrary has aggravated its internal imbalances. It is for this fundamental reason that the project of the centre-left government is seen by the Italian Communists as a hopeless one: the rationalization of capitalism is not to be fought because it is undesirable but because it is Utopian. As Giorgio Amendola put it:

> It seems to me that those who asserted the bourgeois democratic nature of questions such as that of the agrarian reform or of the South, and who thought that a solution would be found through capitalist development, are now victims of the neo-capitalistic mirage and are not able to see the knot of new and old contradictions into which monopolistic expansion resolves itself . . .[17]

This thesis meant that the Italian Communists could fight for an agrarian reform not separately but in connection with a struggle for the industrialization of the South. This type of demand would bring immediately to the fore, as Ingrao pointed out in the above citation, questions of fundamental importance such as the control of monopolies and of their investments. If the working class could impose its hegemony in such a way as to determine the general pattern of investment, then it would really be trying to impose its control at the level of accumulation. As early as May 1957 the 'Assemblea Meridionale' called by the PCI proposed, in its final resolution, that the struggle for the South should no longer be confined purely to the defence of existing levels of occupation. It advocated concrete objectives such as the utilization of State enterprises for the creation of an industrial base in the South, the use of compulsion to force large monopolies to invest part of their profits in the South, the use of incentives in favour of small- and medium-sized industry and the granting of incentives to the large groups providing the direction of their activities were governed by politically defined goals, that is defined by the State in conjunction with working class organizations.[18]

The Communist rejection of the 'capitalist rationalization' thesis in agriculture is clearly illustrated by this passage from the resolution of the Central Committee meeting of April 1961:

> The devastation of agriculture and of the South has been and is the first condition (and not a marginal and hence eliminable consequence) of a rapid process of capitalist concentration and centralization which has allowed monopoly capital to enlarge its economic and political dominance.[19]

The consequence of this process, according to the resolution, is a restriction of the home market. A pauperized South, in fact, cannot constitute a proper home market for Italian goods. This was partly due to a long-term tendency of the Italian economy towards insertion into the international market. This feature, which the Italian Communists, having

rejected autarkic solutions, considered positive, had, however the consequence of putting Italy at the mercy of an international economic
conjuncture it would not control on its own. Thus an organic policy of
economic development, in the Communists' analysis, had to be based on
a parallel increase in the size of the market and not on the compression
of wages and the increased exploitation of the labour force. This was to
be achieved by an agrarian reform which would free the agricultural
sector from the condition of inferiority in which monopoly capital had
placed it and which would favour an improvement in the purchasing power
of the peasant masses and the development of small peasant enterprises —
both necessary factors for an enlargement of the home market and, in
turn, a condition for further industrial development. At the same time, the
Communists' objective was not a mere defence of peasant property but the
development of associated and co-operative forms of farming towards
agricultural enterprises of sufficient size to permit the rational utilization
of technical advances.

It is this analysis, and the strategy which follows from it, which constitutes the real basis for the alliance between the Northern proletariat
and the Southern peasantry and which makes of the South the dominant
problem facing the Italian Communists. Thus the Communists reaffirmed
the centrality of the Southern question against those (both in the ranks
of the PCI and in the left in general) who considered the Southern question
on its way to resolution due to the concentration of capital in the South
and who believed that the slogan of agrarian reform was increasingly out
of date because the traditional latifundi had been liquidated.

The rejection of the 'rationalization of capitalism' thesis remains substantially unchanged throughout the period under examination. The crux
of the position is a condemnation of policies aimed at rationalizing
capitalism by liberating it from 'backward' relations which are seen as an
obstacle to its growth. The development of Italian capitalism, according
to the PCI, does not solve traditional conflicts, but reproduces them.
Furthermore the strategy of the Italian Communists is not one which
merely aims at splitting the ruling historical bloc, so to speak, 'at the top',
that is, at the level of the coalition of monopolistic and 'feudal–pre-
capitalist' interests. The destruction of the bloc necessitates rather the
appropriation on the part of the working class of the various social forces
which have been aggregated through the political dominance of the
Catholic party (the DC) and its 'inter-class' ideology: the peasantry, the
urban and rural middle strata and even small-scale entrepreneurs.

Finally, given the particular intertwining between monopolies and the
'backward sector', it follows that the anti-monopolistic struggle cannot

be seen 'as an isolated fact, but must be conceived in the framework of all the contradictions which the monopolies create and aggravate'.[20]

The polemic against the 'rationalization thesis', which is essentially a polemic against reformism and a defence of the strategy of structural reforms, intensifies in the early sixties concurrently with the initial stages of the political construction of the centre-left. Togliatti, in particular, was to attempt to locate the explanatory key of the new DC project in their application, in the sphere of the economy of the formula of 'inter-class' (*interclassismo*), defined as an ideology which refuses to examine the class nature of the economic order and is therefore led to attempt a series of compromises between varying social interests without having examined the structures of the social relations which determine, in whatever mediated a form, the range of apparent interests.[21] Togliatti points out that when a special force attempts a project of rationalization of the economic structures it cannot but deal with a number of problems each of which affects in different ways different social strata. The project of Italian Christian Democracy is to be the mediator between these social groups through the use of the State machinery, at the same time avoiding, however, the adoption of a unifying stand. The result of these inter-class policies of collaboration between the State and a sector of monopoly capital could not accelerate the growth of State monopoly capitalism, 'the most advanced form of capitalist development'.

What is of interest here is not so much whether Togliatti's analysis is correct but the fact that he refused to characterize the DC as a traditional conservative or capitalist party. What he condemns is the practical impossibility of the 'inter-class' project, that is, of the possibility of conciliating in the long-run fundamentally disparate class interests.

The Communists' position was then essentially one which attributed a Utopian character to projects of rationalization of capitalism, because the removal of backward sectors and of obstacles to development could only be achieved through an organic anti-monopolistic intervention at the point of accumulation, at the level of structures and not at the level of the effects of those structures.

Furthermore, the dominating characteristic of structural reforms, that is their organic quality, is that they are never about purely quantitative factors, but point, at every moment and in accordance with a particular situation, to politically-determined objectives. Let us take, for instance, the question of public expenditure. A policy which simply demands an increase in public expenditure would fail to be a structural reform unless it had a definite anti-monopolistic direction, that is, unless it sought to change the existing relations of forces. As Amendola put it in 1960:

We must state that a policy of economic development cannot be based on an undifferentiated increase in public expenditure. It is not merely a question of the state spending more, but of deciding in which direction must the state spend and in whose interest.[22]

The question then is: what is the political principle which guides the formulation of a criterion directing structural reforms? This principle can only be derived from an examination of the conjuncture and the consequent isolation of the main enemy. On this point there is little doubt that the continuity in the party policy throughout the entire post-war period is remarkable: the main enemy is monopoly capital and a policy of structural reform can only be an anti-monopolistic policy. This is repeated in all the party theses at the various congresses and is often re-stated by Togliatti. It is here that the link between structural reform and the alliance strategy of the party is at its closest: the anti-monopolistic nature of the PCI's policy establishes at one and the same time the form of the structural reforms the party must propose and points to the new historical bloc to be constructed, a bloc which must be made up of the various non-monopoly classes and strata. It is this characteristic which permits the Italian Communists to claim that their policies are in *the national interest*, defined as the interest of a potentially anti-monopolistic collectivity.[23]

If the strategy of structural reforms is a revolutionary strategy, it entails a view of revolution as a process, an acceptance of a certain gradual development. Within this 'it is difficult', as Togliatti wrote in his report to the Tenth Congress, 'to establish precisely when the qualitative jump takes place'.[24]

Here two issues arise: first, is the qualitative change a consequence of a quantitative increase? Is it a Hegelian-economistic position which assumes that the sheer accumulation of reforms will provoke at a certain point in time a crisis during which either the revolutionary party can intervene or there occurs a spontaneous passage to a new social order? A close reading of the context would show that for Togliatti the question of the 'qualitative jump' is not a theoretical question but a practical one: it is not possible to theorize *a priori* the moment of the revolutionary break. These are moments which manifest themselves in the course of the struggle. It is clear, in any case, that Togliatti envisaged a long-term strategy, necessary, as he says, for advanced capitalist countries with a well-rooted democratic system. During this period the working classes operate to build their hegemony (e.g. through the struggle for the extension of democracy and for structural reforms) and this struggle opens the possibility (only the possibility, not the mathematical certainty) of a radical change in the social structure. What he clearly specified is that this struggle cannot be reduced to the conquest of 51 per cent of the votes in Parliament; this, he says, 'would be naïve' because the 'dominant bourgeois class can always succeed in stopping this conquest'.[25]

Rossanda, following Togliatti, asserts that the theoretical basis of the strategy of structural reforms lies in the rejection of necessarily conceiving the taking of power at a single moment, as a revolutionary 'jump'; it is rather a *process* which is characterized by a set of objectives which are neither immediately socialist nor transitory demands as in Lenin. In Leninist theory transitory demands are tactical stages rapidly culminating in a revolutionary situation while structural demands are permanent strategic conquests.[26] In so doing, however, Rossanda seems to eliminate completely the qualitative rupture still envisaged by Togliatti.

So far we have discussed the strategy of structural reforms, but not the actual reforms which the PCI put forward in the period we are examining. In analysing these we immediately encounter a problem: not all demands made by the PCI can be termed structural demands, some are in fact short-term immediate demands (in the Italian terminology 'conjunctural demands') yet we are never given the criterion with which to distinguish between the two.

For instance, in a motion on anti-inflationary policies presented by the PCI in the Chamber of Deputies on 10 January 1963 (one month after the Tenth Congress), we find demands put forward as part of a general economic plan (it is this in particular which would give them organic characteristics and hence establish them as structural demands). They are:

1. Agrarian reform.
2. State intervention in the distribution sector.
3. A reform of retail associations in the agricultural sector.
4. Public control of the quality of the production of the food industry (especially the canning industry).
5. Land and housing reform.
6. A fiscal reform.

To these long-term demands the resolution also added specifically 'conjunctural' demands, namely, price and imports control.[27]

Let us compare these demands with a resolution of the PCI executive committee of October 1963. Here all the demands are presented as immediate ones, but they include demands which in the Chamber of Deputies motion were presented as long-term: agrarian reform and land reform. Moreover, even the other demands have undoubtedly the characteristic of long-term structural reforms: the demand for an entire new system of State participation in industry, a radical reform in the pharmaceutical sector, the constitution of a single institution for the management of the real estate portfolio of all welfare institutions (some are semi-private) and, finally, the development of collective consumption in order to achieve a different composition of aggregate consumption.[28]

What this comparison tells us is that clearly there was a manifest confusion in the PCI as to the nexus between immediate 'conjunctural' demands and structural ones. The general principles were clear enough: there must be an organic connection between immediate demands and structural ones in the sense that the former must constitute the initial stages of the latter. The problem was the practical application of this principle. As long as the party tended not to press coherent short-term demands to counterpose the government's short-term plans, structural demands could not but be seen as a propagandist exercise removed from a situation which urgently requested immediate decisions.[29] In the dialectic between centre-left government and Communist opposition there was a clear asymmetry. On the one hand the government was unable to formulate organic long-term proposals for the solution of fundamental structural disequilibria, or when it actually did so they were unrelated to its day-to-day policies. On the other hand the opposition seemed to be able to counterpose little except long-term proposals. The reason for this confusion in the PCI policies should not only be blamed on the Communist rank and file, whose tendencies towards agitation and propaganda rather than realistic proposals was in part the heritage of a certain type of conception of the battle for socialism, which could not but affect the leadership. A deeper reason could be found in the traditional inability of Italian Communism (and Italian society) to devote to the economic analysis of the empirical the energies and resources it devoted to problems of culture and theory. In a sense the PCI was still marked by the anti-scientific tradition of Italian culture. However, the recognition of this confusion must not obscure the fundamental importance of having established general principles of political analysis which could be, and indeed were, a guide to the Italian Communists in the pursuit of their strategy. These principles eventually allowed them to escape to a certain extent from the abstract quality which tends to characterize the behaviour of opposition parties in other countries with different traditions.

The practical use of these principles can best be seen at work in the approach adopted by the PCI towards the issue of nationalization.

The organic link between the struggle for reforms and political power had been established by Togliatti in his report to the Ninth Congress (1960) in which he said:

> We know very well that a single nationalization or a certain intervention of the state for a rational economic development or an extension of political autonomies or even an increase in welfare does not change at all the nature of the regime and of the society in which we live.[30]

He went on to say that something would change, if not in the nature, at least in the relation of forces, if these actions were part of a wider struggle. It is precisely this wider struggle which is a feature of the revolutionary process.

A similar organic conception appeared in an editorial, again by Togliatti, in 1962:

> The extension of the economic action of the state, nationalization, attempts at economic planning, etc., do not guarantee by themselves either the safety of democracy or its development, necessary today and demanded by the working masses. A democratic life, in all fields of social and economic activity and, consequently, a closer control and access of the masses to the management of power must accompany the economic process.[31]

Togliatti had made it clear that nationalization must not be undertaken for ideological reasons. He pointed out that the PCI had never asked for wholesale nationalization. On the contrary it had rejected the idea that even at the moment of the transition to socialism there should be measures of general nationalization, as they envisaged the possibility of the coexistence of a nationalized sector with private initiative.[32]

Thus the reason for demanding a particular nationalization is 'to contrast, limit and possibly break the growing and suffocating powers of monopoly capital . . . It is not the area of private initiative which we want to reduce but the area of power . . . of monopoly capital. Nationalization is a means of accomplishing this operation. . . .' So nationalization *per se* does not necessarily contain any progressive elements. What is evident so far is that the significance of nationalization depends on its political content.

The discussion on nationalization was not divorced from ongoing economic policy. The projected policies of the centre-left coalition included in fact the nationalization of electricity. The law which created the new State electricity company (ENEL, *Ente nazionale energia elettrica*) was passed by Parliament on 6 December 1962 with the votes of the DC, the Republicans, the Social Democrats and the Socialists while the Communists abstained.[33]

The Communists, as we have seen, had never put forward a general plan of nationalization, but the State take-over of electricity had always been in their proposals.[34] During their Eighth Congress they listed electricity, public services, and the sugar and chemical industries (Montecatini) in their specific nationalization proposals.[35]

In accordance with their views on the undesirability of a strategy of nationalization which would not be part of a wider set of measures[36] the PCI, in March 1962, established the conditions for their support of the projected nationalization of electricity.[37] We can read these as conditions which would give their reform a structural character.

The first condition was that the compensation to be paid to the shareholders should not be such that it would constitute too great a burden of repayment for the new State electrical company. Secondly, the new public corporation should have a 'democratic structure'. Finally, and this is the third condition, it should have a policy which should radically depart from the policies of the old electrical monopolies. In other words, it should operate in a discriminatory sense in favour of small and medium business, of the agricultural sector and for the redevelopment of the South. The new public corporation would have to become 'the servant of collectivity' in a clearly politically-defined manner, that is, in an anti-monopolistic direction.

What we see here at work in this resolution is a concept of the 'primacy of the political', that is, the emphasis is not on nationalization *per se*, but on the form, the political sign which this nationalization should take — the system of alliances and the 'historic bloc' which would direct it.

None of the conditions listed above was met by successive centre-left governments. The PCI economist Pesenti recognized that the way in which the nationalization of the electrical sector occurred undoubtedly hit the finance capital sector because it withdrew from it a source of accumulation. However, because the State paid generous compensation and because of the lack of any anti-monopolistic control of investment, the vast sums thus released enabled finance capital to extend its dominance in other sectors.[38]

Hence without an appropriate policy of investment control any nationalization would tend to 'free' money capital and would facilitate the growth of finance capital.[39] It is for this reason that the anti-monopolistic struggle had to be organic, that is, constituted by a strategic unity which would take into account the various forms in which monopoly capital rekindles itself.

Thus a nationalization can become a part of a policy of structural reform only when it is connected to a policy of price controls, investments and profits and to a 'democratic' monetary and credit policy — all these to be co-ordinated by a plan of economic development.

In his 'Yalta Memorandum', Togliatti notes that the question of economic planning is 'on the agenda in the entire Western world' and he adds:

> It is evident that the democratic and labour movement cannot ignore this question. We must fight on this terrain too. This requires a development and a co-ordination of immediate working class demands with proposals of economic structural reforms (nationalization, agrarian reform, etc., etc.) under a general plan of economic development to counterpose to capitalist planning. This would not yet be a socialist plan, because the conditions of it are not there, but it would be a new form and a new means of struggle to advance towards socialism. The possibility of an advance (to socialism) in a peaceful way is today closely linked to the approach and solution to this problem.[40]

Economic planning, which, under the impact of the reformism of the centre-left government, was increasingly debated in the PCI, is, in essence, the key to structural reforms. It is the co-ordinating element which can give a politically-defined organic characteristic to the various demands put forward by the PCI. A central role is not given to economic planning until the Tenth Congress of 1962. The Congress Theses defined economic planning as a 'new terrain' on which the popular forces are called upon to fight.[41] This terrain is not determined by ideological reasons but by an objective situation. What the Theses reject is 'planning aimed at guaranteeing the maximum monopolistic profit and at rationalizing for this purpose public spending'. To this the working class 'should not simply counterpose . . . a type of planning devised to maximise productivity and aimed only at preventing . . . the imbalance which this may cause'. The type of planning envisaged by the Communists would determine a 'different quality in the accumulation of capital, developing and directing investments towards a different sectorial and territorial distribution'.[42]

The general aims the PCI would want to give to such an economic plan are 'the major concrete and historically-determined issues . . .: the conditions of the working class, the problem of its liberty and emancipation, the situation of the peasantry, feminine emancipation, the Southern question, education and public services'.[43]

Here we should note that the plan is not conceived as a socialist one: capitalist accumulation is not in question, but only its direction and composition. There remains the fact, however, that the PCI introduces in the same context the question of the emancipation of the working class as an objective of a 'democratic' plan. This would tend to indicate that the plan itself is not seen as completely bound up within capitalism, but that it would constitute a basis (or part of a basis) for a transition to socialism. This interpretation is based on the Italian Communist conception of revolution as a process and their stress on the links between democracy and socialism with no 'Chinese wall' in between. There is little doubt, however, that the PCI wanted to emphasize that their conception of planning did not entail a socialist society and that it could be put into practice in the existing system; hence the term 'democratic' planning counterposed to 'socialist' planning.

Democratic planning as such is not meant to operate at the economic level alone. Togliatti, in his report to the Tenth Congress, explained that a transformation of the structures of the State and, in particular, the creation of the regional councils and the strengthening of local autonomy was a necessary creation for a policy of democratic planning.[44] He added:

> Democratic economic development and political democracy thus co-incide in an articulated system of studies, debates, decisions, realizations and controls.[45]

The specific conditions for the existence of a democratic plan (as opposed to a mere series of government measures of economic intervention) were to be fundamentally political. A plan can actually exist, in Togliatti's view:

> . . . when there is not only the initiative of a public institution for the development of determinate economic activities but also a social orientation of this initiative; that is, when there is a struggle directed against the capitalistic and monopolistic ruling groups for the purpose of controlling them and for the limitation of their privileges.[46]

Naturally, the PCI had to develop its ideas on planning against the background of the activities of a government which was deeply committed to planning. Thus the important question of the relationship between the 'conjunctural' policies and the longer-term objectives of the plan came to the fore in an analysis by Eugenio Peggio of the programme of the Moro government of 1963–4.[47] This administration, the first with socialist ministers, had proposed a two-stage programme.

The first stage was supposed to deal with the most pressing questions posed by an adverse conjuncture (the anti-conjunctural stage), the second with economic planning proper. In separating the two stages in this way, the Moro government adopted the first stage measures which, if fulfilled, would have diminished, according to Peggio, the possibility of a successful economic plan. The anti-conjunctural measures, aimed mainly at reducing the rate of inflation were: (1) an incomes policy; (2) cuts in public spending; and (3) a reduction of public investment programme. All three measures, which in any case failed, would have had the effect of increasing the self-financing capabilities of the large monopolies and would have thus reduced the possibility of successful economic planning. Peggio's conclusion is that it was never in the intention of the Moro government to enter the second stage and that the proposed centre-left economic plan was never more than a propagandist instrument in the hands of the DC to convince the PSI to accept an incomes policy.[48]

The point which is important here is that Peggio, through a critique of the Moro government, is in fact asserting the inseparability of 'anti-conjunctural' policies and structural reforms: both must have the same political and strategic content, that is an anti-monopolistic one. To some extent this constitutes, as we have seen, a self-criticism of some tendencies within the PCI which emphasized structural reforms without always being able to propose short-term measures.

The Moro government and many of the economic experts of the centre-left coalition had linked incomes policy and economic planning. The control of wages was seen as a necessary anti-inflationary measure needed to create the conditions for an economic plan. Once an incomes policy had been put on the agenda it was necessary for the PCI, very much on the defensive in this period, to fit it within its strategic framework.

An appropriate starting-point is provided by one of Togliatti's last writings, an article in *Rinascita* on the question of the relation between democratic planning and incomes policy.[49] According to Togliatti incomes policy and democratic planning are contradictory terms. In other words they denote deeply contrasting modes of economic management.[50] He defined an incomes policy in a one-sided way, that is, as a policy which tends to compress working class incomes so that their expansion does not disturb the economic equilibrium of the system. Democratic planning, on the other hand, is defined as a policy which, through a set of controls in the sphere of the economy, seeks to destroy positions of superprofit and speculations as well as of rent and which would thus serve to transfer gradually important decision-making powers to the collectivity.[51]

Togliatti discounted a possible counter-argument, namely the existence of a form of control of incomes in socialist countries, by insisting that the situation is so different that there could be no valid parallel. Nevertheless it is far from clear in which way an incomes policy and democratic planning are mutually exclusive alternatives. What Togliatti did was to set up a position (which he alleged to be that of the Governor of the Bank of Italy, Guido Carli), according to which the fundamental problems of Italian society would be solved if there were some sort of official check on the increase in wages.[52] To this position he contrasted democratic planning. But having done so he still had not proved that a voluntary incomes policy enjoying the agreement of all the workers' organizations could not coexist with a programme of structural reforms within the framework of economic planning.

In fact the case could be made that the only reason why workers should accept a limitation to wage increases is precisely the existence of a government which effectively represents their interests and is prepared to redirect the Italian economy in an anti-monopolistic direction. Here Togliatti seems to have put forward a thesis — that of the contradictory nature of incomes policy and democratic planning — in a manner which is substantially conditioned by ongoing polemics. It reflected Togliatti's profound conviction that the centre-left government was not in a position to implement any structural reforms whatsoever and that hence a Communist acceptance of the principle of an incomes policy would have simply disorientated its trade union following. Politically Togliatti was proved right even though the case he made for the incompatibility between economic planning (and hence structural reforms) and incomes policy is far from convincing.

The net opposition of the PCI to incomes policy was also linked to the CGIL's intransigent rejection of any form of control (the Catholic trade union — CISL — however, maintained that there should be a correlation between productivity and wages). However, among the Communist leaders of the CGIL we can note a more differentiated approach.

One of the leaders of the powerful engineering section of the CGIL, Bruno Trentin, a Communist and a representative of the 'left' both within the party and the CGIL, in an interesting article in *Critica Marxista*, analysed the experiences of the European labour movement towards forms of wage control. He came to the conclusion that if the only alternative was between a rigid opposition to incomes policy (for whatever reason, even the most corporative) and a subordination of trade union activity to a vague and 'mythical' conception of State intervention and planning subservient to private accumulation, then rigid opposition was amply justified.[53]

It is clear that not all conceptions of planning had to be 'mythical'. What then should the attitude of the trade unions be to a 'democratic' plan? Trentin did not answer this directly but suggested that the trade union movement should not simply wait for this type of planning to be developed, but that it should actually contribute to its formulation. The unions themselves would have to provide the necessary intellectual tools for an operation of this scale.[54]

Clearly the traditional sphere of trade union activity is remarkably enlarged: the separation between an economic struggle, which is the prerogative of the trade unions, and a political struggle, which is the appropriate sphere of competence of the political party, is challenged. This proposal is put forward in a context which seeks to re-affirm the autonomy of the trade union movement from all parties: it should not delegate to a friendly government the tasks of delivering the goods in exchange for a pre-emptive offer of a wage truce (the British experience). Trentin asserted that for all intents and purposes wages should be considered an independent variable at least in the initial stages of the plan.[55] Only subsequently and only if the effects of the plan have been favourable to an increase in real wages would trade unionists take into consideration these factors in formulating their demands.

There are, of course, 'obvious' reasons why the PCI was hostile, even though not in an intransigent manner, to an incomes policy: the special relationship it had with the trade unions, the refusal to 'freeze' the existing distribution of income, the realization that an incomes policy would tie the trades union to the orbit of a government which, in their view, was not committed to an anti-monopolistic policy, and many other factors which would necessarily lead a working class party to take a less than friendly attitude to anything which would limit the ability of the workers to increase their standard of living. There is, however, another reason closely linked to the relatively new line which the PCI was taking on the question of productivity. The PCI had come to the conclusion that the economic miracle had been due to a large extent to the stimulus provided by the economic class struggle. This view finds one of its first official expressions in the Theses of the Ninth Congress (1960) which read in part:

> The wages struggle and the systematic increase in the standard of living of the working class has today a decisive importance not only as a factor in the expansion of the home market but because it favours basic consumption. This is qualitatively important for a real economic development both as a unique stimulus in directing productive investment and as the objective basis of a specific increase of the importance of the working class as a guide in the general action against the powers of the monopolies.[56]

This line found a leading supporter in Giorgio Amendola. His positive evaluation of Italian economic development, a development which had had the merit of transforming the economic structure from 'agrarian–industrial' to 'industrial–agrarian', led him to point out that the growth of the Italian economy was the result of certain 'democratic facts' imposed by the 'struggle of the people' against the ruling class.[57]

These 'democratic facts' include the salvaging of Italy's industrial base immediately after the war, the beginning of reconstruction, the Constitution and, when the national unity coalition was broken in 1947, the Labour Plan and the struggle for the land. These 'facts', in Amendola's view, all contributed to an increment in the standard of living of the Italian people through an increase in real wages. This was the precondition for the rise of an internal market for Italian industry which was the basis of the economic miracle (he thus rejects the thesis that Italian economic development was fundamentally export-led).

This view was elaborated at the 1962 conference on the tendencies of Italian capitalism. In Amendola's view Italian capitalism, under the pressure of the trade unions, has been forced to abandon its traditional role of simply protecting backward positions and to engage itself in a dynamic growth based on improved technology and fast economic development.[58] In this sense there is no doubt that the 'structure' has changed. But this does not entail a structural reform in the sense in which it has been defined by Italian Communists, including Amendola. Unless one accepts the reductivist and economist position that any form of economic development brings the socialist revolution nearer, structural reforms can only be considered as a working class strategy which seeks to modify the relations of forces to its advantage. It is true that Amendola did not say that what has occurred is a structural reform; he simply pointed out that any change of the economic structure is a result of a determinate class struggle. Here, among Marxists (but not only among Marxists) there is no possibility of disagreement. Economic development is not to be attacked *per se*. In Amendola's view, it was a historical fact that the workers had been on the losing side for the past decade and one of the reasons was precisely the failure to recognize consciously this aspect of the battle.

It is significant that the possibility of a new direction and composition of production under an economic plan did not arise out of ideological considerations but out of the realization of the existence of a specific interconnection between the economy and the State which the Communists characterized as state monopoly capitalism. The Theses of the Tenth Congress stated that public industries, once they were withdrawn from the sphere of influence of the monopolies, could be an important instrument

in the anti-monopolistic struggle. The Theses added that this public intervention, however, could not be of a purely centralist nature but had to
rely on a broad articulation of different levels of local power.[59]

The Theses also specified that state monopoly capital could become
an instrument of intervention in a variety of fields: in the general direction
of the economy by intervening in the energy sector and in basic industries,
in the field of investment through the direct and indirect effect it could
have on both its composition and position, in the field of anti-monopolistic
activity through a support of middle and small enterprises, etc.[60]

Considering the importance attributed by the PCI to State monopoly
capitalism, it is all the more remarkable that, in the period we are examining,
there is a serious lack of a theoretical investigation of such central concept.

In an article published in 1966 on the problem of state monopoly
capital, Luciano Barca admitted that not only, when the PCI appeared on
the scene in 1945 as a mass party, had its elaboration on state monopoly
capital not advanced since Lenin, but that to a certain extent 'this gap
still persists today'.[61] It is true that, in practice, the entire strategy of the
PCI from the days of the Resistance had implied the acceptance of the
possibility of a democratic utilization of the state sector. It had been this
implicit acceptance which led the PCI to oppose any attempt to dismantle
the IRI (the state holding company created by the fascist regime in the
1930s). This, however, does not invalidate a criticism of the absence of
theoretical work in this field.

Only in 1956 do we find a first explicit mention of the possibility of
democratic utilization of the state sector. The 'Elements for a Programmatic Declaration' presented at the Eighth Congress, state:

> Even the forms of state monopoly capital can open the road to socialism,
> provided these are accompanied by a democratic political struggle
> which would ensure the participation of the working classes in the
> direction of the state and allow them the effective control of public
> affairs. The economic apparatuses of the state must be withdrawn from
> the dominance of the monopolistic groups, must be organized and must
> act in a democratic manner in order to follow the cause of the anti-
> monopolistic struggle and of the democratization of the whole of
> economic life.[62]

The Theses of the same congress also attempted to clarify the interconnection between capitalism and the State:

> This reinforced subordination of the entire national economy to the
> power of direction of the monopolies is expressed today more and

more through the direct utilization of the State apparatus by the dominant groups of finance capital in the forms of state monopoly capitalism.[63]

This is seen as the characteristic element of indirect political and economic control over society. Political power over the economy is exercised not only with traditional instruments (such as fiscal and monetary policies), but also through public corporations (such as ENI and IRI), public forms of marketing associations (such as the *Ente Risi* — Rice Marketing Board) and new instruments such as the Fund for the South (*Cassa per il Mezzogiorno*), and a host of special institutes and bodies which have the dual task of increasing the interconnection between the State and finance capital and of increasing the political power of the Christian-Democratic Party by the creation of a myriad of state jobs for its supporters and by the strengthening and ramification of state clienteles.[64]

The consequence of this process in the social and political field is extremely complex. According to the party Theses it has caused the deterioration of the conditions of some of the middle strata which had become increasingly dependent on monopoly capital, thereby losing their traditional autonomy and their job security.[65]

Also heightened is the contradiction between the city and countryside expressed by the deterioration in the living conditions of the agricultural population and their consequent mass exodus from the country. This question is situated in the context of the traditional feature of the development of capitalism in Italy: the disparity between the North and the South (the Southern question). The most recent tendencies of monopoly capital in Italy were, according to the Theses, an attempt to obtain an intervention of the State in the South in order to create better conditions for private investment in the southern regions.[66]

These processes are seen as constituting the principal cause for the strengthening of monopoly capital in Italy, but they are also responsible for some divisions which appear to intervene in the bourgeoisie itself:

The most reactionary of the entrepreneurial groups, in particular the landed ones, and a section of the clerical leaders, are orientated towards defending to the very last the dominant positions of the privileged classes and reject any concessions. Other groups of finance capital, on the contrary, thanks to their more dynamic productivity and a stronger economic position are not reluctant to undertake reformist and paternalistic initiatives in order to overcome the situation.[67]

Thus it seems that the Communist analysis, in applying a differentiated method of investigation, succeeded in individuating (although in a very schematic form, and our account is, of necessity, even more schematic) the component parts of the social system in their basic political and economic divisions. The tasks of the Communists had then to be that of formulating policies which would utilize these divisions: a strategy of alliance.

Notes

1. G. Vacca, *Saggio su Togliatti*, Bari, 1974, p. 373.
2. P. Togliatti, 'Rapporto all'VIII Congresso', reprinted in *Nella democrazia e nella pace verso il socialismo*, Rome, 1963 (henceforth cited as 'Rapporto VIII'), p. 44. In the course of his report Togliatti listed only three reforms: the agrarian reform, the fiscal reform and the nationalization of the large industrial and financial monopolies (p. 44). To these he added (p. 60) the improvements in the conditions of life of the working classes, the fight against unemployment, the creation of a welfare system and regional autonomy.
3. 'Elementi per una dichiarazione programmatica del PCI' in *VIII Congresso*, p. 909.
4. P. Togliatti, 'Rapporto VIII', p. 45.
5. In *Opere scelte*, p. 1105; see also p. 1107.
6. See R. Rossanda, 'Note sul rapporto riforme-rivoluzione nella elaborazione del PCI' in *Critica Marxista*, No. 2, Mar.–Apr. 1963, p. 35.
7. See R. Garaudy, 'A propos de la "Voie Italienne vers le socialisme" ' in *Cahiers du Communisme*, Vol. XXXIII, 1 (January 1957), pp. 35–56. It appeared in *Rinascita*, No. 1, January 1957, under the title 'Osservazioni critiche ai dibattiti e alle posizioni del nostro Congresso'. Togliatti's rebuttal followed in the same issue with the title 'Postilla'.
8. P. Togliatti, 'Comunismo e riformismo', originally in *Rinascita*, No. 13, 28 July 1962, now in *OS*, p. 1066.
9. Ibid., p. 1067, where he says that in Italy 'The road to reforms cannot be taken without reforms which alter more or less radically the very structure of capitalism'.
10. P. Togliatti, report to the Tenth Congress in *OS*, p. 1109. The positive aspects specifically mentioned by Togliatti were the proposals to nationalize the electricity industry and the decision to adopt an economic plan to regulate the economy.
11. Ibid., p. 1108.
12. 'Theses' in *VIII Congresso*, p. 931.
13. Ibid., pp. 933–4.
14. P. Ingrao, 'Risposta a Lombardi' in *Rinascita*, No. 21, 23 May 1964. See also Ingrao's 'Democrazia socialista e democrazia interna di partito' in *Rinascita*, No. 17, 25 April 1964.
15. P. Ingrao, 'Risposta a Lombardi' in op. cit., p. 198. This is, of course, a development of Togliatti's remarks in his 'Comunismo e riformisto' in op. cit., discussed above.
16. P. Ingrao, op. cit.
17. G. Amendola, 'Il monopolio nemico principale nel quadro dell'azione anti-capitalista' in *Rinascita*, No. 12, 21 March 1964.
18. 'Risoluzione dell'Assemblea meridionale del PCI' (Naples, 12 May 1957) in Barca, Botta and Zevi, *I comunisti e l'economia italiana (1944–1974)*, Bari, 1975, p. 246. This collection of documents will henceforth be cited as *Barca–Botta–Zevi*.

19. 'La riforma agraria condizione necessaria del processo della agricultura' from the resolution of the Central Committee of the PCI (Rome, 29 April 1961) in *Barca-Botta-Zevi*, pp. 296–7.

20. 'I compiti dei comunisti nelle lotte della classe operaia', resolution of the Central Committee of the PCI (1 March 1957) in *Barca-Botta-Zevi*, p. 233.

21. P. Togliatti, 'Passare dei programmi all'azione per una effettiva svolta di sinistra' (report to the Central Committee, 12–14 February 1962) in *OS*, p. 1044.

22. G. Amendola, 'La II Assemblea dei comunisti nelle fabbriche' report to the Central Committee meeting of 1–3 March 1960 in *Barca-Botta-Zevi*, p. 291.

23. Theses of the Ninth Congress of the PCI in *Barca-Botta-Zevi*, p. 274.

24. P. Togliatti, report to the Tenth Congress, in *OS*, p. 1111.

25. Ibid., p. 1112.

26. R. Rossanda, op. cit., p. 19.

27. The text can be found in E. Peggio, 'Aspetti della politica economica italiana dal 1961 ad oggi' in *Critica Marxista*, No. 4–5, July–Oct. 1964, p. 302.

28. 'Per una soluzione democratica dei problemi economici e della crisi politica' (Rome, 16 October 1963) in *Barca-Botta-Zevi*, pp. 320–1.

29. This criticism, cogently expressed by Claudio Napoleoni and Franco Rodano in 'Significato e prospettive di una tregua salariale' in *Rivista Trimestrale*, No. 10, June 1964 was accepted by PCI economist E. Peggio, op. cit. pp. 315–15.

30. P. Togliatti, report to the Ninth Congress in *Nella pace e nella democrazia verso il socialismo*, pp. 147–8.

31. P. Togliatti, 'Obtorto collo', *Rinascita*, No. 19, 30 June 1962.

32. Togliatti (report to the Central Committee, February 1962) op. cit., in *OS*, p. 1043.

33. Strictly speaking, the centre-left government was launched on 4 December 1963 with Aldo Moro as Prime Minister; however, the Fanfani government (22 February 1962 – May 1963) could be considered as the first centre-left government as it enjoyed the external support of the PSI.

34. However, it should be pointed out that on 26 June 1946, the PCI had put forward a government plan which specifically mentioned the nationalization of electricity together with the chemical sector, public services, insurances and big banks (see *La politica economica italiana 1945–1974*, PCI (ed.), Rome n.d., p. 25). By the late 1950s the nationalization of electricity was supported by a large sector of informed public opinion.

35. Theses in *VIII Congresso*, p. 964.

36. These views are made official in the Theses of the Ninth Congress (1960), which stated that some nationalization was indispensable, particularly in some decisive sectors of industry and credit, but these measures had to be undertaken only as part of a wider policy which would include control of investment, prices and of profits of the large enterprises; in *Barca-Botta-Zevi*, p. 274.

37. 'Per una politica anti-monopolistica dell'energia', resolution of the Exec. Comm. (Rome, 27 March 1962) in *Barca-Botta-Zevi*, p. 301.

38. A. Pesenti, 'Sul "capitale finanziario"' in *Critica Marxista*, No. 3, 1963, p. 85. The size of compensations was such (2,000 milliard lires in ten years plus interest) that it caused the ENEL to be in a precarious financial situation from the very beginning. See E. Peggio, *Capitalismo italiano anni '70*, Rome, 1970, p. 190.

39. A. Pesenti, op. cit., p. 86.

40. In *OS*, p. 1175.

41. Theses of the Tenth Congress, in *Barca-Botta-Zevi*, p. 307.

42. Ibid., p. 307.

44. P. Togliatti, report to the Tenth Congress, in *OS*, p. 1107.

45. Ibid., p. 1108.

46. Speech, Chamber of Deputies, 18 July 1958 ('Contro la minaccia di guerra. Contro il programma reazionario di Fanfani').
47. E. Peggio, 'Aspetti della politica economica italiana dal 1961 ad oggi', *Critica Marxista*, No. 4–5, July–Oct. 1964.
48. Ibid., p. 306.
49. P. Togliatti, 'Programmazione o politica dei redditi?' in *Rinascita*, No. 24, 13 June 1964, now in *OS*.
50. Ibid., p. 1158.
51. Ibid., p. 1159.
52. Here Togliatti must be referring to Carli's report of May 1963. To a certain extent the 'incomes policy' of the centre-left government was an attempt to redress the relationship between wages and profit which had been upset by the wave of union struggles of 1962–3.
53. B. Trentin, 'Politica dei redditi e programmazione' in *Critica Marxista*, No. 1, Jan.–Feb. 1964, p. 49.
54. Ibid., p. 51.
55. Ibid., p. 55.
56. In *Barca-Botta-Zevi*, p. 275.
57. G. Amendola, 'La II Assemblea dei comunisti nell fabbriche' (report to the Central Committee meeting of 1–3 March 1960) in *Barca-Botta-Zevi*, p. 292. This report was accepted by the Central Committee thereby becoming official party policy.
58. Amendola, *Lotta di classe e sviluppo economico dopo la Liberazione*, Rome, 1962, p. 22.
59. In *Barca-Botta-Zevi*, p. 275.
60. In ibid., p. 315. See also G. Napolitano, *Movimento operaio e industria di stato*, Rome, 1962.
61. Luciano Barca, 'Per lo sviluppo dell'analisi teorica sul capitalismo monoplistico di Stato' in *Critica Marxista*, No. 5–6, Sept.–Dec. 1966, pp. 54, 56. For an interesting and critical discussion of the communist analyses of state monopoly capital from 1920 to 1945 see E. Sereni, 'Fascismo, capitale finanziario e capitale monopolistico di stato nelle analisi dei comunisti italiani' in *Critica Marxista*, No. 5, Sept.–Oct. 1972.
62. In *VIII Congresso*, p. 916.
63. In Ibid., p. 935.
64. See also the declaration of the PCI of 26 February 1958 in *Barca-Botta-Zevi*, p. 250.
65. In *VIII Congresso*, p. 939.
66. Ibid., pp. 939–40.
67. Ibid., p. 945.

9. Alliance Strategy

The traditional form of alliances established by the Soviet revolution was that between workers and peasants. This Leninist lesson was 'translated' into Italian by Gramsci in an unfinished manuscript of 1926 in which he wrote:

> The proletariat can become a directing and dominant class only in so far as it is able to create a system of class alliances which would permit the majority of the working population to mobilize against capitalism and the bourgeois state. In Italy, this entails, given the existing class relations, the consensus of the broad peasant masses. But in Italy, the peasant question is historically determined; it is not the 'peasant and agrarian question in general'; in Italy the peasant question, because of a determinate development of Italian history, has acquired two typical and peculiar forms, the Southern question and the Vatican question. The conquest of the majority of the peasant masses entails then, for the Italian proletariat the comprehension of these two questions from the social point of view, the understanding of the class needs they represent, the incorporation of these needs in a transitional revolutionary programme and the demands formulated in the course of the struggle.[1]

Thus while Gramsci maintained the worker–peasant alliance as the basis of the strategy, he also analysed the *specific form* this alliance takes in Italy (note the insistence on the Italian peculiarity): a socio-economic dimension with a geographical element (the Southern question) and an ideological one (the Vatican question). But Gramsci did not ignore a third dimension: the political one. The political representative of the peasant masses and of Catholic ideology was the Popular Party, founded in January 1919, something which Gramsci considered as 'the most important event in Italian history after the Risorgimento'.[2] Gramsci is, of course, critical of the Popular Party but recognizes that it had the merit of organizing the Catholic masses hitherto excluded from political life.[3]

Whatever specific alliances were proposed by Gramsci in 1921 or in 1926 they cannot necessarily be considered valid in a successive period.

What is important is the methodological criterion of differentiating alliance at the socio-economic level (class and other social groups), at the 'ideological' level (e.g. alliance with the Catholics), and at the political level (i.e. alliance with political parties).

We shall use this methodological criterion in our discussion of the alliance strategy of the PCI in the period 1956–64.

The first element to bear in mind is that in the post-war period the specific form of class alliance pursued by the PCI was not reducible to the classical worker–peasant alliance. Already in his 1946 conference, 'Ceto medio e Emilia rossa', Togliatti introduced the factor of the 'middle strata'. The importance of these strata was underlined again in 1956, at the Eighth Congress, but with a particular emphasis on the specificity of the Italian situation: in Russia, Togliatti declared, the alliance which was formed was that between the working class and the peasantry. In China even the national bourgeoisie took part in the construction of socialism while in Italy

> . . . around the working class, historical opponent of capitalism, are to be grouped the large peasant masses including the small and medium independent farmers, a very large productive urban middle strata and we cannot exclude the adhesion in the anti-monopolistic struggle of numerous small and medium industrialists.[4]

As we can see here, the language is couched entirely in terms of alliance with social forces.

The importance of this type of alliance was further stressed by Pietro Ingrao who, in discussing the 'opening to the left', accused its proponents of envisaging this line as a formula for particular agreements to be reached at the political summit without involving the base in the struggle. What was needed, he added, in what clearly amounted to polemics against a section of the leadership group of the PSI, was a 'combined struggle at the base and at the top, in Parliament and in the country over questions and themes which would subtract new sections of the middle strata, peasants and workers from the power of the monopolies . . .'.[5]

Having thus established the necessity of a combination of social and political alliances over merely political ones, he also stressed that it would be harmful to concentrate on the base without being able at the same time to propose an alternative government. Thus the duality we have described between the two levels of alliance was maintained in the analysis.

In a sense Ingrao, and with him the PCI as a whole, avoided the old counterposing of the 'united front from below' versus the 'popular front'.

What is envisaged is an articulation of social, political and ideological alliances, its specific form, that is, its heirarchy and priorities being historically determined in a definite situation.

It is clear that the definition of a system of class alliances can only be arrived at through the definition of the main enemy (in turn a result of an analysis of the existing situation).

As the previous section made clear, the strategy of alliances was to have an anti-monopolistic direction. However, PCI economist Luciano Barca pointed out that the dividing line the PCI was trying to establish was not between the state sector and the private sector, but that the real 'enemies' were:

> . . . those forces which impede a healthy industrial development, an accumulation directed towards production and which suffocate and distort the market. These three enemy forces are agrarian rent, monopolistic rent and the superprofits derived from speculation.[6]

It is remarkable that monopoly capital as such is not mentioned, although it could be argued that the three 'enemies' listed by Barca are all manifestations (in the Italian situation) of monopoly capital.

The system of class alliances proposed by the PCI was not particularly original. The majority of European Communist Parties have had a programme based on an anti-monopolistic coalition at least since the Second World War. The originality of the Italian Communists consists in devising a strategy of political and ideological alliances corresponding to the class alliances. The PCI never considered this correspondence from an economistic point of view: no one party ever necessarily corresponds to a single class:

> . . . while we recognize and underline the class origins of political groups (parties) we do not reduce *every* difference between parties to a class difference: there can be more parties which have their origin in the working class and the construction of a united political will can also be the result of a dialectic between them.[7]

In particular the PCI did not assume to be the only 'real' working class party. For Amendola the Communists were not the only non-social-democratic working class party. He specifically stated that the centre-left government was an attempt by the monopolistic groups and by the DC in particular to transform the PSI into a social-democratic party. The transformation would take the form, in the Italian context, of a reversal of alliances from PCI–PSI to DC–PSI.[8] Thus the reconstitution of a unity of purpose between the PSI and the PCI would be the specific form in which the attempt to integrate the working class could be defeated.

This is an important point because it underlines the non-correspondence of social and political alliances: the political alliance with the PSI entails the unity of the working class and hence it does not correspond to a social alliance, while an alliance with the DC would involve an alliance with other social strata (unless it were a pure 'summit' operation).

The PCI — or at least those Communist leaders who more often than others would emphasize fundamental principles — was conscious of the specific problem which an alliance with a Communist party posed to other parties.

> . . . the question of the alliance with us is the question of the alliance with a force which is opposed to the system. The other political forces are perfectly aware of that.[9]

Here Ingrao reaffirmed the fundamental principles of Communist action as if to stress that a strategy of alliances with different political parties and varying social strata does not indicate a change in the fundamental objectives of Communism. He then added, significantly, that the construction of a society no longer divided by classes did not entail the reduction of the whole of society to a single social organism (party totalitarianism) and that this is indeed a 'correction of some of the schematic interpretations of our doctrine'. He hence acknowledged that the unity of political direction of a socialist society could be realized through co-operation among different parties.

There is, of course, the problem of the guarantees the PCI could or should give to other political forces. Strictly speaking the problem does not exist: no political force can give precise and exact guarantees that it will or will not engage in a determinate course of action. Of course, it may be able to convince others with reasoned arguments, or with recourse to its past history, or by drawing parallels with similar situations or by emphasizing the particularities of the national situation. These arguments may be more or less convincing but they do not amount to 'exact and precise guarantees'.

Ingrao offered three reasons for the Communist acceptance of the principle of the alteration of political power (i.e. the right of the minority to become the majority) and of the principle that the political rights of individuals and groups who are not socialist will be recognized. The first reason is that this is necessary to reach agreement with other political forces (that is, for a policy of alliances); the second is that a battle for democracy is also a battle against the power of the monopolies (and this is the connection already discussed between socialism and democracy and structural reforms), but the most important reason, according to Ingrao, is that

> . . . we are becoming increasingly aware that determinate limitations of political freedom open up a problem also for the internal dialectic of the labour and socialist movement: these limitations can be used for authoritarian solutions which would suffocate the internal democracy of the socialist forces.[10]

The reference to the Soviet experience could not have been more explicit.

It is now possible to turn to the specific question of the alliance with the middle strata. We can use as a starting-point Gramsci's thesis (quoted above) that the specific forms of the peasant question in Italy are the Southern question and the Vatican question. We shall turn to the Vatican question when examining the problem of alliance with ideological forces and deal now with the Southern question.

For the Italian Communists the Southern question was not an element extraneous to Italian capitalism, a sort of tumour which was in the way of its development and which could be eradicated by a policy of capitalist modernization; on the contrary, as was stated at the Eighth Congress:

> . . . the backwardness of the South, the imbalance between the southern regions and the islands and the other regions of Italy with serious consequences for the working masses of the countryside and the towns, for the middle strata and also for a section of the property owners, are inherent in the economic and political structure of Italian capitalism.[11]

Thus there could be no distinction between a strategy for the North and one for the South, they are bound up together.[12] It followed that, as Giorgio Napolitano pointed out, the growth of monopoly capital in Italy could not but aggravate further the 'historical contradiction, the economic and social contrast between the North and the South'.[13] Thus the struggle for the renewal of the South was essentially synonymous with the struggle against the monopolies and for structural reforms.[14] It was, in other words, part of the struggle for an Italian road to socialism.

The fundamental point of the struggle for the renewal of the South was based on the slogan 'land to those who till it'.[15] This was not to be a purely 'democratic' slogan, valid, that is, only for a situation characterized by the maximum extension of democracy compatible with capitalism. Here the 'Political Motion' of the Eighth Congress firmly specifies that 'modern socialist agriculture . . . will be based in Italy on the proprietorship of the land of those who work it'.[16] The 'Elements for a Programmatic Declaration' confirms this: 'The small farmers (*coltivatori diretti*) will be guaranteed, in a socialist society, the absolute possession of their property.'[17] Clearly collectivization was not on the agenda. The novelty of the proposal was stressed by Emilio Sereni, the leading party expert on agriculture, in a passage we quote in full:

> A contribution to our efforts for the conquest of the small peasantry in the alliance with the working class is given in an entirely new and open perspective offered in the statement contained in our congressional documentation according to which the proprietorship of the land of those who work it can become and remain in our country the basis for the construction of socialism in the countryside. This is, without any doubt, a new directive, not only in the Italian socialist movement, but also in the international labour movement. There may be some comrades from fraternal parties, here present, who will remain puzzled, perhaps even upset by this new direction. But our affirmation regarding the proprietorship of the land of those who work it as the basis for socialist construction is certainly not based on an abandonment of the principles of Marxism–Leninism, but, on the contrary, it is based on the effort to apply these principles scientifically to the conditions of our country: a country where monopoly capital itself has shown us how the economic control and the direction of agricultural production is possible independently of the particular forms of property of the land. If, in the exclusive interest of a few financial tycoons, the dominant monopolistic groupings succeed in controlling and orientating the production of millions of peasants and of small agricultural producers, even forcing them — to the detriment of the national agriculture — to restrict or enlarge the cultivated areas of particular crops, I do not see why the proprietorship of the land of those who work it should stop a socialist state from organizing and orientating (in the interest of the entire collectivity and first of all in the interest of the peasants themselves) the labour of millions of producers who, as owners of their own land, would be able to exercise their agricultural activity in an individual or associated form as they freely decide.[18]

This declaration, which reflected the consensus of the Congress, at one and the same time constituted a break with the policies of agricultural development followed by the socialist countries coupled with a determination to present the change as being in accordance with the tradition of

Marxism. It was fully consistent with the proclamation of the 'permanent' feature of the alliance with the middle strata and with the Catholics of which the independent farmers were an important component.

The general implications of Sereni's statement was a criticism of the forced nature of collectivization of the agricultural sector in most of the socialist countries. Thus, the Italian Communists offered a 'guarantee' to the peasantry: they would be left free to choose between individual farming and co-operative farming although it was quite obvious that the Communists would favour the formation of co-operatives. The distance from the Eastern pattern was emphasized by the trade union leader Di Vittorio who approved Togliatti's condemnation of

. . . the forced development of co-operation and collectivization of small agricultural enterprises in flagrant violation of the principles established by the great teachers of socialism . . . And Lenin defined *as pure stupidity* any attempt to force peasants to any form of collectivization which can come only when the peasants themselves through their own experience come to prefer of their own free will a particular form of associated enterprise. Here we find it difficult to understand why certain communist parties persist in this 'pure stupidity' of which Lenin was talking, causing grave economic and political damage.[19]

'Land to the tillers' was, of course, an old slogan, but to put it forward with as much force and clarity as was done during the Eighth Congress was an indication that the party was aware that its relative weakness among southern peasants was partly due to a 'doppiezza' in its organization. The traditional sectarianism of the southern cadres had taken its toll and the post-war attempt to include in a single organization landless labourers and small peasants had increased the deeply-held fear of the latter that Communism entails the collectivization of the land. Thus the slogan had also the intention of taking these feelings into account. The fundamental objective of the strategy was, however, the destruction of the so-called 'rural bloc'. This was the term given by the PCI to the rural structure towards which the policies of the Christian Democratic Party were directed: the division between workers and peasants and the inclusion of agricultural labourers and small agricultural producers in a 'rural bloc' dominated by large landowners and monopolies and under the ideological influence of the Church.[20]

There was also the objective fact that monopolistic development was destroying peasant property without creating an efficient agriculture. The typical small capitalist farm of the Po Valley was fast disappearing and — in Sereni's opinion — the forms of oppression of the petty peasantry were becoming more and more direct. These new forms of oppression came from monopoly capital through the control of the price of fertilizers and land as well as through the control of rent payment, mortgages, etc. Increasingly the large landowner and monopoly capital ('closely inter-twined') faced not only the farmhands and the sharecroppers, but also the smallholder as a hostile force.[21]

Given this situation it would appear that the slogan 'land to the tillers' is excessively restrictive from the point of view of an alliance strategy which would also include the rural middle strata, that is, the land-owning peasants. This relatively narrow position was revised in the early sixties when new themes around questions of democratic planning emerged.

An important resolution of the Central Committee of the PCI of 29 April 1961 stated that the three conditions for a rebirth of Italian agriculture were land to the tillers, voluntary associations of peasants and public investments and technical assistance.[22] The introduction of the third condition which is nothing but the introduction of a form of state planning in agriculture is meant not only to contribute to the viability of new peasant enterprises but also to that of the old ones. Thus the strata to be mobilized by the agrarian policies proposed by the PCI were not only the landless labourers, the salaried hands, the sharecroppers and tenant farmers but also

> . . . the great mass of small peasant owners [who] are today gravely hit . . . by policies of monopolistic expansion and of concentration of public investments, condemned by degradation to ruin and to the abandonment of the land . . . sacrificed by the DC of which they constitute such a large part of its mass basis. These masses can and must become participants of a policy of agrarian reform which would allow them not to defend the little land they possess but which would give them the means and help to guarantee the technical and economic progress of their farmers associated in a common effort of common transformation and modernization of agriculture.[23]

We are thus presented with a new way of conceiving the alliance with the peasantry, not merely − as Alfredo Reichlin pointed out − on the basis of 'land to the tillers' but as a bloc of organic alliances for a new agrarian economy which would have to defend itself from the encroach-ment of monopolies with the help of 'new and original and democratic forms of state capitalism and of economic planning'.[24]

However, as we have pointed out, the alliance between workers and peasants is no longer sufficient in the new stage of capitalist develop-ment. The Eighth Congress, in reconnecting its analysis to the post-war period, so rich in strategic elaboration, advanced the thesis that the middle strata are among the driving forces of the revolution.

After 1956 these groups, seldom rigorously defined, would always be included among the potential members of an anti-monopolistic alliance. Within these middle strata one should, of course, distinguish at least between the small- and medium-sized rural producers and the urban middle strata. It is the latter which were to constitute a new source of support for the PCI after the failure of the centre-left and the social unrest of 1968-9. In this period the Communist appeal to the middle strata was still subdued and mainly concerned with tranquillizing them with words such as the following from the Theses of the Ninth Congress: 'The structural reforms we propose . . . do not mean the destruction of the middle strata, the end of all individual initiative, the imposition of bureaucratic planning and an amorphous egalitarianism.'[25]

In the development of this perspective the PCI was partially impeded by the remnants of a certain schematism which took the form of assuming that a given objective necessity for a particular alliance would solve half the problem: the subjective basis would arise sooner or later. Thus Scoccimarro in 1959 stressed the 'objective' basis of an alliance between the working class and the middle strata. This basis was brought about by the activities of the large monopolies which hit not only the working classes but also the middle strata.[26] We find here the assumption that immediate economic interests (in this case the threat from the monopolies) automatically engender political interests similar to those of the proletariat. Clearly there is here a reductionist problem which assumes an immediate reflection of the economic level in the political level. What also remains hidden is the fact that the contradictory mass called 'middle strata' cannot be moved by an appeal to economic interest alone.

The context of the social alliance with peasants and middle strata in Italy presented a peculiar feature engendered by the presence of the ideological dominance of Catholicism. This necessarily entailed an elucidation of the Catholic question and hence of the Communists' relation to the Roman Catholic Church.

This had always been a constant problem in Togliatti's reflections, stretching back to the period of the Resistance and later to the PCI attitude to Article 7 of the Constitution which enshrined the Concordat in the law of the Republic, and to the 1954 appeal to the Catholics 'for the salvation of humanity'.

In an analysis presented by Togliatti at the Central Committee meeting of September 1956, the Catholic world was then described in terms of a contradiction between its dominant political ideology (called 'Catholic integrality') and its social base. The function of Catholic integralism was that of ensuring an ideological hegemony along clerical lines which would facilitate the establishment of a consensus for the development of monopoly capital.[27] However, this ideological movement is forced, according to Togliatti, to take into consideration the self-evident needs of the Catholic masses whose consciousness 'is largely a class consciousness'. Having thus acknowledged the existence of a potential conflict within the Catholic movement, Togliatti indicated that the task of the Communists was to fight any attempt to 'clericalize' the State, that is, any attempt to substitute for the lay republican order a conception of the State which rested on the directives of religious authorities. A fertile terrain for this struggle could be established in alliance with left-wing Catholics: this was to be the basis for a Communist–Catholic dialogue.[28]

The proposal for a dialogue is reiterated with greater force in Togliatti's report to the Eighth Congress:

> The search for an Italian road to socialism will necessarily have to include a political alliance with those Catholic forces which, starting from a generic anti-capitalist position have reached the point at which they are ready to do what is necessary in order to force the capitalist structures of Italy to undergo certain indispensable profound changes.[29]

Even though the words 'political alliance' occur in the above passage, there is no direct evidence that they refer to some sort of alliance with the Christian Democratic Party or even with a section of it. The general direction of the proposals is for a collaboration with an ideologically defined group representing various classes and strata. At the same time it is unlikely that what is implied is a mere entry into the ranks of the Communist electorate of a large number of Catholic voters: this would not represent an 'alliance', for alliance infers compromise.

The problem is left unresolved but what is clear is that, given the existence of anti-capitalist feelings in the Catholic masses and of a real contradiction between these and the political party which 'represents' them (electorally), the DC, there is a possibility of dialogue, a possibility which the Communists must cultivate. The organizational forms which anti-capitalist Catholicism wanted could not be predicted or delineated at this stage. All that could be registered was the fact that the Communists were ready for collaboration and that they considered this collaboration as one of the necessary conditions for the implementation of their strategy.

But at this stage what is still taken into consideration is not the 'Catholic world' *per se* but rather its actual class composition. The tendency is to stress the class and economic interests of certain Catholics and to base an appeal on these elements rather than on their religious feelings as such.

A real change occurred at the Ninth Congress (1960) whose 'Theses' declared:

> . . . because the victory of socialism in Italy is connected to the forma-
> tion of a bloc much wider and more articulated than the worker–
> peasant alliance, the policy of entente with the Catholic world must
> be conceived as an aspect of the Italian road to socialism, as a long-
> term perspective of unity-orientated battles and of alliances not only
> with the popular Catholic masses but also with their organization.[30]

What is important here is that the Communist policy of alliance with the peasants and the middle strata had to be achieved through an under-standing with the Catholic world. This means that it is no longer a question of approaching the peasants and middle strata purely as economic group-ings with an 'objective' class interest. Nor is it a question of recognizing that a Catholic peasant is a peasant and can be won over as such, but that his Catholicism is part and parcel of his political outlook and acti-vity. By the Tenth Congress the religious aspect would even be seen as a positive element:

> The aspiration to the socialist society can not only evolve in religious
> people but such aspiration can even find a stimulus in a religious
> conscience which faces the dramatic problems of the contemporary
> world.[31]

This is consistent with a characteristic trait of the PCI in its ideological struggle: what it usually challenges is not the form of ideologies but their political content. It uses the unavoidable ambiguities they contain to extricate their progressive elements. In so doing it often exacerbates the internal contradictions of its opponents/potential allies. This charac-teristic, which at times gives rise to accusations of scheming and oppor-tunism, is the particular form in which the PCI conceives its battle for hegemony, a hegemony which does not entail the elimination of non-socialist ideologies but the ability to influence them towards politically-defined social goals. This is not of course applicable to all ideologies, but to the extent that most ideologies have to take into account some interests which are common to the whole of society, the Communists are able to stress the points of convergence. This is even easier, contrary to common belief, in the case of religious ideologies. In attempting to influence the Church into adopting 'progressive' stands, the Communists would facilitate the gradual adaptation of an institution and a move (which, in any case, have already adapted themselves to a variety of social orders) towards the transition to socialism.

In the early sixties, the Roman Catholic Church, at the end of a conservative and anti-Communist papacy, began, in the person of the new Pope John XXIII, to examine its own relation to an increasingly secular world. In the encyclica *Mater et Magistra* the new Pope examined the questions posed by 'neo-capitalism' and took an essentially reformist position in the sense that it adopted some elements present in the writings of Catholic reformist economists (somewhat influenced by Keynes) who had contributed to the economic proposals of the centre-left government. The real innovation, however, had to come with the *Pacem in Terris*, particularly where it dealt with the question of world peace and with the question of the dialogue between the Catholics and the 'others'.[32] The 'others' are the non-believers, in Italy the Communists. In complete contrast to the *Divinis Redemptoris* of Pius XI, which condemned Communism as 'intrinsically perverted', and to Pius XII, who excommunicated all Communists as well as their friends and supporters, Pope John's *Pacem in Terris* made a distinction between the 'error' and 'he who errs' and between 'false ideologies' and the movements which are inspired by them. With these movements, the Pope wrote a *'rapprochement* or an encounter on questions of a practical nature is possible . . .'.[33]

Togliatti, of course, took advantage of the new situation. In a preelection television broadcast, on 25 April 1963, he underlined the similarity in views between the Pope and himself on the question of peace and peaceful coexistence.[34] A more complete statement on the entire question of the relations with the Catholics was, however, given during a conference held in Bergamo (near Pope John's birthplace) a few weeks previously entitled 'The destiny of mankind'.[35]

Togliatti began by establishing that the alliance with the Catholics did not take the form of a compromise between ideologies.[36] Catholics and Communists, continued Togliatti, must be seen in terms of a complex of real forces: states, governments, organizations, individual beliefs, social movements, etc. It is on this basis that one should study the question of the mutual recognition of doctrines and principles and hence whether there was the possibility of an agreement 'necessary for the whole of humanity'.

For Togliatti the basis of the alliance was not only the question of peace and the universal fear caused by the existence of thermo-nuclear weapons, but also the new problems connected to the 'consumer society', the alienation of modern man, the destruction of the family unit in industrial society without a new set of values arising from it, the oppression

of women, etc. And here Togliatti offered the vision of a socialist society
which could not fail (or at least so he thought) to offer people a new
dignity in a new qualitatively superior material and spiritual affluence
(i.e. culture, literacy, etc.).[37] And he concluded by saying: 'It is not true
that a religious spirit would be an obstacle to the understanding of these
tasks . . . on the contrary.'[38]

We can now return to the question raised in the Theses of the Tenth
Congress where 'a long-term perspective of unity-orientated battles and
of alliances not only with the popular Catholic masses but also with their
organizations' was mentioned. Implicitly included among these organizations were the Catholic trade union federation (CISL), the organization
of Catholic workers (ACLI), as well as the so-called 'white' co-operatives,
sports organizations, etc. But it is also clear that the alliance with the
Catholics was not a mere 'united' front from below; it entailed some forms
of co-operation with political parties and not just with the PSI for, as we
shall see, 'popular frontism' had been ruled out. At the same time the
PCI had made it clear that it did not conceive of the possibility of solving
the Italian crisis on the basis of one party. As Togliatti put it at the Central
Committee meeting of February 1962: '. . . we have always maintained
that a single party cannot solve the crisis.'[39] In his electoral broadcast
on television of 25 April 1963 he affirmed that just as the Resistance
had not been the work of a single party so the tasks of ensuring economic,
social and political progress could not be the task of a single party. He
added, however, that it would not be possible to change the present
direction of public affairs without breaking up the conservative bloc
'which has as its core the existing leadership group of the DC'.[40]

It should be noted that Togliatti referred only to the 'leadership group'
of the DC as being the core of the conservative bloc. The entire DC was
not seen as a conservative bloc. This differentiation has important consequences: never in the years 1956–64 would the PCI rule out a co-
operation with the DC as a *matter of principle*, although often there was
a tendency to distinguish between 'right wing' and 'left wing' and to
assume that the separation of these two wings would give a 'progressive
bloc' the necessary political (and not merely electoral) majority with
which to pursue a policy of structural reforms.

At the Eighth Congress the DC was seen as the leading party of the
Italian bourgeoisie.[41] But this is only the beginning of a more differentiated analysis, for the 'party of the Italian bourgeoisie' also represents
a wide range of social forces (middle strata, peasants and also a section
of the working class). Thus the situation was potentially extremely fluid
and represented a proper terrain for a Communist party ready to intervene

politically using every available space for manœuvre. The 1958 elections gave the DC 12 million votes which constituted, in Togliatti's view, 'the real electoral basis of the capitalist bourgeoisie in Italy . . .'.[42]

The DC had in fact emerged from the elections of 25 May 1958 as the real victor. It had increased its votes by 2.27 per cent reaching 42.35 per cent of the votes for the Chamber of Deputies.[43] This was considered to be a success for the 'integralist' platform of its general-secretary Amintore Fanfani whose long-term project was the organic unification of the Italian bourgeoisie.[44]

In an analysis of 'Fanfanismo' published towards the end of 1957, Reichlin, then one of the leading Communist commentators on Christian Democratic affairs, came to the conclusion that Fanfani was neither the expression of the most backward sectors of Italian society nor that of a new reformism of the DC.[45] The chief characteristic of 'Fanfanismo', continued Reichlin, was that it was the first attempt to achieve an organic relationship between the Catholic world and the most advanced sector of Italian capitalism. This political project involved the end of any attempt to counterpose the Catholic world to the State, an attempt which was often conducted in a demagogic manner and, at times, under the banner of *'laissez-faire'*.

With a good deal of political perception Reichlin characterized the new phase of development of the Catholic world as an attempt to penetrate the state machinery, particularly in its economic ramification such as ENI and IRI. Thus with Fanfani the DC became the instrument of 'neo-capitalist' reformism, that is, of an attempt to capture the economic instruments of the State and to use them for capitalist development.

However, an alliance with the DC was not ruled out. Pietro Ingrao, in an article written in 1958, wrote that the PCI had never denied the necessity of a policy of co-operation with the masses organized by the DC. This co-operation could be achieved even before these masses detached themselves from the 'organized Catholic movement'.[46] He then added:

> No one can believe in a sudden mirage whereby all of a sudden the DC votes in Parliament can be added on to those of the Communists and the Socialists to form a new majority. It is evident that this new political coalition can only be determined by an intense struggle of the masses which would win over and move a great part of the workers now under the influence of the Catholic movement and which would push them to overthrow the existing leadership group of the DC.

There is little doubt that around 1958 the PCI considered that the overthrow of the 'existing leadership group' of the DC depended in some measure on the existence of a left-wing faction which should be supported. Togliatti explicitly said so when he explained the conditions which would be required for any working class party to co-operate with at least some sections of the DC:

> Is there within the Christian Democratic Party a faction, a man . . . which understands the need to modify the present trends in foreign policy or in economic and internal policies? No working class party would not be prepared to be understanding and helpful.[47]

It is remarkable that these attempts to forge a dialogue occur in a period of bitter polemics with the DC. With the passing of time the bridge-building exercise could not but be intensified. The grounds for this policy was the recognition of the existence of popular forces within the DC and the possibility of utilizing the 'political awakening' of some Catholics in a progressive direction.

It could certainly be argued that modern Conservative parties because of their mass basis always have to rely on the support of popular strata and classes, but that this does not make them possible partners of parties committed to socialism. Yet reading the debates in DC circles on the issues of economic planning, reforms, rationalization, one cannot escape being struck by the similarity between this problematic and a social-democratic one, particularly on the question of state intervention. The rhetoric characteristic of Conservative parties such as the British one is non-existent. Moreover the commitment to capitalism does not rank very high in the language of Italian Christian Democracy. Nevertheless it was a party which had been second to none in its anti-Communism and whose commitment to democracy had not always gone very deep. Could the PCI actually propose an alliance with its main enemy?

In the period we are examining this proposal is not made but the ground is certainly being prepared. Reichlin, for instance, warns: 'The critique we must make is not, in our opinion, the critique of the principle of a compromise with the DC. . . .' The question which he thought should be asked was whether a compromise with the DC entailed the abandonment of a socialist perspective. Clearly here the door is left open: a compromise with the DC which would not be an abandonment of socialism but which would entail the construction of a united mass movement and a new bloc of forces is acceptable.[48]

What is actually being discussed here by Reichlin is the PSI, or rather the PSI 'compromise' with the DC, and what Reichlin wanted to make clear was that the PCI objected to the contents of the PSI–DC compromise (the centre-left government), not to the existence of the compromise.

It is a paradox of history that the PSI decision to break its ties with the PCI had positive effects for the PCI.[49] In a sense it allowed the PCI to re-examine its strategy of political alliances unemcumbered by a 'special relationship' with the Socialists. This, of course, does not imply at all that the Communists did not consider the actions of the PSI as a considerable threat to the long-term perspectives of socialism in Italy and did not remain convinced that the unity with the PSI was the political form the unity of the working class was to take.

Togliatti, at the Eighth Congress, had reaffirmed his conviction that both parties were working-class parties and shared similar ideological positions. The co-operation of the past twenty years was, in his opinion, a fundamental factor in the successes obtained by the labour movement; such co-operation, however, could assume different forms in different periods and could not be limited to the 'frontism' of the 1948 elections.[50]

It is thus clear that the continuation of the collaboration between the PCI and the PSI was seen as the basis for a strategy of alliances: the political unity of the working class was seen as 'the starting point . . . for the slogan of a democratic government of the working classes'.[51]

The belief in the overall importance of the PCI–PSI alliance for a transition to socialism did not last long. In 1961, when Nenni declared that it was no longer possible to have with the PCI a 'general political alliance', Togliatti answered that there should be a distinction between a 'general political alliance' and a 'political agreement'. The general alliance is something which will eventually be reached, but it is not on the agenda: 'We prefer today to speak, more modestly, of a reasonable political agreement because this is the perspective which corresponds to modern conditions and to the foreseeable future.'[52]

There is little doubt that the 'modest' proposal was forced on Togliatti by the rapid *rapprochement* between the PSI and the DC. None the less, it is more and more evident that the Communists, while not yet able to elaborate a comprehensive alliance strategy at the political level, would no longer place at the centre of their long-term aims an organic strategy with the PSI alone. But the door would be kept open for a continuation of a PCI–PSI dialogue. This was all the more important in the absence of formal links.

The particular caution exercised by the Communists is evident in that the attacks on the PSI would often be directed against the party's 'right wing'. Togliatti, in his report to the Central Committee of April 1964, criticized only the right wing of the PSI for not having been able to develop any strategy for socialism and for having simply offered 'an empirical and improvised' number of temporary slogans and proposals.[53]

The Communists' concept of alliances becomes clearer when we examine the criticisms levelled at the PSI. Thus Amendola, in 1963, wrote that the *rapprochement* of the PSI to the DC was conceived by the socialists as an operation 'at the top' without any mobilization of the masses.[54] He further added that the PSI, because it underestimated the strength of the masses and overestimated the strength of the bourgeoisie, negotiated with the DC from a position of weakness. Thus the PSI had been forced to accept compromises which did not correspond to the real relations of forces.[55] From this we can derive that:

1. Alliances between parties cannot be reduced to mere agreement at the top but must involve a mobilization of the masses, hence the alliance must involve different levels.

2. Negotiations and compromises must correspond to the relations of forces and must therefore be entered into only with a clear understanding of the real relations of forces.

This is the recurrent theme of the strategy of the Italian Communist Party. The 'real relations of forces' single out the anti-monopolistic alliance. This, in turn, defines a political programme of structural reforms specific to Italian society. The 'real relations' or, amounting to the same thing, the Leninist 'concrete situation', destroy the acceptability of imported models of revolution and of model states. We said how polycentrism — defined in terms of the autonomy of the PCI — was the necessary mechanism for the full acquisition of strategic freedom, a mechanism which permitted the development of a democratic road to socialism. There is one remaining element to analyse: the development of the Italian Communists' considerations of the chief instrument with which to achieve its tasks: the political party. It is to this development that we now turn.

Notes

1. A. Gramsci, 'Alcuni temi della quistione meridionale' in *La Quistione meridionale*, Rome, 1970, p. 135.
2. A. Gramsci, *Scritti giovanili 1914–18*, Turin, 1958, p. 349.
3. For an analysis of Gramsci's position on the religious question in Italy, see Hugues Portelli, *Gramsci et la question religieuse*, Paris, 1974.
4. P. Togliatti, 'Rapporto VIII' in *Nella pace e nelle democrazia verso il socialismo*, Rome, 1963, p. 45.
5. 'Intervento di Pietro Ingrao' in *VIII Congresso*, p. 180.
6. L. Barca, 'Per un programma di sviluppo economico', *Rinascita*, No. 6, June 1959.
7. P. Ingrao, 'Democrazia socialista e democrazia interna di partito', *Rinascita*, No. 17, 25 April 1964, now in *Masse e potere*, Rome, 1977, p. 183.
8. G. Amendola, 'Unità e autonomia della classe operaia' in *Critica Marxista*, No. 1, Jan.–Feb. 1963, p. 18.

9. P. Ingrao, op. cit., p. 182.
10. Ibid., p. 186; Ingrao added, significantly, 'In this sense we accept some elements of liberalism'.
11. This statement occurs in both the Theses and the Political Motion of the Eighth Congress, in *VIII Congresso*, pp. 969 and 889.
12. S. G. Tarrow, in his *Peasant Communism in Southern Italy* (New Haven, 1967), however, attempts to show that the Italian road to socialism is exclusively a 'Northern' strategy.
13. Speech to the Eighth Congress in *VIII Congresso*, p. 254.
14. Ibid., p. 255. Napolitano's point is that because the Southern question and monopolistic development are part of the same political problem it is not possible to consider the struggle for the renewal of the South as simply democratic: it also has a socialist content.
15. Theses, *VIII Congresso*, p. 960.
16. Political Motion, ibid., p. 895.
17. 'Elementi per una dichiarazione programmatica del PCI' in ibid., p. 915.
18. 'Intervento di Emilio Sereni', in ibid., p. 128.
19. 'Intervento di Di Vittorio', in ibid., p. 434.
20. E. Sereni, 'Gli obiettivi di lotta dei contadini italiani contro il "blocco rurale" conservatore', *Rinascita*, No. 3, March 1958.
21. Ibid.
22. In *La politica economica italiana 1945–1974*, Rome (n.d.), p. 143.
23. Ibid., p. 145.
24. A. Reichlin, 'Aspetti della politica unitaria col Psi', *Critica Marxista*, No. 4, July–Aug. 1963, p. 21.
25. In L. Barca, F. Botta, A. Zevi (eds.), *I comunisti e l'economia italiana 1944–1974*, Bari, 1975, p. 277.
26. M. Scoccimarro, 'Nazionalizzazione e controllo democratico', *Rinascita*, No. 3, March 1959.
27. 'Le conclusioni di Palmiro Togliatti' in *Documento per l'VIII Congresso del PCI. Un partito piu forte e rinnovato*. Supplement of *Voce Comunista*, No. 38, 4 October 1956, p. 20.
28. Ibid., p. 29.
29. P. Togliatti, 'Rapporto VIII' in op. cit., p. 59.
30. Quoted in L. Gruppi's introduction to Togliatti, *Comunisti socialisti cattolici*, Rome, 1974, pp. 21–2.
31. Theses of the Tenth Congress quoted in G. Chiarante, 'L'Enciclica, i comunisti e il laicato cattolico' in *Critica Marxista*, No. 3, May–June 1963, p. 52.
32. These remarks are based on G. Chiarante, op. cit., in particular pp. 40–1.
33. The *Pacem in terris* was published on 12 April 1963. This was preceded a month before by an important symbolic gesture: the Pope received Khruschev's son-in-law, a gesture which had upset the right-wing hierarchy of the Church particularly as the elections were approaching. The *Pacem in terris* was John XXIII's last major act; he died on 3 June 1963.
34. The text is in *Opere scelte*, pp. 1141–6. See in particular p. 1142.
35. See 'Il destino dell'uomo' in *OS*, pp. 1123–35.
36. Ibid., p. 1123. This is practically the same proposition contained in John's *Pacem in terris*. The coincidence in timing is remarkable. While a (divinely-inspired?) convergence is perfectly possible, the more sceptical will remain suspicious.
37. Ibid., p. 1132.
38. Ibid., p. 1134.

39. In *OS*, p. 1048.
40. In *OS*, p. 1145.
41. Theses in *VIII Congresso*, p. 942.
42. P. Togliatti, speech to the Chamber of Deputies of 18 July 1958.
43. See Celso Ghini *Il voto degli italiano*, Rome, 1975, p. 170. The PCI was practically stationary, increasing its strength by only 500,000 votes corresponding to an increment of 0.09 per cent. Considering that these were the first elections after the Hungarian events and after the defection of many leading Communists, this arrest in the general growth of the PCI's electoral strength was far from being negative.
44. A. Reichlin, 'Il "riformismo" integralista di Fanfani, prodotto di una crisi della politica di centro-sinistra e strumento di un regime clericale' in *Rinascita*, No. 8, August 1958.
45. A. Reichlin, 'Legame odierno tra l'integralismo clericale e l'odierno capitalismo italiano', *Rinascita* No. 10–11, Oct.–Nov. 1957.
46. Ingrao, 'Il problema dell'unità della classe operaia nell' attuale situazione politica', *Rinascita*, No. 5, May 1958.
47. P. Togliatti, 'Invito ai socialisti', *Rinascita*, No. 1, January 1959.
48. A. Reichlin, 'Aspetti della politica unitaria col PSI', *Critica Marxista*, No. 4, July–Aug. 1963, p. 28.
49. The steps of this rupture were the following: on 27 August 1956 Nenni met Saragat at Pralognan; the purpose of the meeting was to prepare the ground for a closer relation between the PSI and the PSDI. On 6 October 1956, Socialists and Communists cancelled their pact for 'unity of action' and signed a 'consultative pact' which was shortly afterwards repudiated by Nenni. The 32nd Congress of the PSI, held in Venice on 6–10 February 1957, upheld Nenni's decision. This position was further confirmed at the 34th Congress of the PSI (Milan, 14–20 March 1961). The short-lived unification between PSI and PSDI took place only in October 1966.
50. P. Togliatti, 'Rapporto VIII', pp. 67–8. An implicit rejection of 'frontism' had already been made by Togliatti at the Central Committee meeting of March 1956 where he explained that even though the alliance with the PSI '. . . is an important thing, it is not everything' and urged the development of policies directed towards the social-democratic *masses*, the middle strata and the Catholics. See Togliatti, 'Le diverse vie verso il socialismo' in AA.VV. *Il PCI e il movimento operaio internazionale*, Rome, 1968, pp. 19–20.
51. P. Togliatti, 'Rapporto VIII', p. 69.
52. Togliatti, 'Ancora su socialismo e democrazia', *Rinascita*, No. 5, May 1961, in *OS*, p. 1027.
53. P. Togliatti, 'Per l'unità del movimento operaio e comunista internazionale' (report to the Central Committee of 21–3 April 1964) in *Sul movimento operaio internazionale*, Rome, 1964, p. 346. There is probably a good dose of tactics in Togliatti's differentiation between a 'right' and a 'left' on this question. The left of the PSI had by then already split and formed the PSIUP (*Partito socialista italiano di unità proletaria*).
54. G. Amendola, op. cit., *Critica Marxista*, No. 1, Jan.–Feb. 1963, p. 34.
55. Ibid., p. 35.

10.   The Political Party

> The question of internal party democracy and, more generally, the question of the internal dialectics of the communist movement came to the fore in full strength, 'erupted', when the Twentieth Congress operated a drastic critical revision of Stalinism.

So wrote Pietro Ingrao in 1964.[1] It was inevitable that the crisis of Stalinism which, at the time, engendered a crisis in the Communist movement, generated deep fractures and divisions. To quote Ingrao again, it seems to be true that, whereas on the whole the working class components of the party accepted loyally the changes, then occurred

> . . . a crisis in the relationship between the party and some of the middle strata components (particularly in the towns; things went differently in the countryside) which were hit at the same time (this should not seem to be contradictory) by Khruschev's violent criticism of Stalin and by the events in Hungary and Poland.[2]

There also occurred a crisis in the relationship between the party and some of its intellectuals who moved towards a 'reformist' position. The difficulties of the party were compounded by the fact that some groups within it remained solidly 'Stalinist' and refused to acknowledge the realities of the new situation.[3] But the emergence of these trends into the open was in turn due to more fundamental causes, as Aldo Natoli, the secretary of the Roman federation of the PCI, wrote:

> Here we have seen coming to the surface perplexities, doubts and even mistrust. These do not depend only on the novelty of these formula- tions, but reflect the ways in which these, in the last years, have come to the attention of comrades (that is from the outside and from above) and reflect . . . a deep incomprehension of the political line of the party since the 'Salerno turning-point' . . .[4]

This exemplifies the fundamental problem which was to persist for a long period of time: the dichotomy between a political strategy elaborated at the top and its distorted reception at the base. This problem required for its solution a fundamental rethinking of the application of the principles of democratic centralism within the PCI and a theoretical analysis and an elaboration of the political strategy itself.

By the time the 'secret speech' (see Chapter 6) was made known to all, demands came to be expressed by more and more Italian Communists and this was reflected in an article written by Pietro Ingrao which was published before the beginning of the Polish crisis.[5]

Ingrao located in what he called *praticismo* one of the fundamental erroneous tendencies of the PCI. *Praticismo* takes for granted once and for all the general political line of the party and limits research to its modes of operation in its practical adaptation to local conditions:

> Instead of political discussion . . . there is local analysis, organization, propaganda with the result that the relation to the political level remains detached from the debates.

This causes the development of two levels, one where the political line of the party rests 'in a state of sleep and undiscussed' and the other level where the day-to-day struggles are examined. These two levels of operation reproduce themselves throughout the party including the highest echelons up to the Central Committee. This split between the elaboration of a political strategy and the day-to-day activities of the party had had a dual effect:

1. 'A weakening of our political research and our criticism of essential aspects, precisely when important changes were taking place in the internal and international situation.'

2. '. . . the denial of the contribution that the base of the party is asked to give to the debate and to the elaboration of the political line, and hence a limitation of the development of democracy within the party.'

These errors of *praticismo* and their consequences resulted in, among the rank and file, either insufficient understanding of the political line or a hidden disagreement towards it. This meant that while the line was propounded, its actual application, far from flowing from the line itself corresponded to a different strategy and a different experience:

> . . . the slogan of a new party remained, for a part of our leading cadres, only a mythological perspective, an exhortation, behind which the schemes and modes of a restricted organization divided in a heterogeneous manner between a daily reformist struggle, propaganda and the expectation of a miraculous occasion which would solve the problem of socialism in Italy.

There is also, continued Ingrao, a practical problem: the new generations of militants who are in need of developing their ideological formation are drained of all their energies in continuous activism and have little time for ample debates and studies: 'How much time is left for our militants to think about and discuss things other than immediate practical needs? How many books are they able to read?' Ingrao reaffirmed the need for the unity of the party according to the principles of democratic centralism. However, he maintained that this unity was not a once and for all conquest, but it was an aim for which one must constantly strive and it was the conclusion of debates and struggle of ideas, 'otherwise unity would be reduced to a formal, militaristic discipline' which is what had happened within the party. This, according to Ingrao, was one of the causes of the 'personality cult'. As long as there was a separation between the formulation of a political line and its implementation there would be a tendency to expect from the leadership a solution to all problems. This problem was not just internal to the party, continued Ingrao, and he asked:

> The unity of the party is an essential component of its strength, its influence and its capacity to attract among the masses. But how does a large section of public opinion perceive our internal debates resolving themselves in the unity and cohesion of all members of the party? Let us be frank: they perceive them in an unreal and false manner (and this is a fundamental self-criticism of our press); the party appears to many Italians as a great force, serious, severe and monolithic, whose internal laws, however, they do not understand.[6]

These statements are remarkable for their frankness and for their ability in examining in some depth the fundamental problems which are exemplified by the Italian expression *doppiezza*. *Doppiezza* here does not mean 'duplicity' in the sense of a deception, but in the sense of a dichotomy between the party's political line and the way in which this political line is understood by the base. The result is that the party's official line may be at odds with the thinking of its militants who, however, follow it out of a sense of duty and party unity. Although this may function in the case of small organizations engaged in a limited range of activities, for instance terroristic squads, in the case of a mass party seeking to intervene at all levels of society *doppiezza* is a major liability.

There is, however, a further element in Ingrao's thought. There is the idea that a unity which is formalistic is not a true unity. A party whose political line is dogmatically accepted by the membership is not a united party however much it may appear to be so. Here too we have the problem of bringing into correspondence the form of the party unity with its content. This correspondence, far from weakening the party's structure, strengthens it and the party becomes a more formidable weapon in the class struggle. Thus the argument for democracy, as put forward by Ingrao, is not in contradiction with unity but on the contrary is a condition of political unity.

Discussion on democratic centralism was to continue throughout 1956 and we shall examine this in the context of the debates immediately preceding the Eighth Congress, the so-called pre-congressional debates. However, we shall first discuss an example of the 'revisionist' tendencies which erupted throughout the summer of 1956: the so-called 'Onofri case'.

Onofri was a member of the Central Committee and was in charge of the party school in Bologna. He had been at odds for some time with the Executive Committee of the PCI which he accused of excessive bureaucracy and of failing to follow the strategy of the Italian road to socialism to its logical conclusions.[7] At the June meeting of the Central Committee he tried to bring up the question of Cominform interference in the affairs of the Italian Communist Party, but the time allotted to him was too short. He therefore prepared an article for *Rinascita* which was published shortly afterwards.[8]

The article, highly critical of the political strategy of the post-war years, appeared with a title imposed by Togliatti: 'An Unacceptable Attack on the Policy of the Italian Communist Party'.[9]

Onofri, in the first few paragraphs of the article, took up Ingrao's point (but does not mention Ingrao by name) about the error of *praticismo* which is alleged to have pervaded the party. The root of the problem, affirmed Onofri, was not in *praticismo*.

The root of all our defects and of all our weaknesses . . . is in my opinion this: at a certain point, and precisely towards the end of 1947, our fundamental slogan — the struggle for the opening of an Italian (democratic) road to socialism — was abandoned.[10]

Togliatti replied in the same issue refuting Onofri point by point.[11] The exchange had a significance far greater than its contents. Togliatti's answer was a way of signalling the limits of permissible dissent, dissent that should be expressed in a 'constructive manner' without the harsh polemical tones Onofri had used. He had also intended to establish firmly that the Italian road to socialism was not a new invention which was sparked off by the Twentieth Congress, but that it had been in operation for a long period of time.

This point was all the more important as the pre-congressional debates leading to the Eighth Congress were being prepared. The participants had to take stock not only of the Twentieth Congress and of the polemics which ensued, but also of the momentous international events which had taken place. The starting-point was the Central Committee meeting of September 1956.

In his introductory speech Longo pointed out the twin deviations to eliminate: the 'generic revisionism' which, in its desperate search for the new, challenges everything which is 'old' and its mirror image: dogmatism.[12] The stress, however, is on the need to combat revisionism which seems, at this stage, to be considered the major danger probably because the real need for renewal is seen as containing the seeds of possible revisionist attitudes.

The differentiation between the two forms of deviation did not preclude self-criticism and the definition of what Longo called 'the biggest defect of the party':

> Our party still finds difficulty in going from the position of resistance and affirmation of itself . . . to a constructive activity, to proposals with a new and wide content, to the organization of a permanent pressure which would succeed in making the entire movement progress by obtaining one conquest after another.[13]

This criticism had already been made by Togliatti in the previous session of the Central Committee and by other leading figures. It indicated the partial lack of success of Togliatti's directives of 1944–5 which stated that the party should abandon a position of pure propaganda and pure opposition and become a 'party of government'. Longo's declaration was an admission that this task had not been completely achieved. This failure was particularly evident, added Longo, on the question of feminine emancipation:

> The struggle for the emancipation of women − for the abolition of the juridical, economic and moral conditions of inferiority which Italian society has inflicted on women − is an integral part of the struggle for democracy and socialism, and cannot be conceived as a simple ensemble of propagandist themes. It must be put on the same level with all the structural transformations which are connected to constitutional principles. It must therefore be put in terms of struggle. We must recognize that the policy of feminine emancipation has not been completely understood by the party. There is a political and ideological resistance which has the same root as the other obstacles to

the proper understanding and implementation of the political line of the party.[14]

This point was taken up, for instance, by the Executive Committee of the Milan federation of the PCI which stated that the conditions of inferiority of the feminine masses was one of the essential instruments used by the monopolies to maintain their privileges.[15] The Milan Communists specified in the same resolution that on this point in particular there existed within the party elements which had not understood the political line or which paid only lip service to it:

> The problem of feminine emancipation is a typical example of a problem on which there has not been a political unity within the party. In fact on this problem in particular there has been an attitude of formal approval of the party line without a real adhesion to it in practice.

This was a frank admission of *doppiezza*, a symptom which, in any case, was increasingly recognized within the party.

For Aldo Natoli, for instance, writing in *Rinascita*, *doppiezza* consisted in not having explained with clarity that the Salerno policies of 1944 were perfectly in accordance with communist principles.[16] Here *doppiezza* ceases to be simply a 'sickness' of the rank and file: the responsibility for it is placed squarely on the shoulders of the leadership. Thus Togliatti's ideas and policies were not clear at all to 'a great part of the directing cadres of the party'. To this criticism Natoli added another one: it is perfectly true, he continued, that the Salerno policy of democratic unity against fascism was successful, but the party should recognize that, though this policy had been valid for the defence of conquered positions, it had not been successful for progress involving the destruction of the roots of fascism. It was true that this was due to the opponents of the PCI breaking the unity of the anti-fascist forces, but, Natoli added, the party should not simply reiterate this. He thus implied that the actions of the years 1945–7 were far from being successful and that the PCI could have improved its position in those years.[17]

It is clear that the question of deviations, *doppiezza*, and the ability to carry out the party line and to understand it turned round the fundamental problem of internal organization to that of the concept of democratic centralism.

It is no surprise that in the course of the 'unforgettable 1956' period even this concept would come to be questioned. As far as the leadership was concerned, though, democratic centralism was to remain the principal organizing concept of the Communist Party. Nevertheless there would be important attempts to revise this aspect of the Leninist doctrine, in particular by Alberto Caracciolo, who would eventually find himself compelled to leave the party.[18]

Caracciolo began his contribution with two observations: first, that the principle of democratic centralism had not been developed since Lenin; second, that it had become a rigid formula which had been institutionalized in the catechetic formulations of Stalin's *Short Course*.[19] Caracciolo proceeded to discuss those points which, he claimed, had been left unanswered so far in all debates on democratic centralism. These questions were:[20]

1. On which questions can there be an interplay between majority and minority within the party?
2. To what rights and guarantees are the minorities entitled, whenever these minorities emerge?
3. When can discussion take place without damaging the need to apply the directives of the majority?
4. How can the minority become a majority?

Caracciolo did not provide clear answers to these questions (he offered them for discussion), but stressed that the bureaucratic infirmities with which the Communist Parties were plagued could be removed, at least in part, if it were openly recognized that there was a need for an open and permanent political struggle at all levels of the party structure and if this declaration were followed by the removal of all obstacles that prevented the possibility of new tendencies throughout the party.[21] Thus the fetishism of unity had to be broken, and more publicity had to be given to debates for this would allow the minority to become a majority.

Caracciolo's contribution to the pre-congressional debates, together with other interventions, only highlights the extent of the discussions which had occurred in 1956. A deeper analysis of these debates would only confirm the fact that very few of what were the accepted principles of Marxism–Leninism had been left completely unchallenged. These debates were but symptoms of a general malaise which existed not only in the PCI but thoughout the international communist movement. In Italy it was the task of the Eighth Congress to resolve some of the questions which had been raised. The Congress, however, acted as a general systematizer of a diffuse desire for change and re-examination and attempted to offer a clear political line which was consistent with the ideological reactions to the principal events of 1956.

The Congress debates were characterized by a refreshing frankness, particularly in those contributions which referred directly to the internal organization of the party.

The significance of the debate was that it drew lines of demarcation between those who wanted a radical change of the party's line, a change which entailed the termination of the special relationship with the CPSU, and those around Togliatti who advocated a development of the Italian road to socialism which did not put the PCI in open conflict with the CPSU. For the advocates of the second position it was necessary to maintain the view that the development of the Italian road had continued more or less harmoniously for more than ten years and that there was no need for major ruptures. Thus Di Vittorio maintained that:

The Italian road to socialism is not for us an absolutely new direction. It is the development — made possible by the changes occurring in the general situation — of the fundamentally correct policy followed by our party ever since the famous speech in Naples in 1944 by Comrade Togliatti (but we could go even further back).[22]

Even the changes in the party's constitution were presented by Longo as being in the spirit of developing the features of the 'new party' along the lines originally expressed by Togliatti in Salerno in 1944.[23]

The affirmation of the basic continuity in party policy implied that what was happening was not due to a real change in policy, but rather to the realization that many cadres had not understood the party line until the events of 1956 had forced it out into the open. The problem was to link this phenomenon of *doppiezza* to the two deviations which were said to characterize the PCI: 'sectarianism' and 'reformism'. According to the Theses of the Congress, 'sectarianism' was the political deviation which was the most rooted within the ranks because of the 'old traditions of our movement'.[24] Nevertheless, 'reformism' was considered a more dangerous deviation because it led to passivity and 'extinguishes revolutionary ardour'. The link between the two was a result of the assumption that a party which is closed and sectarian cannot fight properly against reformism, in other words, sectarianism helps reformism. Sectarianism is considered inevitable in a party which is not convinced of the validity of its own political line (but this point was not elaborated further and thus remained vague); thus *doppiezza* (in the Italian case) is closely linked to sectarianism. Furthermore, another correspondence was made between reformism and sectarianism by Togliatti himself:

> At the centre of the work of renewal of the party is the struggle for
> the party line and for an Italian road to socialism. What can prevent us
> from proceeding along this path? There are two principal obstacles:
> maximalist sectarianism and reformist revisionism. The former is with-
> drawn within itself waiting for the 'great day'. The latter kneels before
> capitalism in the expectation that it will turn into socialism. Both
> renounce revolutionary action for the conquest of socialism.[25]

Thus the political consequences of both deviations, according to Togliatti,
are identical. It is now possible to state that, in the analysis of the Italian
Communists, *doppiezza* provides a terrain for the development of the
sectarian deviation, and through that it is linked to the reformist deviation.

Togliatti, as Longo before him, offered, as a significant example of
doppiezza, the question of the emancipation of women ('one of the
central questions of democracy and the advance towards socialism'),[26]
a question which had met enormous resistance and to which many Communists had paid only lip service. This revealed, declared Togliatti, 'a
party which approves correct policies, but part of which does not implement them or, worse, does the wrong things. Is it only disregard or in-
capacity, or is it the absence, even if not obvious, of adhesion to the
political line?'.

The chief cause of *doppiezza* was seen to be the excessive centralization of the party bureaucracy. This was clearly stated by Giacomo Ferrari
in his official report on the activities of the Central Control Commission.
In an eight-point statement he summarized the principal defects of the
organization of the party, all centred on the question of excessive centralism.[27]

The persistence of *doppiezza* was not denied. Yet there was no doubt
that for Togliatti *doppiezza* was a disease of the rank and file.

But, while insisting on the continuing validity of its strategy, the
party recognized that there were serious faults in its internal life. It attributed this in great part to the fact that in the immediate post-war period
the construction of the party took place 'from above'. This favoured
'old methods of personal direction' or, at least, insufficient collective
direction. These methods (and the criticism here is more likely to have
been directed against Secchia and Longo rather than against Togliatti)
were an offshoot of the partisan war. Thus the methods used in the period
of illegality survived in the period of legality. This is not a new theme.
It had emerged after the cadres-orientated direction of Pietro Secchia,
but obviously could have come to the fore only after the 1956 crises. In

fact, in that year, a great number of leading local cadres (secretaries of federations and other local officials) were removed from office. It was the formation of this entrenched middle level which had resulted, as the Theses admit, in 'organizational blocs' which had become an 'obstacle to a more rapid circulation of ideas and energies'.[28]

While there was a tendency both within the party and from without to attribute this bureaucratization to democratic centralism as a form of organization, the leadership group, in the person of Luigi Longo, suggested, in the report on the new statute, that it was because the principles of democratic centralism had not been fully respected that there had been a tendency to transform it into bureaucratic centralism:[29]

> The lack of an intense democratic life within the party, and the prevalence of 'bureaucratism' leads to the separation between the directing organs and the masses of the party and between the party and the masses it should guide in action and struggle.[30]

This feature, which, as we can easily see, is connected to the entire question of *doppiezza*, is hence acknowledged without reticence. Thus, although democratic centralism 'remains the fundamental principle which regulates the internal life of the party',[31] some important modifications are introduced in the statute. These aim at a decentralization of the party and are an attempt to involve more and more members in its organizational life. Other reforms were adopted, but Longo made it clear that the fundamental principles of organization of the Leninist party were not going to be modified. On the contrary, as Giuliano Procacci has shown, the Eighth Congress statute is a backward step when compared with the preceding statutes and has a narrower, stricter conception of the internal life of the party.[32] On the controversial issue of the right of factions Longo, in dispute with Giolitti, said:

> . . . Comrade Giolitti has recognized that a decision taken regularly by the leading organs must be accepted in practice by all comrades. However, he adopts the pretension of safeguarding, even after the decision has been taken and has become mandatory, the right for those not in agreement to continue to debate in public against the decision taken. This is unacceptable . . . There is little sense, then, in a Communist party talking about the right of the minority to become majority, as somebody has already said. The dialectic which is proper to bourgeois parties, within which there are diverse social groupings struggling against each other with diverse immediate objectives and different possibilities for action, cannot exist within a homogeneous and united

party which fights for well-determined objectives, as the PCI is and wants to be.[33]

Lacking, however, an internal opposition which might have the positive function of signalling possible errors in the party's political line and political practice, the PCI had to have a mechanism which would partially check the proper functioning of democratic life within the party ('partially' because it is quite obvious that the real effective checks can only be political). Longo indicated that this mechanism must lie in a reconstructed and hence 'new' Central Control Commission:

> The new Central Control Commission must, like the one which has existed so far, control the application of the statute, the respect of democracy in the internal life of the party, and discipline at all levels and of all members, and solve the various instances of irregularities. But the new Control Commission must also take the initiative in these various fields, must try to prevent ruptures and wrong turnings by indicating them in time to the directing organs so that they may try to prevent them.[34]

These are the most important institutional changes which took place at the Eighth Congress on the question of internal democracy. It may be observed that these do not amount to much and certainly one cannot say that there had been a major institutional upheaval.

The reforms which were promulgated were thus purely functional in the sense of helping the transition from the existing trend towards bureaucracy to real democratic centralism. But the fundamental factor in this transition could only be political, that is, the adoption of the correct political line by the *whole* party. It is in this sense that we can talk of the primacy of the political as the organizing force of all the aspects of Italian Communism. Thus studies of the organizational or 'structural' aspects of Italian Communism that fail to understand the strategy of the party in its complexity cannot but give us partial and distorted images.

The problems of bureaucracy existent in all organizations, political or otherwise, increase tenfold in the case of mass parties and one does not need to adopt Michels' determinism to accept this. Thus it was the mass nature of the PCI which posed these problems and yet the tasks it had set itself to accomplish necessitated a mass party, a 'new' party.

Then arose the problem of how to organize the relations between the national and the local leadership groups, between these and the active members or cadres and the mass of relatively non-active members. In the period we are describing the problem was not solved in a more simple, provisional manner but, and this was the innovation, it was tackled more decisively than in the past. In previous years the question of internal organization was seen mainly as a question of efficiency. Now there was a realization that internal democracy was one of the chief determinants of efficiency.[35] There was no doubt that the prevalent relation within the party was one of faith on the part of the rank and file. In this sense Giolitti was right to attack the fetishistic relation between the militant and the party and the conception of the party as a Church, 'sole depository of an absolute and all-knowing truth'.[36] However, these debates were too late to repair the damage done by the events of 1956. The reaffirmation of the prevalence of the democratic moment did not and could not stop the exodus of members from the party. This exodus, however, was in general confined to intellectuals, involving all the generational 'strata' of the party: from those who were leading members since the foundation of the PCI to those of the clandestine period, of the beginning of the war and of the Resistance. It is estimated that the net loss of membership due to the 1956 events was in the region of 200,000 members. In the period 1954–61 party membership dwindled from 2.1 million to 1.7 million.

The exit of intellectuals was primarily attributed to sectarian tendencies which still pervaded the party (although the intellectuals too were far from being immune from such tendencies).

Pietro Secchia, in his speech at the Eighth Congress, went as far as saying that intellectuals did not feel at ease in the party.[37] There were thus attempts to break the barriers which existed between intellectuals and workers. As Longo explained there existed a certain separation

> . . . not only organizational but also political between the various strata in the party: the workers are organized in factory branches . . .; the intellectuals can usually be found in branches of particular areas.[38]

It is quite possible that it was this separation which had led, in many instances, to the formation of sectarian attitudes particularly with regard to the questions of Hungary and Poland over which in general the proletarian basis of the party had remained firm in its loyalty. It was Secchia, the man who was considered to have been the leader of a 'workerist' tendency, who attacked this deviation:

> We need serious and able intellectuals because they are able to contribute to the progress and the enrichment of Marxist culture, and because they can link us directly and indirectly with a large section of the people. This is why we must have a great understanding of

the needs and the specific interests of intellectual comrades; because of this we must reject any remnants of workerism.[39]

This somewhat paternalistic and instrumental note reveals the reaffirmation of the need for 'organic' intellectuals of the working class who on the one hand would develop Marxist theory and on the other would operate on the front of culture in order to weave an ideological pattern which would allow the Italian working class to affirm its cultural hegemony in Italian life. This was the reason, in Secchia's words, why all 'workerist' conception had to be abandoned: they were an obstacle to any possibility of alliance with the middle strata.

The party's relations with the intellectuals remained for a long time a major problem. Eight years later, in 1964, Rossana Rossanda, then in charge of cultural affairs, noted the ever growing gap between the rise of the PCI influence in Italian culture and its failure to improve its capacity to win over intellectuals:

. . . our criticisms influence and condition them, they are willing to co-operate, sometimes very easily: we are a determinant force and they recognize us as such. However, seldom are we able to win them over politically.[40]

But the question of the internal life of the party could not be reduced to modifications intended to retain the consensus of specific groups whether formally inside or outside the party, or to deal with the twin 'deviations' (left and right) which characterize the history of the Communist movement. The problem was to discover which form of internal organization suited a mass party engaged in the struggle for socialism in an advanced capitalist country. This entailed a functional view of the party, a view of the party as a means, as an instrument, put succinctly by Gerratana:

. . . it is not possible for a democratic mass party to separate the problems of internal life from the elaboration of its political line. The construction of a mass democratic party cannot precede nor follow the elaboration of the political line because the organization of the party is never (unless it is transformed into a pure power apparatus) an *instrument* indifferent to the sort of politics it is called upon to follow, but it can only be the expression and the functional *organ* of a determinate political strategy for which it inevitably bears the consequences, negative or positive.[41]

Thus, the question of internal organization had to be recast in terms of the concrete situation which faced the Italian Communists and the strategy which flowed from the situation. It had hence to involve the relation between the party and mass organizations such as the trade union movement.

The relation between party and trade unions (or any other mass organization) posed the question of the character of the discipline which should bind the Communist trade unionist. The old question of whether the Communist trade unionist owed his first allegiance to his trade union or to the party could only be solved by recasting the relation between the party and the trade union as a whole. In Italy this particular question was connected to the division of the labour movement into three trade union federations and to the alliance strategy of the Communist Party which sought to unite Catholics, Socialists and Communists. It was quite obvious that this alliance strategy entailed the reunification of the trade union movement. Accordingly the Theses of the Eighth Congress proclaimed that it was the duty of Communist militants to work for the creation in Italy of a new united trade union organization with the Republican Constitution as its programmatic basis.[42] It followed that the Communists could not assert any special or privileged links between their own party and the trade union movement, be it a future united movement or the existing CGIL.

This new political line gave rise to the definitive and official abandonment of the so-called 'transmission belt' principle which had hitherto determined the relation between the party and the trade union movement. This principle, which had its origin at the Stuttgart Congress of the Second International (1907), had established that the trade union movement should function as a 'transmission belt' for the decisions of the political party. Thus the trade unions were seen in an essentially instrumental role as a force bringing the political line of the 'vanguard party' to the masses at the 'base'. It was this principle which, according to Di Vittorio, could no longer be adhered to and, therefore, any attempt at political interference with the trade union movement constituted an attack against its unity.[43]

The practical indications of the new policy for Communist trade unionists relied more on their political flair than on the establishment of specific rules. The Communist trade union militants had to consider, in taking a particular decision, that the general requirements of a united trade union movement would, in general, take priority over a rigorous implementation of every detail of the party line.[44]

This indication of priorities could and did cause at different times a discrepancy between the decisions of the party and those of Communist elements in the trade union movement. The solution of these problems was not facilitated by the fact that for the entire period under examination it was considered compatible to hold positions of leadership in both the CGIL and in the PCI and even to be a Communist deputy in Parliament as well.

The new official line embodied in the decision to abolish the conception of 'transmission belts' also signalled the attempt to terminate the Church-like devotion of the militant to his party, a devotion which was a heritage from the days of Stalinism. It signalled the fact that in the complexities of Italian society, characterized by a rich articulation of different levels and fields of battle (e.g. the political party, the mass organizations, the trade union movement), it was not sufficient for the militant to follow blindly a political line which arrived from above. The new situation required a new type of militant, disciplined and loyal, yes, but also aware that the party could only indicate the general policies and not the steps to be taken in everyday struggles.

The general re-examination of the entire question of the strength of the party and its internal organization reached a new height in 1963–4. The general trend was to contain the debate within the parameters of democratic centralism understood in terms of an organic relation between the principles of democracy and centralism. These general principles are usually firmly historicized by making the actual form of organization dependent on a determinate historical situation and even on a particular conjuncture.

As we have found so often, the process of adaptation which the Italian Communists chose for the general principles that guide their activities was deeply entrenched in tradition. In this case too the Togliattian principle of change in continuity was followed to the letter. Thus Natta and Pajetta defended democratic centralism from the accusation that it was the principal cause of the deterioration of democracy in the Soviet Union. Democracy, they claimed, cannot be reduced to a technical matter of formal guarantees: 'Democracy even in the Party, is always first of all a political fact before it can also be the codification of statutory norms.'[45]

The balance between the democratic moment and the centralist one is determined by 'tactical necessities' and 'strategic ends'.[46] What cannot be altered is the necessity of democratic centralism itself. The suggestion that the PCI, like the other Italian parties, should accept the formation of internally-organized factions was rejected firmly on the ground that they would be an obstacle to the unity and to the democracy of the party.[47]

The demands for a return to factionalism, which came particularly from the Socialist Party and the Social Democratic Party, had certainly a rather hypocritical ring about them. Those very parties were at the same time trying to get rid of their own internal factions.[48] In the history of the Italian Socialist Party there is, for instance, a continuous recurrence of the demand to do away with factions. It should also be added that the formation of organized factions within the major Italian parties did not contribute in the least to their democratization. Within the PCI the demand for an acceptance of factions was minimal. The question was, rather, as Ingrao put it, to render more apparent and more visible the processes whereby a particular decision was arrived at, 'so that the political organism and the individual member called upon to decide can really participate in the decision, be aware of the consequences and of the problems that such a decision implies . . . The opposite, therefore, of a formal participation, this is a road which attempts to arrive as much as possible at a common endeavour, that is, exactly in the opposite direction of factionalism . . .'.[49]

In fact, neither the Eighth Congress nor the new policies on socialism and democracy had cancelled the traditional Communist resistance to reveal internal differences. In a situation of legality, internal democracy certainly required the maximum possible information. The Central Committee, for instance, invariably approved resolutions put in front of it with a unanimous vote. Ingrao pointed out that the PCI attempted to solve the internal differences which arose in its leadership group not through counting votes but mainly through a thorough debate on controversial points until an agreement was reached, but he added: '. . . we should, however, ask ourselves: why are we so reluctant to make public some dissenting opinions?'[50] The answer Ingrao gave is twofold: the reluctance is partly due to the weight of history and tradition which even (or, we would suggest, especially) a Communist party finds difficult to get rid of and, secondly, to the fact that the opponents of the PCI have always been ready to exploit any internal party difference (but, one could reply, this is an inevitable part of political struggles). The recognition of the causes of a certain secrecy is not used in order to justify it. Ingrao pointed out the risks implicit in continuous unanimity and in the fact that the party theses are not sufficiently discussed in pre-congress periods and, consequently, that the base does not contribute sufficiently to the elaboration of the party line.[51]

This 'fictitious unanimity', as Amendola called it, contributed to a tendency on the part of the Italian Communists to present their debates as smooth events which inevitably terminated in complete unanimity,

their political line as developing without ruptures or difficult moments
and their political activities as triumphantly hitting the right target at
the right moment. It was this situation which caused Amendola to
write:

> The moment has come to get rid of, once and for all, an optimistic
> and superficial vision which we adopted for propagandist and electoral
> reasons according to which social development always follows a uni-
> linear path . . . in which defeats, errors, crises, retreats and moments
> of stagnation disappear. If that were true, the parties of the working
> class could do without the pains and suffering of criticism and self-
> criticism. But when these disappear a Communist party loses its
> essential Leninist character, becomes bureaucratic and fossilized and
> ceases to be a revolutionary party.[52]

In addition to these apparently purely 'internal' problems there was
the realization that the presence in Italy of a mass progressive movement
(as evidenced by the decisive popular reaction to the formation of the
Tambroni government in 1960) had not generated a corresponding increase in the membership of the PCI.[53] What had occurred over the years
was that the electoral strength of the PCI had increased more or less
continuously but its membership had decreased both in absolute terms and
in relation to its vote, as can be seen in the table following.

Election year	Membership	Votes	% of members to voters	Ratio of voters to members
1946	1,676,013	4,358,243	38.5	2.6
1948	1,798,722	(5,077,517)*	35.4	2.8
1953	2,134,285	6,121,922	34.8	2.8
1958	1,826,098	6,704,706	27.2	3.6
1963	1,615,112	7,768,288	20.8	4.8

* This is a very rough estimate derived from the number of Communist deputies
elected in 1948. In 1948 the Communists and the Socialists joined in an electoral
front which obtained 8,137,047 votes.

Thus, while in 1953 every party member could 'capture' an extra 1.8
votes, by 1963 a member had to 'capture' 3.8 votes. In other words,
only one in five PCI voters was sufficiently committed to the ideas of the
PCI to wish to be in its ranks.

Even though the number of members increased until 1953–4, this aggregate number hides the fact that the serious membership losses which had occurred in the North in the period 1950–1 had been compensated by a remarkable increase in membership in the South. Towards the end of the fifties losses began to occur in the South, too, without the balance being redressed by a corresponding increase in the North.[54]

A particularly negative aspect of the decrease in membership was constituted by the decrease in the number of Communist factory workers which fell from 856,000 in 1954 to 543,000 in 1962. This was all the more worrying when one considers that the total number of factory workers in Italy increased remarkably in these years. In percentage terms this meant that while in 1954 23.5 per cent of factory workers were members of the PCI, in 1962 this figure was reduced to only 12.3 per cent.[55]

Macaluso, in his report to the Naples organization conference of 1964, noted not only the gap between membership and votes and the manifest wearing down of the party organizations in the factories, but also the more than proportionate decrease in the numbers of women and young people and the continuing weakness of the party in the Christian Democratic strongholds of north-eastern Italy.[56]

But there were more problems. E. Berlinguer, then in charge of party organization, estimated that, while the actual number of active Communists increased, daily political activities in the organizations at the base (branches, cells, etc.) had decreased. This meant that an increasing number of Communists were active in the trade unions, in local government, in cultural and recreational organizations, in the schools, etc., while the party branches were increasingly deserted.[57] Berlinguer also noted the slow growth of new cadres which was part of the reason for the trend towards an increase in the average age of the party.

The decline in recruitment in the new generation is not specifically explained. One reason, however, can be derived from the analyses we have presented in the previous sections which showed that, even though the post-1956 years was a period of great elaboration and development in the party strategy, the PCI had not been able to dominate politically the new reality which was emerging in Italy. The party succeeded in understanding it but with difficulty and it proposed a set of policies which it had to elaborate rapidly against a difficult background but often reacting to developments outside its control. The presence of ambiguities in its political line extracted a price: the loss of its monopoly on left-wing culture, a loss which would become manifest in the years 1968–9 when an entire new generation would embrace Marxism without entering the

Italian Communist Party and often in bitter polemics with it. The new cadres which were to emerge in the early 1970s, particularly those who belonged to the middle strata, were often not 'born' into the party, but had joined it after a painful and tortuous process of intellectual development. This can, of course, only partially account for the problem raised by the 'ageing' of the party.

There were, of course, also 'technical factors' accounting for a decrease in the South that was undoubtedly due, at least in part, to internal and external emigration. Between 1951 and 1960 2.8 million workers (including presumably many Communists) went abroad.[58] Furthermore, in the same period more than 13 million people changed their residence in Italy, the bulk of them moving from the South to the North. However, it was clear that the PCI had not been able to grasp satisfactorily that the process of formation of a political conscience among the new proletarians could not take place in the relatively unproblematic manner of the previous years.[59] The new conditions of work, the assembly line, overtime, the greater distance between the home and the place of work and the new forms of cultural domination were many obstacles to a willingness to devote one's time to political work. The PCI had also failed to understand the new forms of working class organizations within the factories, the modifications which had taken place in the agrarian sector and the new aspects of the social stratification of the middle strata.

It is clear that many of the defects listed were not only dependent on party organization but on the ambiguity of the PCI political elaboration as well as on the changing structure of Italian society. However, in so far as internal organization was defective and the existing structures impeded the participation of the rank and file in the elaboration and implementation of the party strategy, a general reorganization of its internal life was required.

The recognition of the need to adapt the organizational forms to the new situation had to be the starting-point for a set of specific proposals.[60] Most of these can be reduced to the decision to 'decentralize' the party. This decentralization was to take the form of the development of new organizational levels which would have the task of co-ordinating the party work in socially identifiable geographical areas.[61] These new structures called, according to the area, Municipal Committees (*Comitati comunali*), City Committees (*Comitati cittadini*) and Area Committees (*Comitati di Zona*), would have the task of elaborating policies and applying them to sectors of Italian life to which the traditional organs (federations, branches and cells) could no longer be suited. The constitutions of these committees would take into account the social and structural composition of the area in question and would also attempt to co-ordinate more effectively the work of the traditional organizations. In this way it was thought that the classical vertical organization could be integrated by horizontal co-ordination.[62]

The new proposals were not meant to create a federated structure or to weaken the existing traditional organs. It was a practical attempt to resolve some of the problems and weaknesses which had been acknowledged so openly. It certainly did not go to the roots of the problem and, anyway, even these modest proposals encountered endless difficulties.

We do not possess here the necessary elements either to examine the practical implementation of the policy of decentralization nor its results. However, we can draw a general conclusion from an examination of these policy changes and the causes which determined them. This can be reduced to the principle of the historical tradition of the political party, that is of the necessity to understand at every point in time what sort of party is both necessary and possible. The recognition of the historical determinations of the forms of political organizations of the working class cannot coexist with a Bordighist conception of the political party which sees the party only as the organizer of the masses from the outside and as their 'teacher'.[63] For Bordiga the party could 'dominate' history, it could be the subject of history. In Togliatti, as well as in Gramsci the revolutionary party cannot become the form of the revolutionary process, cannot be identified with the revolution and not even with the State which emerges during the revolution.

In fact one of the chief characteristics of the Togliattian conception of the party is in his definition of it not only as a vanguard but especially as a *part* of the working class.[64] It is significant that as early as 1925 Togliatti warned the PCI (the actual target was Bordiga) not to commit the mistake of separating the party from 'the objective situation in which it constitutes itself and operates and to consider . . . its tactics as independent of (the situation), of the modifications of the situation and of the shifts which occur within the working class'.[65]

Against the Bordighist maximalist conception of the party as an element separated from the working class, Togliatti in that now distant text of 1925, had written that the problem of the conjunction of party and class in a moment of crisis did not exist for revolutionary Marxism because 'we maintain that the party must be with the working class through all the intermediate positions this goes through up to and including the last one — that which precedes the struggle for power. And "to be with" means to adapt one's slogans and tactics to these positions.'

This constant reference to the historical determinations of the party —

the true line of continuity in the elaboration of the PCI's strategy in the post-war period — implies the recognition of the eventual disappearance of the party itself, a recognition present in Gramsci too:

> It is true that one may say that a party is never complete and fully-formed, in the sense that every development creates new tasks and functions, and in the sense that for certain parties the paradox is true that they are complete and fully-formed only when they no longer exist, i.e. when their existence has become historically redundant . . . it is obvious that the party which proposes to put an end to class divisions will only achieve complete self-fulfilment when it ceases to exist because classes, and therefore their expression, no longer exists.[66]

Notes

1. P. Ingrao, 'Democrazia socialista e democrazia interna di partito', *Rinascita*, No. 17, 25 April 1964.
2. P. Ingrao, 'Il XX Congresso del PCUS e l'VIII Congresso del PCI' in AA.VV. *Problemi di storia del Partito comunista italiano*, Rome, 1971, pp. 161–2.
3. Ibid., p. 162.
4. A. Natoli, 'Il dibattito sul XX Congresso nella Federazione di Roma', *Rinascita*, No. 5–6, May–June 1956.
5. P. Ingrao, 'La democrazia interna, l'unità e la politica dei comunisti', ibid.
6. Ibid.
7. See G. Bocca, *Palmiro Togliatti*, Bari, 1973, p. 623.
8. D. L. M. Blackmer, *Unity in Diversity*, Cambridge, Mass., 1968, pp. 74–5.
9. 'Un innamissibile attacco alla politica del PCI', *Rinascita*, No. 7, July 1956.
10. Ibid.
11. P. Togliatti, 'La realtà dei fatti e della nostra azione rintuzza l'irresponsabile disfattismo', *Rinascita*, No. 7, July 1956.
12. 'La relazione di Luigi Longo' in *Documenti per l'VIII Congresso del PCI. Per un partito più forte e rinnovato*. Supplement of *Voce Comunista*, No. 38, 4 October 1956, p. 4.
13. Ibid., p. 13.
14. Ibid., p. 15.
15. *Risoluzione del Comitato Direttivo della Federazione Milanese* (PCI Milan), 15 October 1956. The Milan Communist Party was undergoing a severe shake-up. Traditionally a stronghold of sectarianism, it now produced a younger and more 'Togliattian' leadership.
16. A. Natoli, 'Potere operaio e libertà democratiche', *Rinascita*, No. 10, October 1956.
17. Here Natoli was clearly following Togliatti's lead. The PCI leader, in his reply to Onofri's argument that the party had abandoned the Italian road to socialism and had adopted a mistaken strategy after 1947, stated that, on the contrary '. . . in the first two years after the victory against fascism our mistake was that we moved too slowly . . . At the beginning we were not able to move on the terrain of economic struggles because we feared to break the [anti-fascist] unity . . .', in op. cit.

18. A Caracciolo, 'Il centralismo democratico e la vita interna dei partiti operai', *Società*, No. 6, Nov.–Dec. 1956, p. 1037.
19. Ibid.
20. Ibid., p. 1051.
21. Ibid., p. 1055.
22. 'Intervento di Giuseppe Di Vittorio', *VIII Congresso*, p. 431.
23. 'Intervento di Luigi Longo sullo Statuto', ibid., p. 573.
24. Theses, ibid., p. 977.
25. Togliatti, 'Rapporto VIII', in *Nella pace e nella democrazia verso il socialismo*, Rome, 1963, p. 75.
26. Ibid., p. 72.
27. 'Relazione di Giacomo Ferrari sull'attività della Commissione Centrale di Controllo', *VIII Congresso*, pp. 567–7.
28. Theses in ibid., p. 976.
29. 'Il rapporto di Luigi Longo sullo Statuto', ibid., p. 55.
30. Ibid., p. 559.
31. Ibid., p. 554.
32. G. Procacci, 'Appunti sugli statuti del PCI dopo la Liberazione', in *Critica Marxista*, No. 6, 1978, p. 69.
33. Longo, op. cit., pp. 561–2. Giolitti had said: 'I think that democratic centralism must be conceived and applied in such a manner that, while the rigorous observance of the directives elaborated by the majority must be assured in so far as their execution is concerned, the debate of opinions and ideas, an indispensable condition for true democracy, is kept open. Only thus is the real unity of the party ensured' in *VIII Congresso*, p. 232. Longo's references to those who had asked for a proper interplay between majority and minority within the party can also be taken to refer to Caracciolo's article ('Il centralismo democratico e la vita interna dei partiti operai') already discussed.
34. Longo, op. cit., p. 565.
35. Longo, for instance, explained the complete paralysis of the Hungarian CP in terms of the lack of a democratic life within the party, in *Revisionismo, nuovo e antico*, Turin, 1957, p. 61.
36. A. Giolitti, *Riforme e rivoluzione*, Turin, 1957, pp. 43–51.
37. In *VIII Congresso*, p. 344. This is one way of interpreting this statement: 'Those comrades who are also intellectuals must feel more and more at ease in the party, the party of the working class and of the workers, which is their party'.
38. L. Longo, 'Rapporto sullo Statuto', ibid., p. 569. The new statute established that members of factory cells were expected to frequent their local cell as well.
39. 'Intervento di Secchia', ibid., p. 344.
40. R. Rossanda, 'Appunti per una discussione sugli intellettuali e il partito', *Rinascita*, No. 11, 14 March 1964.
41. V. Gerratana, 'Forme e contenuti della democrazia nei partiti politici italiani', *Critica Marxista*, No. 5–6, Sept.–Oct. 1963, p. 135.
42. Theses, *VIII Congresso*, p. 982. See also Di Vittorio's statement supporting the same point, p. 437.
43. 'Intervento di Di Vittorio' in ibid., p. 437. The proposal to revise the 'transmission belt' thesis originated in an article by Di Vittorio in *L'Unità* of 1 August 1956 ('Fermenti di unità nazionale').
44. In *X Congresso — Atti e Risoluzioni*, Rome, 1963, p. 730.
45. A. Natta and G. C. Pajetta, 'Il centralismo democratico nella elaborazione e nell'esperienca dei comunisti italiani' in *Critica Marxista*, No. 5–6, Sept.–Dec. 1963, p. 119.
46. Ibid., p. 118.
47. A. Natta and G. C. Pajetta, op. cit., p. 126.

48. The Christian Democratic Party, whose history is a history of factional struggle, has in its statute a specific ban on factions: '. . . groups or organized factions are not allowed within the party' (Art. 10, second paragraph, quoted in V. Gerratana, op. cit., p. 151).
49. P. Ingrao, 'Democrazia socialista e democrazia interna di partito', *Rinascita*, No. 17, 25 April 1964, in *Masse e potere*, p. 196.
50. P. Ingrao, 'Discussione e ricerca dell'unità', *Rinascita*, No. 27, 4 July 1964.
51. Ibid.
52. G. Amendola, 'Movimento e organizzazione delle masses' in *Critica Marxista*, No. 5–6, Sept.–Oct. 1963, p. 167.
53. Amendola, op. cit., p. 165.
54. See Longo's report to the Central Committee meeting of April 1962 in *L'Unità*, 27 April 1962.
55. E. Berlinguer, 'Lo stato del partito in rapporto alle modificazioni della società italiana', *Critica Marxista*, No. 5–6, Sept.–Dec. 1963, p. 197.
56. E. Macaluso, *L'Unità*, 13 March 1964.
57. Berlinguer, op. cit., pp. 200–1.
58. Ibid., p. 202.
59. Ibid., p. 203.
60. Thus wrote Togliatti in 1961: 'Our political organization like any other tends at a certain stage to become ossified in a stabilized form even when this no longer corresponds to the required tasks and situation. It is for this reason that we insist so much on renewal and we make this the keystone of the development and strengthening of our entire party', in 'Tesseramento e reclutamento', *Rinascita*, No. 4, April 1961.
61. Berlinguer, op. cit., p. 210.
62. See Longo's speech to the Fifth Conference on organization in *L'Unità*, 14 March 1964.
63. F. de Felice, *Serrati, Bordiga, Gramsci e il problema della rivoluzione in Italia 1919–20*, Bari, 1971, p. 232.
64. P. Togliatti, 'La nostra ideologia', originally in *L'Unità*, 23 September 1925, now in *Opere Complete*, Vol. 1, Rome, 1974, pp. 651–2, qutoed in Vacca, op.
65. P. Togliatti, 'La nostra ideologia', originally in L'Unità, 23 September 1925, now in *Opere Complete* Vol. 1, Rome, 1974, pp. 651–2, quoted in Vacca, op. cit., p. 496.
66. A. Gramsci, *Selections from the Prison Notebooks*, London, 1971, p. 152.

PART III   1964–1980

11.   Towards Eurocommunism

Throughout the sixties and seventies the Italian Communist Party sought to challenge the 'logic of the blocs' which had characterized international relations since the end of the Second World War. This entailed a process of further autonomy from the CPSU – and we have seen how painful and difficult that was – and, at the same time, a struggle which would direct the PCI towards becoming one of the foremost assertors of European unity. The creation of a zone of disengagement from Cold War politics in Europe involved the phasing out of the two power blocs and hence a process of détente which would facilitate the reacquisition of autonomy as far as Italy was concerned. We have seen that the PCI's initial attitude towards Europe was a hostile one. But in the period 1963–9 this hostility gradually turned into outright acceptance of the EEC.

Throughout the 1960s the PCI explored the possibilities of widespread action (both in Italy and in Europe) which would encourage the development of a democratic alternative to the existing forms of community institutions. In particular it attempted to find an alternative policy to both the 'American' conception of Europe and the 'Gaullist' one.

The necessity of constructing a strategy on the European level entailed the development of forms of collaboration with other political forces. At the same time it was felt necessary to struggle for the entry of the representatives of the PCI into the European Parliament and of the CGIL on the Economic and Social Committee of the EEC. This could not be done without attempting to convince other European Communist Parties, and the French in particular, to join forces.

Togliatti's successor, Luigi Longo, in a declaration to the West German weekly *Stern*, specifically stated that all European Communist Parties, and not just the Italian one, should be represented in the European Parliament.[1]

Accordingly Longo tried to involve the French Communist Party in common initiatives towards the EEC, in successive meetings between the two parties in Geneva (1965) and San Remo (1966). The result of this operation, if it did not eliminate the deep-felt suspicions that the PCF had towards the EEC, certainly contributed to some important changes: it helped the PCF to initiate a policy of co-operation with the French Socialist Party.

The attempt to find a European level for their own strategy was further developed by the Italian Communists at every international gathering of the Communist movement and particularly at those which took place among the Western Communist Parties.

A definition of a possible European strategy was delineated by Ugo Pecchioli, the Italian representative at the West European Communist Conference held in Vienna in May 1966. According to Pecchioli, the difference existing in Europe should not obscure the fact that the problems and the processes taking place in this 'region' have common roots and determine common tasks for the European left. The characteristics of the situation in Europe was one of extreme fluidity in which the directing groups of European capitalism were divided between two roads, one of increasing subordination to American capital, and the other, the 'French road', which attempted to reconquer for European capital a world role.[2] In this situation the task of the Communists was one of intervening in these ongoing processes in order to favour the development of what Pecchioli called a 'democratic alternative'. This alternative was based fundamentally on the proposal for the phasing out of the blocs — a proposal which could be implemented through controlled disarmament, agreements for nuclear control, recognition of the two Germanies and of the present boundaries in Europe and an end to all foreign bases. At the economic level it is necessary to go beyond the simple demand for increasing East–West trade and to examine the possibility of a system of European economic co-operation (involving both Eastern and Western Europe). How could this alternative be achieved? Pecchioli emphasized that the recognition of the objective tendency towards economic internationalization must imply the recognition of the abstract nature of a position on which 'for too long some sectors of the European working class have remained anchored', i.e. the position of simple condemnation and rejection of European economic integration. The steps to the democratic alternative thus necessarily must begin with a rejection of past erroneous positions. Secondly, the new strategy presupposes the development of a united struggle with those democratic forces within each country which, though critical of the EEC, continue to support it. Thirdly, the new strategy demands the recognition by every Communist party that the development of monopolistic integration across Europe poses problems which can only be solved on the basis of co-operation with the progressive forces in Western Europe.

This remains the basis of the PCI strategy for Europe at the present. But any strategy based on the creation of a united Europe free from political commitments to a bipolar world poses the question of the Atlantic alliance. Until 1974 PCI policy on NATO was based on a unilateralist vision; the slogan was 'Italy out of NATO, NATO out of Italy'. However, it should be noted that at the Twelfth Congress of the party (1969) Luigi Longo, then still party secretary, while reaffirming his unilateral rejection of NATO, declared that the party's policy 'was not the disintegration of the Western bloc in favour of the Eastern bloc', but the simultaneous dissolution of both the Atlantic Alliance and the Warsaw Pact.[3] A few years later, at the Central Committee meeting of February 1972, Enrico Berlinguer envisaged a Europe which would be 'neither anti-USA nor anti-USSR'.[4] By the Thirteenth Congress the unilateral call for a withdrawal from NATO appears neither in the party's programme nor in Berlinguer's report nor in Amendola's intervention on foreign affairs. It is already evident that some policy changes were under way: Berlinguer warned that the question of NATO should be seen 'in a dynamic way and not in the static manner of the Cold War years' and declared that the question of Italy's membership of NATO could not be reduced to a simple pronouncement in favour of or against the alliance.[5]

It took some time for the full implications of these silences and Berlinguer's veiled pronouncement to emerge. By December 1974, in his Central Committee report which was the basis for the debates leading to the Fourteenth Congress (March 1975), Berlinguer announced the new NATO policy: 'As Italy is concerned we do not put forward as a precondition the problem of the Italian withdrawal from the Atlantic Alliance.'[6] And he then added:

> We make it clear that we too believe that the Italian government must not propose to undertake a unilateral action which would alter the military strategic equilibrium between the Atlantic Pact and the Warsaw Pact, and with as much clarity and firmness we assert that the Italian people has the right to decide freely, according to the principles of the Republican Constitution, the political directions of its internal life, the parliamentary majorities and the governments called to lead the country.[7]

The realization that the 'NATO question' could not be isolated from the 'Warsaw question' and that a unilateral exit from NATO would bring no benefit but would be, on the contrary, a harbinger of crisis was not the only motive for the change in the PCI's NATO policy. A few days before the general elections of 20 June 1976, in an interview to the *Corriere della Sera*, Berlinguer declared:

As Italy does not belong to the Warsaw Pact: there is, from this point of view, the absolute certainty that we can proceed along the Italian road to socialism without constraints. But this does not mean that there are no problems within the Western bloc: indeed, we are forced to demand from within the Atlantic Pact (which we do not question) the right of Italy to choose her destiny independently.[8]

And to the question of whether NATO could also serve as a shield for the construction of socialism with freedom, he answered positively: 'I want Italy to remain in NATO "also" for this reason and not only because our withdrawal would upset the international balance. I feel safer on this side, but on this side too there are serious attempts to limit our autonomy.'

The context of these changes in a policy which had been in existence for so long is not only the result of a new international conjuncture but also the explicit bid of the PCI to form an entente with the DC. The unity of the Resistance (the first 'historic compromise') was broken principally because of the internal division of the world into two power blocs as a result of the Cold War. Thus no strategy could ignore the fact of the presence of Italy in the American sphere of influence. As we have shown, it was thought at first that Italy could unilaterally withdraw from this sphere. This view was based on a rigid interpretation of the 'Italian road to socialism' as a manifestation of Italian autonomy. What eventually emerged was the gradual understanding that this withdrawal from the US sphere of influence had to take into consideration not only internal but also international relations of forces. Thus the unilateral approach was rejected in favour of a policy of a gradual, reciprocal phasing out of the power bloc through multilateral negotiations and the defence of the process of détente.

The autonomy of the PCI (and of Italy), however, is not only restricted by political considerations. The process of economic integration, the unification of the European market, and the formation of the EEC was an obstacle to a purely Italian road to socialism, but it was an obstacle which, the PCI believed, could not nor should be removed because it was convinced that the development of the productive forces in Italy could only take place on the basis of European economic integration. The only way to tackle this apparent obstacle was to extend the strategy to the European level: a European road to socialism, i.e. what later came to be known as 'Eurocommunism'.

The existing political trend of economic integration (i.e. subjection of European capital to American capital) did not tend to develop the 'productive forces in general', but only those which would ensure the monopolies a profit rate adequate for the reproduction of the social relations within which they operated. In other words, the limitations to the development of the productive forces are not determined by factors which are 'outside' capitalist development (e.g. 'pre-capitalist' forms acting as an obstacle to capitalism) but by the concrete process of capitalist accumulation. Thus, in order to create at the economic level the conditions for the unimpeded development of the productive forces and, at the political level, the possibility for a mutual and reciprocal phasing out of the power blocs, it is necessary (in the Communist view) to fight for European autonomy. Such autonomy, or at least an advance towards it, would be the political precondition for a democratic type of economic integration. The European working class must see it as being in its interest to favour the development of common policies (transport, energy, scientific research, etc.), because no country in Europe can obtain rapid economic growth without the development of these common policies. This cannot be separated from political autonomy because, for instance, in the field of energy (crucial to Italy, a country with poor energy resources) any common action implies a foreign policy decision (as was evident after the Middle East War of 1973).

If the development of the productive forces is part of an advance to socialism and if this development depends on the creation of an autonomous Europe, that is, of a new relationship between Europe and the USA, then it follows that it is no longer possible to conceive (in Europe) of an advance to socialism on the basis of one nation. The European question becomes of primary importance: the logical conclusion of Togliatti's polycentric vision is drawn.

This new emphasis on Europe is increasingly evident. The programme of the PCI approved at the Thirteenth Congress (1972) stated that, in the context of the international collocation of Italy: 'The question of Europe, of its security and of the democratic transformation of the Economic Community . . . is decisive.'[9] Berlinguer, at the same congress, said in his opening remarks: 'Our attention is particularly concentrated on Europe' and in his conclusion he explicitly stated that the novelty of their position on the international front was 'The particular emphasis we want to give to our commitment in Europe and to the role of the democratic and labour movement of Western Europe'.[10] Finally, Amendola in his speech entirely devoted to international questions also pointed out that the theme of Europe was a new direction and that it would be a central element on the platform of a government in which the PCI would be a leading force.[11]

This deep interest in Europe cannot in any way be deemed a tactical move. After 1972 in particular the European theme appeared in practically every important foreign affairs article in the theoretical and political weekly *Rinascita*. An Italian advance to socialism can no longer be assumed to be a real possibility outside a European context. Thus the search for a strategy for socialism in the West and the characteristic features socialism should assume in the West become a fundamental terrain in which the forces of the left in Italy are compelled to operate. As Alfredo Reichlin wrote:

> . . . the fact that the crisis of our country is also an aspect of the larger crisis of Europe and of Western capitalism, and, more generally, of the international structure and order which are the results of the Second World War makes us more aware that *there can be no merely national solution for the Italian crisis*. From this follows the necessity to strengthen and extend the links with the international working class movement and with the other democratic forces in Europe [my emphasis].[12]

The terrain for this development was seen, then, to be particularly favourable because there appeared to be more and more divergencies between Europe and the USA over a whole range of questions both economic (monetary, energy, etc.) and political (relations with the East, the Middle East, South East Asia, etc.) This is a point often emphasized by Berlinguer:

> There is a sharpening of the contradictions between the capitalist states in a way which had not occurred since the end of the Second World War. The recent American decisions on the dollar will accentuate the tendencies of the other capitalist states towards a major autonomy *vis-à-vis* the USA.[13]

The strategy of left unity would intervene in the space created by these contradictions in order to develop an autonomous European policy. The crucial problem is to find the appropriate forms of co-ordination among European Communist Parties as a pre-condition for a wider system of alliances which would include also non-Communist parties.

To talk about common organizational forms within the Communist movement brings back the memories of the Comintern and the Cominform, i.e. of unacceptable models. The Italian Communists emphasized that they did not want to create any 'directing centre': their programme was to 'give consistency and continuity to the relations of co-operation among the parties of Western Europe'.[14] The basis of these forms of co-operation can only be given by the common acceptance of a set of principles which are particular to European Communism. These must be principles which are not necessarily those of other Communist movements outside Europe, they are not therefore 'Communist' in the traditional sense; but they represent the essential features a socialist society must and can have in Europe. All these principles centre on the question of the relationship between socialism and democracy: the affirmation that socialism is a development and a full application of democracy, the recognition of the value of personal freedoms, the principles of the non-confessional nature of the State, of the autonomy of trade unions, of religious, cultural and scientific freedom and in particular the principle of a pluralism of parties.

These principles provide the basis for the unity of the Communist movement in Europe; they also provide strategic indications: the defence of democratic freedoms, the fight for structural reforms and a strategy of alliances, while the acceptance of the plurality of parties even in the period of the transition to socialism had been explicitly accepted by the Italian Communist Party since their Eighth Congress in 1956; its proclamation at the time was not made with a European conception in mind but from the point of view of an Italian road to socialism.

By the 1970s the principle of the plurality of parties is explicitly recognized to be valid for the whole of capitalist Europe. This recognition was partly determined by the political possibilities opened by the objective process of economic integration and the growing awareness of the impossibility of socialism in a single European country; and it was facilitated by other European Communist Parties recognizing this principle as well. At every meeting with the representatives of other Communist Parties the Italian Communists have re-asserted the fundamental importance of pluralism in the construction of a socialist society. On 11 July 1975 the Italian and Spanish Communist Parties jointly declared their strategic and not merely tactical belief in the possibility of a democratic advance towards socialism in Western Europe on the basis of personal and collective freedom as well as a plurality of political parties. And with the French Communist Party, the PCI declared:

> The French and Italian Communists declare themselves for the plurality of political parties, for the right of existence and activity of parties of opposition, for the free formation and democratic change between majority and minority.
>
> All liberties whether they are the fruits of the great democratic-bourgeois revolutions, or of the great popular struggles of this century, headed by the working class, must be guaranteed and developed.[15]

When, after a long period of negotiations, the Berlin Conference of European Communist Parties took place in June 1976, the differences within the international communist movement came to the fore as they had never done previously. Not only did the Rumanians and the Yugoslavs reaffirm their independence in stronger terms than before, but two major West European Communist Parties, the French and the Spanish, took a position which, on all the 'questions of principles', was essentially identical with that of the Italian Communist Party. And what is probably even more important is that the position of the PCF and of the PCE was arrived at 'autonomously and independently'. The unity which had been reached was not imposed by any new form of organization. This was the most authentic sign of what the international press called 'Eurocommunism', an expression which, in spite of its geographical imprecision, came to characterize the new 'ghost' haunting Europe. But to be fully effective Eurocommunism had to be based on new conceptions of internationalism far removed from the 'proletarian internationalism' associated with Soviet foreign policy.

The emergence of this new conception was already implicit in the Yalta Memorandum (1964); however, it is only after the Soviet intervention in Czechoslovakia that it began to be articulated in a more explicit way, though still shrouded in some ambiguity. When at the Twelfth Congress (1969) Berlinguer tried to express this new conception, he referred directly to the PCI position on Czechoslovakia asserting that in the PCI judgement the intervention was not a mere 'mistake', but the product of contradictions within the socialist camp and that, from this starting-point, the Italian Communists, while reasserting firmly the principle of non-intervention in the internal affairs of another party, would attempt to formulate a critical and objective assessment of the realities of the socialist camp.[16]

Clearly a purely legalistic concept of internationalism as non-interference could not be acceptable. Nevertheless, the frequent and repeated criticism of the Soviet invasion, a criticism which would not subside even when it was no longer much debated in the non-Communist press, must be taken as an unequivocal sign that the PCI took its policy of phasing out of the blocs seriously. The invasion of Czechoslovakia was characterized by the then Secretary-General of the PCI, Luigi Longo, in his report to the Central Committee of 27 August 1968, as an expression of that 'logic of the blocs' which the PCI had always opposed. He added that 'the boundaries of socialism no longer coincided with the boundaries of the socialist camp'.

It is inevitable that at stake in this debate is not only the important question of socialist internationalism, but also that of the way in which the policy of détente is conceived. Here too we have a marked difference in the approach of the USSR and that of the PCI. The USSR conceives of peaceful coexistence as an international equilibrium guaranteed by the deterrents represented by the might of Soviet armament; from this follows the Soviet attempt to ignore (or even to repress) the contradictions emerging in socialist societies and the under-estimation of the revolutionary potential existing in the capitalist countries.

These considerations were expressed by Enrico Berlinguer at the important international meeting of the Communist Parties held in Moscow in June 1969, where the disagreement between the PCI and the rest of the international communist movement was evidenced by Berlinguer's refusal to sign the final resolution (the only major Communist leader to refuse): he expressed his agreement only with the section on the 'struggle against imperialism'. Moreover, Berlinguer renewed his condemnation of the entry into Czechoslovakia by the troops of the five Warsaw Treaty countries. He stressed that, while there is a need to avoid interfering in the internal affairs of the Czechs,

> . . . there are aspects of the Czechoslovak events which bear upon fundamental questions and are the business not only of the countries concerned but of our entire movement. These are questions of independence and sovereignty, and these are also questions of socialist democracy and freedom of culture.[17]

The Italian Communist leader had thus spelt out the limits to the policy of non-interference: these are constituted by questions of principle which affected the entire movement. This thesis can be taken to constitute the grounds for a new conception of internationalism.

This new conception was not expressed without an explicit criticism of the monolithic concept based on uncritical acceptance of the policies of the socialist camp:

> It is essentially a question of overcoming any gravitation towards a monolithic concept of our movement's unity, a concept which would be not only erroneous but also Utopian.

An important development of this conception, further defining the limits of non-intervention, was made by Berlinguer at the Berlin Conference of the European Communist Parties, on 30 June 1976:

> It is our opinion that respect for the principle of non-interference cannot exclude freedom of judgement on theoretical or political positions taken by other political parties, as well as on particular events in international life and in the workers' movement. Everyone knows for

example that, while we have always emphasized the great advances made by the socialist countries, we Italian Communists have more than once expressed critical judgement both on certain events and situations (for instance over Czechoslovakia) and on more general problems relative to the relationship between democracy and socialism in various socialist countries.[18]

The autonomy of the Western Communist Parties from any 'directing centres' and their acceptance of common principles is a necessary precondition for a united action of the European left which is in turn an element of the struggle for an autonomous Europe, a struggle which is conceived in terms of the possibility of European intervention in the process of détente.

The Eurocommunist phenomenon was thus premised on the development of the process of détente. But this, in the late seventies, came to be increasingly under attack. The non-ratification of SALT II, the NATO decision to locate in Europe a new generation of nuclear missiles, the Soviet invasion of Afghanistan, the American boycott of the Moscow Olympics and the unrelenting development of 'local wars' (China and Vietnam, Vietnam and Cambodia, Somalia and Eritrea, Iran and Iraq) were so many obstacles to the development of Eurocommunism. Internal dissension on the EEC and the breaking up of the alliance between French Communists and French Socialists prevented the transition from Eurocommunism to a new 'Euroleft' which would regroup Communists, socialists and social democrats in Europe. Soon the French Communist Party broke with Eurocommunism with the same suddenness with which it had joined it and ranked itself alongside the USSR over Afghanistan. The Spanish Communist Party which, to some extent, had been the most outspoken proponent of the new line found it extremely difficult to control its internal in-fighting, particularly the opposition to Eurocommunism which originated from its Catalan rank and file. The Italians decided eventually that they could no longer wait for the French and, against Marchais's advice, began a bout of diplomatic activity directed towards the leading socialist parties of Europe with particular regard for the Germans and the French.

The weakness of Eurocommunism had been that it had never succeeded in developing beyond the assertion of common principles. It never developed concrete programmes and concrete policies. Whatever unity was created was essentially of an ideological kind and even that was precarious. While agreeing on questions such as pluralism and democratic rights, the Eurocommunist Parties did not manage to have a common platform on energy, unemployment, North–South dialogue, the EEC and many other issues.

Notes

1. *Stern,* 10 November 1964.
2. U. Pecchioli, 'Le forze democratiche e l'Europa del Mec', in *Critica Marxista,* No. 3, May–June 1966, pp. 3–14.
3. Luigi Longo, *XII Congresso del Partito comunista italiano — Atti e Risoluzioni,* Rome, 1969, p. 63.
4. E. Berlinguer, *La Questione Comunista,* Vol. 2, Rome 1975, p. 548 (henceforth cited as *La QC*).
5. *XIII Congresso del Partito comunista italiano — Atti e risoluzioni,* Rome, 1972, p. 72.
6. *La QC,* Vol. 2, p. 878.
7. Ibid., p. 881.
8. *Il Corriere della Sera,* 15 June 1976.
9. *XIII Congresso,* Rome, 1972, p. 547.
10. Ibid., pp. 25 and 477.
11. Ibid., p. 98.
12. 'Il Pci e l'Europa' in *Rinascita,* No. 30, 25 July 1975.
13. *La QC,* Vol. 1, p. 347.
14. Ibid., p. 360.
15. See *l'Unità,* 18 November 1975.
16. *La QC,* Vol. 1, pp. 7–8.
17. See Berlinguer's speech in *International Meeting of Communist and Workers Parties,* Moscow, 1969, p. 389.
18. See report in *The Times,* 1 July 1976.

12. Towards the 'Historic Compromise'

We have examined the developments of PCI's foreign policy and have stressed the gradual evolution of a conception of international relations whose central feature is a multi-polarization of the world. This conception brings into question not only the monolithism of the traditional Communist conception of the world as a gigantic struggle between *the* form of socialist rule and *the* form of capitalist domination, but also the very nature of an advance towards socialism according to the classical model.

Togliatti's achievement had been the recognition of differential paths to socialism. His successors would have the difficult task of rendering this recognition concrete and practical. At the same time the death of Togliatti meant also that the party had lost a figure who could guarantee the homogeneity of the leadership group. Togliatti had the unique advantage of being a man of the Third International who had understood the limitation of that intellectual and political tradition. He could move forward towards new territory while maintaining a continuity with the past.

None of Togliatti's successors could aspire to maintain this union of the old and the new in the same way. Formally the new leader was Luigi Longo. But there was never any doubt that Longo could be no more than a caretaker leader. The struggle for the leadership took the form of the struggle between Pietro Ingrao and Giorgio Amendola, although neither of them would in fact become the new Secretary General — as it happened a generation was 'skipped' and the choice fell on Enrico Berlinguer (the only alternative being Giorgio Napolitano) — but because they both represented alternative projects for a redefinition of the Communist strategy.

With the brutality and the fearlessness which characterized his interventions in inner party debates, Amendola stated in a famous article in *Rinascita* that

> . . . neither of the two solutions offered to the working class in the capitalist countries of Western Europe in the last fifty years, the Social-Democratic solution and the Communist solution, has shown itself to

be successful in the socialist transformation of society . . . A political organization which is unable to achieve its objectives after fifty years and at least three generations of activists must be able to investigate the reasons for this failure and be able to transform itself.[1]

Thus, already in 1964, there was a tendency in the PCI which explicitly affirmed that, given the failure of both Social Democracy and Communism, a 'third way', at least in Western Europe, was necessary. Not that Ingrao would have disagreed with that either. The point of the debate was essentially that once it was decided to operate a break with tradition it was also necessary to begin the long and arduous task of envisaging the specific forms of transitions which a 'third way' strategy to socialism would involve in Western Europe. It is on this point that Amendola's proposal shook the party. Amendola suggested that a way out of the impasse was the constitution in Italy of a 'single' party of the working class, i.e. a unification between PSI and PCI. Clearly the proposal, at least in the short term, was not practical. After all the Italian Socialist Party was then in government and was planning to merge with the anti-Communist and pro-Atlantic Social Democrats of Saragat. But what were the implications of putting forward the re-unification of the two main streams of the Italian labour movement? The real basis of Amendola's project was a strategy which underplayed, if not ruled out altogether, any attempt to shift the centre of gravity of the Italian political system by developing an *entente* with the Catholic masses. The proposal of a single party entailed putting at the centre of the transformation process the unity of the working class. In Amendola's project Italy would come to resemble the rest of Europe: a large working class party would face a large conservative party. The transformation of the Christian Democratic Party into a 'normal' conservative party would involve — as a counterpart — the social-democratization of the party of the working class. Against Amendola, Ingrao would stress the need to elaborate a 'new model of development' with which to fight against the centre-left government's proposals to 'rationalize' capitalism. Such a global challenge would have the purpose of operating a realignment of Italian politics in which the co-operation with the Catholic masses would be a central element. The way in which Ingrao advanced the conception of a new model of development entailed a radicalization of political struggle because it would do away with the characteristic mode of political intervention of the PCI: an empirical definition of priorities determined by the political situation. At the Eleventh Congress of the PCI (January 1966) Longo would reject Ingrao's conception and would be supported by Pajetta, Alicata, Berlinguer and Amendola. Not that the Congress closed with Amendola's victory. His proposals for a single party of the working class had caused such opposition in the party press that it was not even discussed at the Congress.[2]

The defeat of Pietro Ingrao at the Eleventh Congress would have profound effects in the PCI. For years '*Ingraoiani*' and '*Amendoliani*' would continue the debate and some of the followers of Ingrao began to publish a monthly journal called *Il Manifesto*. This would be seen as an attempt to form a faction (which is indeed what it was) and the *Manifesto* group was eventually expelled in 1969.

The Amendola–Ingrao controversy was perhaps only the harbinger of a deeper crisis of Italian Communism which would involve its relation with the intellectual world and first and foremost with the students. Until the mid-sixties the PCI was in the position of not having any political rival to its left and in having something approaching a monopoly of Marxist culture. This situation would come to an end in the years 1968–72. After 1972 the PCI would no longer be able to occupy the entire 'space' of Marxist politics and culture. In the period 1968–72 the Youth Federation of the PCI shrank considerably and was on the verge of dissolution. A plethora of small sects appeared on the political scene. The *Manifesto* group, expelled in November 1969, became a rallying point for a number of students and published a daily paper. Texts such as Marcuse's *One Dimensional Man* challenged the classics of Marxism. The student revolt, more pronounced in Italy than anywhere else on the continent of Europe (including France whose student movement was never to recover from the extraordinary heights of the May 1968 events), was no monolith: its ideology comprehended libertarian and anti-authoritarian streaks coupled with a revival of Stalinism. The PCI was accused of being revisionist and reformist and, at the same time, authoritarian and bureaucratic.

This is not the place for an analysis of the student revolt. Its effects were multiple and long-lasting. The student revolt not only challenged the PCI, but also the entire system of political parties for it was the first time in post-war Italian history that a political force emerged without joining forces with another political party. One should reflect on the significance of this. In Italy the Church is closely connected to one political party in particular: the DC. The divided trade union movement is split along party lines. The Co-operative movement is split into a 'white Co-operative movement' and a 'red Co-operative'. Even sporting associations do not escape from 'colonization' by political parties: the ARCI sports clubs are mainly Communist and socialist while the *Libertas* sports club are organized by the DC.

After the student revolt it would be the turn of the trade unions. Grass-root movements in the factories began to engage in widespread strike actions and soon carried with them the three trade union federations anxious not to lose control. As the 'hot autumn' of 1969 developed the three trade union federations moved closer together and more apart from their respective political parties. In the factories the 'Factory Council', an association of all the workers and not simply of union members became, first *de facto* and then also formally, *the* organization of the workers within the factories.

This dual eruption (students and workers) caused a massive crisis within the Italian political system. The demand for democratization and participation was too strong to be resisted by a rather weak state. The period 1968–9 signalled the crisis of the centre-left, the crisis of the DC and the crisis of the PCI. None of these forces could emerge unscathed from the social earthquake. The centre-left coalition gave way to a centrist coalition as the new united Socialist Party (PSU) split again into its former constituent parts: Social Democrats and Socialists. Those Socialists who had rejected the centre-left and formed their own party merged with the PCI in 1972.

This situation of chronic crisis within the Italian political system led Enrico Berlinguer (who by 1972 had become Secretary General) to give the Italian road to socialism a new and more 'concrete' formulation. The immediate cause of this redefinition was the *coup d'état* in Chile.[3] There, a left-wing government had attempted to rule against strong Christian Democrat opposition and was crushed by a military take-over. Berlinguer drew attention to two central elements: the international balance of forces and the internal relations between political parties in Italy. At the international level Italy was clearly in the American sphere of influence. Its sovereignty was to a large extent a 'limited' one. Any advance of the Communist Party towards the seat of power had to be made with the maximum caution and with guarantees that an international crisis would not ensue. At the internal level the strength of the Christian Democrats was not only a question of votes, but resided also in the fact that the Christian Democratic Party had 'colonized' the State, occupying through its clientele system all the major apparatuses of the State including the credit system and the public sector.

Let us take the international level. Here Berlinguer established that détente is an indispensable condition 'in the final analysis, for reducing the possibility of imperialist intervention in the life of other countries' and later on he added:

. . . we have always given due importance to the basic fact represented by Italy's membership in the politico-military bloc dominated by the United States and to the ways this fact inevitably conditions the Italian situation.[4]

In a sense this did not constitute anything new, although it prepared the ground for that acceptance of the Atlantic Alliance which we discussed in the preceding chapter. Turning to the national aspect, Berlinguer insisted on the centrality of the question of the middle classes for the Italian revolution: 'it is clear that . . . wherever these intermediate classes and strata stand and in what direction they tend to turn and move will prove a decisive factor'.[5] It is only at this stage that we find an attempt to define the analysis which the PCI should make of the new political subject which had emerged in the 1960s and early 1970s: women and youth. As Berlinguer admits it is here that classical class analysis breaks down:

Alongside and often interwoven with these intermediate classes and categories and with the proletariat, there are also in our society strata of the population and social forces which do not as such qualify as 'categories' (for example a large part of the southern and island populations, the masses of women and youth, the forces of science, technology, culture and the arts), but which share a condition in society that to a certain extent unites them above and beyond their professional positions and even their membership in a certain social class.

As a consequence of this:

We do not, then, limit ourselves to seeking and establishing a convergence with already defined social forms and economic categories. We aim rather at winning over and incorporating in a diversified grouping of alliances entire groups, social forces not classified as classes, such as women, young people, the popular masses of the South, cultural forces, movements of opinion, etc.[6]

The essential question then is that of developing a new project for society which would not drive a large section of these intermediate groups and 'social forces not classified as classes' into positions of hostility. Thus a mere electoral or mathematical majority would be insufficient:

. . . it would be illusory to think that, even if the left-wing parties and forces succeeded in gaining 51 per cent of the vote and seats in Parliament . . . this fact would guarantee the survival and work of a government representing this 51 per cent.[7]

In order to achieve a *political* majority it was necessary to achieve an alliance with the Catholic masses and enter into a relation of co-operation with the Christian Democratic Party. Berlinguer stressed that one could not assign the DC a fixed political position. It was a party which in the course of its history had frequently changed position. Besides it was also a party which had to maintain a vast consensus of often disparate forces. It was thus a party which could be pushed and transformed in a progressive direction. This was the political context which called for 'a great, new historic compromise' among the forces that represent the vast majority of the Italian people. Berlinguer's strategy was a pessimistic reading of Italian development. It established the fact that the danger of a right-wing backlash would always be present and that it was necessary to ensure that Christian Democratic acceptance of a reforming government would be a guarantee at both the national and international level that Italy would advance towards a radical restructuring only at a very slow pace.

The strategy of the 'historic compromise' entailed the defeat of the right wing of the DC. The opportunity arose when a group of traditional Catholics collected the necessary signatures for a referendum for the abolition of the divorce law. The then leader of the DC, Amintore Fanfani, embraced whole-heartedly the cause of the referendum. The neo-fascists too joined in the anti-divorce crusade. The PCI mobilized itself and was the centre of a broad lay coalition which also included dissenting Catholics. The referendum was held on 12 May 1974. The results were a defeat for Fanfani's wing of the DC: 59.3 per cent of the voters were in favour of the divorce legislation. At the same time there clearly emerged a right-wing terrorist offensive. A bomb exploded at an anti-fascist rally in Brescia killing eight people. Later on in the year (4 August 1974) a bomb on the express train Italicus caused the death of twelve people and injured many others.

The results of the referendum demonstrated the depth of Italy's commitment to a secular state. This not only constituted a rejection of vulgar anti-Communism but it also reaffirmed the belief on the part of a majority of the Italian population that religion was essentially a private affair and that the State could not legislate on matters of faith. Catholics could go on believing that divorce was a mortal sin and at the same time defend the rights of those who did not share this belief.

The defeat of the Christian Democratic Party (and of its temporary ally, the neo-fascist party) led its leader, Fanfani, to see the local elections of 1975 as a second round in the battle against the PCI. These elections took place in the midst of a profound government crisis and threats of an early dissolution of Parliament which would have made it impossible to hold local elections (by law, a general election would take priority). When the Italians eventually arrived at the polling stations on 15 June 1975 they were to vote for 15 regional councils, 86 provincial councils and 6,345 municipal councils. Yet these elections were of wider significance. The debate on the 'historic compromise' had made the 'Communist question' the central one in Italian political life. Italy had been particularly badly hit by the oil crisis of 1973 and this had posed the question of how Italy was to adapt its economic system to meet the changing relations between the primary producing countries of the Third World and the industrialized world.

The results of the elections stunned Italy. Never in Italian electoral history had such a significant shift taken place:

Parties	Results in per cent	Difference with 1970 elections in per cent
DC	35.29	−2.55
PCI	33.45	+5.59
PSI	11.98	+1.56
MSI (Neo-fascists)	6.43	+0.48
PSDI (Soc. Dem.)	5.60	−1.36
PRI (Republicans)	3.17	−0.28
PLI (Liberals)	2.47	−2.17
PDUP–AO (Far left)	1.38	(no previous results)

In terms of aggregate votes, the gap between the DC and the PCI which had been nearly 10 per cent in 1970 was now reduced to a mere 1.84 per cent. This single datum had remarkable political significance. It then seemed that in the not too distant future, the PCI might well become the largest Italian party. This would put an end to the DC view of itself as the sole 'centre' of Italian political life armed with a permanent mandate to decide the direction of Italian society.

In 1975 the joint PCI–PSI vote obtained a majority in four regions with the Communists obtaining an absolute majority in Emilia–Romagna. 'Red' administrations were also formed in Tuscany, Umbria, Piedmont and eventually in Latium. The PSI systematically opted for the formation of a regional government with the Communists. Even in regions where the left did not have a majority, other parties presented too fragmented a front. The political impossibility of the DC forming a majority with the neo-fascists meant that, in order to govern, the DC needed a majority without the help of the extreme right. Changes occurred in practically all other regions with the institution of so-called 'open' administration. This entailed the participation of the Communist Party in the elaboration of the regional programme in return for Communist abstention or positive support. Politically, the 1975 local elections meant the end of the anti-communist discrimination which had prevailed in Italy for nearly thirty years.

City administration was similarly affected. The left obtained an absolute majority in 29 cities (against 23 in the previous elections) including Genoa, Bologna, Pisa, Siena, Turin, Venice and Florence. A 'red' majority was also formed in eight other cities including Milan and Naples. Elections for the Rome municipality took place a year later, and here too a 'red' administration was formed and an independent on the PCI list became the first non-DC mayor in post-war Rome. When all the regional, provincial and city administrations had been formed, nearly 60 per cent of Italians were living in areas governed by administrations which included the Italian Communist Party.

That the electoral success of 1975 was not a freak result became evident in June 1976 when the general elections were held.

Parties	1976 results in per cent	Difference with 1972 in per cent.
DC	38.7	+0.02
PCI	34.4	+7.21
PSI	9.6	+0.06
MSI (Neo-fascists)	6.1	−2.56
PSDI (Soc. Dem.)	3.4	−1.77
PRI (Republicans)	3.1	+0.23
DP (Far left)	1.5	did not contest
PLI (Liberals)	1.3	−2.59
Radicals	1.1	no previous results.

The dimension of the PCI advance can be comprehended if one considers that while it took twenty-six years for the PCI to increase its percentage by eight points (19 per cent in 1946 to 27 per cent in 1972), it took only another four years to jump by another seven points.

The significance of the Communist advance cannot obscure the fact that the Christian Democratic Party was able to make good its losses of 1975 and return to the percentage obtained in the previous general elections. This recovery was made at the expense of its potential junior partners in coalition: the Social Democrats and the Liberals. The significance of these results in parliamentary terms meant that it was no longer possible for the DC to form a stable governing coalition without the left. Only two options were left open: either the reconstitution of the centre-left, or a government with all democratic parties (i.e. including the PCI and excluding the neo-fascists). The PSI was not alone in refusing to enter any government which rejected the contribution of the PCI. The Republicans and the Social Democrats took a similar stand. Yet the DC was not yet ready for the 'historic compromise' in its governmental form. The DC thus formed a government on its own relying on the abstentions of other parties and negotiating with them the measures to be undertaken to face the crisis.

In July 1976, for the first time since the break-up of the tripartite coalition of 1947 (the first 'historic compromise'), a Christian Democratic Prime Minister (Giulio Andreotti) had to appeal to the PCI in order to guarantee the survival of his government. Furthermore, at the local level, co-operation and agreement between the Communists and Christian Democrats was becoming commonplace and by June 1977 a wide-ranging government programme had been agreed between DC, PCI and the other minor parties. Though not *in* the government, the PCI seemed to have achieved its aim of becoming a party *of* government.

Between 1976 and the end of 1979 Italy was governed by the Christian Democratic Party, whose leaders filled all the government posts. This government was supported in Parliament by the PCI, the PSI, the PRI and the PSDI. It was the period of the so-called 'government of national unity'. This government was seen as a possible stepping-stone towards a fully-fledged participation of the Communists in government.

But this did not happen. In the space of three years the Italian Communist Party lost some of the support and the goodwill it had accumulated in the preceding five years. The policy of compromise was seen as a policy of subordination. The explosion of left-wing terrorism forced the PCI to defend the State. In so doing the PCI was defending the democratic principle of the post-war State, but it could not avoid being seen as the defender of the entire edifice of the Italian State as it had developed since the war with its corruption, its degenerations, its bigotry. In a sense the masterpiece of the DC was that it was able to let the PCI emerge as the stoutest defender of law and order and the principal responsible for and guarantor of the government of national unity. The DC stood apart as if it were not the actual government party, as if it had not 'occupied' the State, as if it had not been the constructor of the clientele system. The DC was able, thanks to its leading light, Aldo Moro, to prepare for itself a strategy which would allow for the incorporation of the PCI in the DC system. This would have been the third stage in the Christian

Democrats' post-war history. After the years of centrist coalition (1948–63), and after the years of the centre-left (1963–9), it seemed inevitable that eventually the DC would have to face the question of alliance and co-operation with the PCI.

For Aldo Moro this alliance was inevitable. The problem was to oversee carefully the timing of this historic encounter as well as the modalities. While for the PCI the alliance with the DC depended on the eventual transformation of this party into a progressive force, then for the DC alliance with the PCI depended on the eventual transformation of the PCI into a mildly reforming machine, whose task would be to bring its supporters and the masses it inspired under the political hegemony of a new governing system led by the Christian Democrats. Thus the DC's strategy was also a strategy of 'historic compromise'. The difference between the two parties was that each gave a different content to the compromise.

At the superficial level it certainly did appear that Moro's interpretation of the historic compromise was prevailing over Berlinguer's. The Communist Party was undoubtedly undergoing a crisis in its relation with its working class base. Berlinguer had declared that 'sacrifices' were needed in order to be able to introduce 'elements of socialism' in Italy.[8] It seemed that the PCI was decreasingly able to maintain the proper distinctions with the DC. But the DC too was in crisis. Moro was able to carry out his policies only to the extent that he was able to hold the entire party together. But the concessions that Moro's approach to the 'historic compromise' entailed were too strong for the rest of his party. The fact was that Italy had become increasingly difficult to govern. The tactic of incorporation could only work as long as the economic situation at both the national and international level was favourable. The DC had been able to maintain its hegemony on the Italian political system precisely because it had used its control over the public purse to acquire a vast popular consensus. With the world-wide crisis caused by the end of dollar supremacy and the increase in oil prices and the crisis of welfare throughout Europe and North America, the DC found it more and more difficult to stick to its traditional mode of political intervention.

The diffusion of left-wing terrorism helped the DC by forcing the PCI to the defensive and by establishing in public opinion a parallelism between terrorists who called themselves 'Communist' and the 'Communism' of the PCI, but it also meant that there was a new political phenomenon which could perhaps be used but which could not be easily incorporated. The dramatic rupture of the 'historic compromise' occurred precisely when the Red Brigades terrorist group kidnapped Aldo Moro in a spectacular operation which took place in the centre of Rome in the middle of the morning of 16 March 1978. After killing the five bodyguards, they captured Moro and held him for fifty-five days. The PCI stood firm against any attempt at negotiation with the Red Brigades whilst the Socialist Party began its long journey towards a reconstitution of a new form of centre-left by distancing itself from the PCI on the very question of terrorism (it suggested that a 'softer' line be taken). Moro was killed and his body left between the headquarters of the PCI and that of the DC. In killing Moro the Red Brigades destroyed the key man who could have paved the way for the entry of the PCI in the government. The target had been chosen with great political accuracy. Had the Red Brigades kidnapped a different leader of the DC, and one more involved in corruption or more visibly seen as an enemy of the PCI, it would have caused great embarrassment to the Italian Communists and would have made it difficult for them to call successfully for the mass mobilization which did occur in those weeks. But by kidnapping Moro and murdering him the Red Brigades effectively killed any hope the PCI had of entering the government. In effect they had killed the 'historic compromise' and permitted the revival of the right wing of the DC.

The PCI did not actually leave the government until the end of that year. The actual excuse was Italy's participation in the European Monetary System. In fact the PCI had already been politically defeated and the results of the general elections of 1979 confirmed this defeat:

Parties	1979 results in per cent	Difference with 1976 in per cent.
DC	38.3	−0.4
PCI	30.4	−4.0
PSI	9.8	+0.2
MSI (Neo-fascists)	5.3	−0.8
PSDI (Soc. Dem.)	3.8	+0.2
Radicals	3.4	+2.3
PRI (Republicans)	3.0	−0.1
PLI (Liberals)	1.9	+0.6
PDUP (Far left)	1.4	no previous results

PCI losses were extremely heavy, particularly if one bears in mind that never in the whole post-war period had the PCI gone down in percentage points in a general election. The DC vote did not change remarkably and hence the DC 'won'. Apart from the PCI losses the main novelty of the poll was the growth of the Radical Party. This party, whose political position remained ambiguous and which behaved essentially as a pressure group on questions of civil liberties, was able to capture the votes of many urban middle-class youth. Its campaign was essentially waged against the PCI, then accused of excessive compromise with the DC.

An analysis of the vote shows that the PCI lost everywhere but it lost in the South far more than anywhere else. While its average national loss was in the region of 4 percentage points, it lost in the Campania region (around Naples) 7.42 percentage points, over 6 per cent in Calabria and Sicily and over 4 per cent in the Apulia, Basilicata and Molise. However, it also lost heavily in working class areas in cities like Turin.

In 1976 the South had accounted for a large part of PCI gains, now it accounted for its losses. The PCI thus paid for its failure, during the period of 'national unity', to dislodge in the slightest way the DC from its southern enclaves where the State is everything and where DC control over state institutions entails control over public resources. The Italian South is not a political chaos, a disintegrated society divided into a myriad of local interest groups. Through the State the Christian Democratic Party has succeeded in organizing these multiplicity of interests. The South is an 'assisted' and 'dependent' society. To tackle this factor the Communist policy of demanding greater local autonomy could not succeed in the South as it could, perhaps, in the centre and in the North. In fact, if we examine the DC vote per region in 1979 we would see that while its vote went down in the North (reaching its lowest point in twenty years) and in the Centre, it actually went up in the South and in Sicily and Sardinia.

The 1979 elections revealed something else, namely that what in the aftermath of the elections of 1976 had been thought to be a tendency towards polarization had been reversed. The growth or stability of the small parties and in particular the success of the Radicals and of the small leftist PDUP meant that the electorate was becoming even more fragmented and that a unifying perspective would be more difficult to arrive at. Italy was undoubtedly more divided; the North from the South, the city from the countryside, the youth from the others.

The crisis of Italian society could not fail to manifest itself in the trade union movement. Its slow progress towards unity was seriously hampered not only by differences in policy and outlook among the three trade union federations, but also because the links between the trade union leadership and the rank and file became more and more difficult to maintain. The trade union had followed a policy which put general economic and political demands and the narrowing of differentials before wage bargaining. The higher-paid workers and the white-collar workers had seen this gap narrowing and the situation became increasingly difficult. The kind of symbolic general strikes (lasting as little as four hours and no more than a day) which had been one of the chief instruments of pressure of the trade unions in demanding a change in economic policy, were no longer as supported as they had been until then.

Finally, the crisis had also overtaken the Christian Democratic Party. The passage from the anti-communism of Fanfani to the policy of 'national unity' had entailed the emergence of a new leadership group headed by Benigno Zaccagnini. With the failure of this group and the killing of Aldo Moro (who was Zaccagnini's main source of advice and encouragement) a new group emerged. But this group was devoid of perspectives and policies. It sought to prepare the ground for a new centre-left and to re-establish the links with the Socialist Party whose new leader, Bettino Craxi (July 1976), had done his utmost to differentiate his own party from the PCI. The kind of coalition which emerged eventually in 1980 was formally a centre-left government, but it had none of the reforming intention of its predecessor of the 1960s and was not accompanied by any of the hopes. Craxi sought to use the crisis of the Italian political system to prepare the ground for an authentic refounding of his own party, breaking decisively with the socialist tradition and challenging the DC in the centre of the political spectrum. As government succeeded government in an endless round of crises, none of the principal 'actors' was able to gain hegemonic control of political terrain.

Finally, in November 1980, after a wave of financial scandals involving the highest echelons of government, a powerful earthquake hit southern Italy causing enormous devastation and killing nearly four thousand people. Government rescue teams arrived late on the scene. Many are said to have died of cold and starvation and not under falling rubble, a sign that they could have been rescued if the machinery of government had been more efficient. The president of the Republic indicted the Italian State for its inability to cope with the situation. It was in this context that the PCI changed its political line.

It is far too early to be able to examine the extent and the implications of the change. The earthquake hit Italy on 23 November. On the morning of 27 November Berlinguer announced that the PCI was ready to form a new government without the Christian Democratic Party. This declaration has given rise to many interpretations. It has been said that the PCI had finally recognized that the 'historic compromise' was truly dead. The PCI pointed out (correctly, as it happens) that the 'historic compromise' was never intended to be a mere co-operation or alliance with the DC, but rather an alliance between the 'Communist, Socialist and Catholic masses' which would provide a basis for a government of radical reforms. The difficulty with providing an interpretation lies also in the fact that the division of opinions within the leadership group of the PCI had by then reached such an extent that different interpretations of the new line were given. It seems that for some leaders a policy of 'left-wing alternative' (that is, a coalition government of the left which would exclude the DC) would pave the way for the definitive social-democratization of the party. In fact in order to establish internal and international legitimacy such a government would have to provide even more 'guarantees' than before, for it would be bitterly opposed by the DC or, at least, by a wing of it. For others, who had never approved of the 'historic compromise' this was the opportunity for a return to a more revolutionary posture.

One thing is clear: the proposal of a left-wing government, at the time when it was expressed, had no practical application whatsoever. Not only did the PCI not have the parliamentary support, but relations with the only possible coalition partners (Socialists and Social Democrats) were greatly depressed. In taking this stand the PCI was in fact recognizing that it had encountered a great defeat and that there was no possibility of its entry into the government for the foreseeable future. In the first place, as we have stated, an alliance with the Socialist Party was not appropriate. The policies of Bettino Craxi did not allow for the construction of a stable alliance. Other parties of the left were not on particularly friendly terms with the Italian Communists. Secondly, the unassailable logic of Berlinguer's famous article on Chile, in which he explained that it was not possible to govern Italy against 50 per cent of the population was still as valid as ever. The DC would still be in control of the overwhelming majority of state apparatuses and institutions. It would be folly to think that it would be possible to reform the Italian State without having either split the DC or ensured its acquiescence: a compromise with the DC is still the only way out. Thirdly, the wave of terrorism, from both left and right, which had hit Italy since 1969 (when a bomb in a Milan bank had killed sixteen people) showed no sign of relenting. In spite of police successes, the Red Brigades and other similar organizations had been able to wage a campaign of terror which constantly threatened to destabilize the Italian political system. Nor had right-wing terrorism disappeared. In the summer of 1980 a bomb devastated Bologna train station killing eighty people. Whether or not the terrorists have been penetrated by foreign secret services (and the Italian press as well as leading politicians of various parties believe this is so), it is virtually certain that an embattled left-wing government would need the support of the overwhelming majority of the population and of the parties which organize it to wage an effective battle against the terrorists. The destabilizing element represented by the terrorists has become a divisive factor in Italian political struggle and not an instance of unification. The beginning of the end of the historic compromise was, after all, the kidnapping and the killing of Aldo Moro. Fourthly and finally, the international situation had turned for the worse for the Italian Communist Party. Three weeks before Berlinguer announced the 'new line' a new president was elected in the USA. His nostalgic anti-Communism and the platform on which he was elected made it virtually impossible for the USA to tolerate the presence of Communists in an Italian government. Obvious distinctions between a Soviet and an Italian brand of Communism would clearly be lost among Washington's leading foreign policy-makers. What is the meaning, then, of the 'new line'? A possible area of speculation is that the PCI is attempting to take the maximum distance from the present crisis of the Italian political system. It seeks to demarcate itself from all other forces, and to establish, or rather to re-establish its own identity as a revolutionary force, though not in the sense of any return to the golden age of the Comintern (the polemic against the USSR continues unabated). The PCI's 'new line' is a declaration that no one should forget that this crisis is a crisis of this system and that the PCI is not only 'in' it but that it is also a force which seeks to go beyond it, that it is the harbinger of something new. Thus it must not allow itself to become part of this crisis, for it must survive it to fight another day, because, quite clearly, it has lost the last great battle, the battle of the seventies, together with, perhaps, the other left-wing forces of Europe.

Notes

1. G. Amendola, 'Il socialismo in Occidente' in *Rinascita*, No. 44, 7 November 1964 and also 'Ipotesi sulla riunificazione', ibid., No. 47, 1964.
2. Amendola got little support from his allies in the PCI and most of the articles published in *Rinascita* were against his proposal. See in particular R. Ledda, 'La riunificazione: come e per che cosa', No. 48, 1964; Luigi Longo, 'La nostra lotta per l'unità della classe operaia e delle forze socialiste', No. 50, 1964; Lucio Magri, 'Unificazione: su qualle linea?', No. 10, 1965.
3. The intervention was published in the form of three successive articles in *Rinascita* (28 September, 5 October and 12 October 1973). An English translation appeared in *Marxism Today*, February 1974, with the title 'Reflections after the Events in Chile'.
4. 'Reflections after the Events in Chile' in *Marxism Today*, p. 41.
5. Ibid., p. 46.
6. Ibid., pp. 46–7.
7. Ibid., p. 48.
8. See in particular his speech to the Assembly of Communist Workers of Lombardy of 30 January 1977. Extracts are available in English in D. Sassoon (ed.), *The Italian Communists Speak for Themselves*, Nottingham, 1978, pp. 132–7.

Conclusion

In his report to the Tenth Congress of the PCI (1962), Togliatti observed that the general strategy of the party and its overall principles had started to develop from the Lyons Congress of 1926 to reach its clearest and most amply formulated expression in the *Dichiarazione programmatica* of 1956. He then added:

> The essential point is to understand that once the general perspective had been established it must not be forgotten nor obfuscated. Then the concrete tasks of our political practice are generated by the existing situation. This situation cannot be foreseen from a great distance in time and demands choices and solutions adequate to the situation itself.[1]

The concrete tasks are not determined by the 'general perspective' but by the 'present situation'. Here Togliatti posed the central question of the connection between the general perspective, the programmatic elements (the concrete tasks) and the real situation. This is the central question of politics. Yet if we were, as we should in this conclusion, to produce a balance-sheet of the post-war developments of Italian Communist policies, it would be difficult to avoid stating that this central question has not always been tackled in a satisfactory manner. In other words, the crucial link between 'principles' and the 'concrete' has often been absent from the practice of the party.

It is therefore not surprising that the difficult situation in which the Italian Communist Party finds itself is in part due to its inability to transform itself fully from a party of opposition to a party of government.

Of course, it is difficult to imagine an objective more difficult to achieve for a political party which does not intend to abandon its revolutionary programme: is it not, after all, on the rocks of the actual practice of government that the majority of left-wing attempts to rule have crumbled? I am not only thinking of those left-wing governments with Communist participation, such as the Popular Fronts coalition of the inter-war years and the governments of national unity of the immediate post-war period or even of analogous instances such as the Portuguese regimes of 1974–5. I am also thinking of social-democratic governments which, even after decades in power, such as the Swedish Social Democrats, have not been able to incorporate the 'general perspective' with the 'concrete tasks'. And I am also thinking of the experience of the first Soviet government, so rich in strategic perspectives and so poor in knowledge and expertise. For not only did the Bolshevik leaders lack the technical qualifications with which to resolve the problems of government of the economy and of society, but also the popular masses whom these leaders and the party were organizing did not possess that 'culture of reform' which was and remains the necessary, though not only, reason for the development of what Gramsci called a 'moral and intellectual' reform. The transformation of subordinate masses into the protagonists of history entails far more than the techniques of the 'revolution from above' whether of Stalinist or Fabian derivation. It is worth recalling the words Lenin addressed to the Fourth Congress of the Communist International when he tackled the problem of the 'great internal political crisis' in 1921:

> . . . in our economic offensive we had run too far ahead . . . we had not provided ourselves with adequate resources . . . the masses sensed what we ourselves were not then able to formulate consciously but what we admitted soon after, a few weeks later, namely, that the direct transition to purely socialist forms, to purely socialist distribution, was beyond our available strength, and that if we were unable to effect a retreat so as to confine ourselves to easier tasks, we would face disaster.[2]

And later he concluded by saying:

> Undoubtedly we have done, and will still do, a host of foolish things. No one can judge and see this better than I. Why do we do these foolish things? The reason is clear: firstly, because we are a backward country; secondly, because education in our country is at a low level; and thirdly, because we are getting no outside assistance. . . .
>
> We now have a vast army of government employees, but lack sufficiently educated forces to exercise control over them. In practice it often happens that here at the top, where we exercise political power, the machine functions somehow; but down below government employees have arbitrary control and they often exercise it in such a way as to counteract our measures. At the top, we have, I don't know how many, but at all events, I think, no more than a few thousand, at the outside several tens of thousands of our own people.[3]

It is precisely when we read Lenin's writings of the period when he was a statesman and a constructor of the Soviet State that we realize how much the problem of the government of the economy was often reduced to the question of the forms of control of the State as an instrument. The vision of the State as a mere instrument of political rule and as an apparatus was already present in the Lenin of *State and Revolution*. And this vision persists in the reports, the letters and the documents of the years after the 'rupture' of October 1917. It is difficult to avoid asking whether the failure to tackle the relation between 'general perspective' and 'concrete tasks' is not at least in part due to the very mode of posing the question: if the State is an instrument, the problem lies in discovering how to develop the knowledge and the technique of its utilization. If the State, however, is 'the ensemble of practical and theoretical activities with which a ruling class justifies and maintains its domination and also succeed in obtaining the consent of the governed', then the problem becomes more complex. In this case one must move away from the search for technical qualifications to the search for the link between scientific expertise and a political strategy of reforms.

In order not only to pose the question correctly, but also to arrive at the concrete solution the Italian Communist Party would have had, in the years of the war and its aftermath, to jump like Minerva from the brains of Zeus, i.e. already fully armed with the concepts and categories which would 'fit' the situation. But Togliatti's 'new party' was, yes, the party of Gramsci, but it was also the party of Bordiga, of Stalin, of Lenin; the party of the Second and Third International, besides being heir to a good chunk of the Italian political and intellectual tradition.

Furthermore, the process of political evolution for a party of this kind could not be a painless one, nor could it be unilinear. It had at one and the same time to abandon an aspect of its own tradition, revise another and develop a whole battery of new answers in the context of an international situation which – particularly in the period 1948–56 – was quite unfavourable, not only because of the Cold War and Christian Democratic hegemony in Italy, but also because the USSR had imposed on that party a restricted margin of movement. This was not the kind of restriction which involved, as is commonly alleged, a direct control from Moscow; but there is no doubt that the mere possibility of condemnation and excommunication would have encouraged the more sectarian elements of the PCI to develop a 'French' political line. 'Doppiezza' inside the PCI was not just a question of the Togliattian 'top' against the Stalinist 'base'. The split was right inside the top, as Pietro Secchia's diaries make it abundantly clear. But 'doppiezza' was also manifest in the fact that a political strategy alternative to the traditions of the Third International was being developed without an open process of ideological revision and without an explicit elaboration of the new alternative strategy.

In the first twenty years (1944–64) of the period we have examined, the PCI did not even begin to tackle two questions which would appear and dominate the successive years: those of 'youth' and 'women'. One should not be surprised, therefore, if, when these problems did explode they took the party by surprise and forced it to accelerate the process of revision. This had to be done in a hurry, but it was probably begun too late. The results revealed that for this hurried approach the political price the PCI had to pay was high.

These two questions could not be tackled from the point of view of the Third International, a point of view which reduces all relations to class relations. But even the PCI's strategy of alliances, though was quite different from that of the Third International, did not allow an examination of the peculiar characteristics of the 'youth' and 'women' categories. The PCI was not in a position to direct the transformation of 'social' subjects such as women and youth into 'political' subjects able to play an autonomous role in the construction of a new state.

There is no doubt that the explosion of these two questions on to the Italian political scene has caused important changes and 'revisions' in the main Italian working class party, but these changes have always occurred too late with respect to the 'explosion'. One should also add that this lateness is typical of the difficulties which Togliatti's party encountered in the course of its political development: it was late in recognizing the reorganization of Italian capitalism which fascism was about to operate towards the end of the 1920s (and hence the optimistic declaration that fascism was about to collapse as exemplified by Gramsci's report of August 1926), and late in analysing the dynamic growth of capitalism in the 1950s.

Moreover these problems concerning the elaboration of the political line were rendered even more serious by the fact that the political line itself was not always understood by the entire party and had not always been able to capture broader and broader strata of Italian opinion. It is true that this sort of criticism could be considered to be unfair because we do not, after all, have in Europe instances of political parties which have been able to comprehend with the cold lucidity required the rapid changes of the last thirty or forty years. But European political parties, on the whole, do not have the ambition of the PCI. They tend to be pure oppositional parties such as the French Communists, mediation parties (such as the Italian Christian Democrats), parliamentary parties (the Labour Party), 'opinion' parties (the British Conservatives, the French Gaullists). These parties do not need the kind of analysis and theoretical elaboration that the PCI requires, unless, of course, they intend to alter radically their mode of being in politics. For the PCI the question of establishing a political line cannot be a pure matter of the 'top'. The question (given the aim of creating a new state) of producing a political line must be connected to the development of internal democracy: the initiative from the top must be articulated with the initiative from the 'bottom'. And this process cannot remain enclosed within the party. The organization of democracy throughout society is part and parcel of the creation of a new state. It is not possible to separate these two questions, unless, of course, one thinks of the State as a mere instrument.

What used to be called the dictatorship of the proletariat has now been revised, following Gramsci, into the formula: the transformation of the working class into a leading class, a ruling class. This transition implies, as we have seen, a conception of revolution as a process. It also implies the revision of the Leninist concept of the distinction between 'bourgeois' democracy (Parliament) and 'socialist' democracy (Councils or Soviets). But is it really sufficient to define the 'Italian road' as a 'revolutionary process'? I do not think that the PCI has moved much further than that. What is necessary is to define the State forms of transition which correspond to the economic forms of transition. For instance: the PCI has declared that it does not think it suitable for Italy and Western Europe to hold the concept of socialism as a centrally planned economy, that the market must have a role, that economic planning must proceed on the basis of the existence of a private sector. But what kind of political mechanisms are necessary for this kind of planning, and what kind of democratic institutions, forms of control, decision-making and spheres of participation would guarantee the political autonomy (from the State-apparatus) of the subjects who are the protagonists? This is far from clear from a practical point of view. The general perspective is clear:

> In the formation of leaders, one premise is fundamental: is it the intention that there should always be rulers and the ruled, or is the objective to create the conditions in which this division is no longer necessary? In other words, is the initial premise the perpetual division of the human race, or the belief that this division is only a historical fact, corresponding to certain conditions?[4]

These indications, however, are only general in nature. Without a precise politico-practical elaboration with concrete contents it is not possible to position the political struggle on to the terrain of the transformation of the State. Of course, one can explain in part the 'backwardness' of the PCI by the fact that the single *practical* example of political forms of transition to socialism was that of the USSR (the 'Party-State'), an experiment which could not be repeated, and by the fact that the single *theoretical* proposal for political forms of transition was the classical Leninist one of the 'State of Councils'. The consequences of this 'backwardness' were visible in the seventies when there occurred in Italy a flowering of new elements of local democracy: factory councils, neighbourhood councils, school councils; hospital councils as well as the regions and other elements of local democracy. These could well have provided the practical basis for the 'self-government of the producers'. These institutions, however, instead of becoming the focus for political reform, only too often reproduced, locally, parliamentary politics. Thus in the period 1976–9 the kind of relations which existed between DC and PCI in Parliament were simply reproduced at the local level. The parliamentary *entente* was simply duplicated all over the country. The inability of the PCI to demarcate itself from the DC in the national assembly was reproduced at the local level.

It is necessary, at this stage, to point out how serious it has become for the PCI not to have been able to elaborate a more solid analysis of the Christian Democratic Party. It is true that there exists a solid basis for such an analysis in the cultural production of the PCI. Nevertheless, on the morrow of the great electoral victory of June 1976, the PCI, in its totality (the leaders and the led), did not have that knowledge of the opponent that would have been necessary for a more vigorous and fruitful struggle at the government level.

I have just mentioned the existence of a 'solid basis' for such an analysis. This basis has been achieved through the results of Togliatti's analysis: the refusal to consider the DC as a mere conservative party, the ability to understand the kind of connection the DC is able to establish with the masses it leads, the identification of the dual nature of the DC as the party of government of the ruling classes and the organizer from on high of broad popular strata through a specific development of the welfare state; the refusal to reduce the 'Christian Democratic question' to the 'Catholic question'; the refusal to reduce the complex reality called DC to a simple question of corruption and clienteles. One should add, however, that this solid analytical basis has not always been understood by the party (both leaders and led).

In the development of a more informed analysis of the DC we have not found anything noteworthy not even in the most recent Congress of the PCI, the Fifteenth Congress held in 1979. Of the ninety-three Theses discussed only one (No. 73) mentioned the DC, and this when the PCI was preparing itself for the general elections of 1979, difficult elections which would test the extent of the failure of the governments of national unity of 1976–9.

On the positive side, one should not fail to recognize that the PCI did not make the mistake of confusing the question of the Catholic masses with that of the DC and hence did not confuse alliance with the Catholics with alliance with the DC. Here the PCI stands well outside the 'third force' ideology (which did penetrate wide areas of the Socialist Party), which saw, and still sees, the tight grip of Catholicism on a large part of the Italian population as yet another expression of Italian backwardness. After all one of the elements that explains the rise to political hegemony in thirty years of Italian history of the DC was precisely the fact that this party was able to appear as the principal guarantor of and the organizing force behind the ideals and aspirations of the Catholic masses. This embodies not only the fruits of the political intelligence of leaders such as Sturzo and De Gasperi: it is also the result of the inability of the leading forces of the Italian Risorgimento to incorporate the Catholic masses into a new power bloc.

Most of Italian history from the end of the Risorgimento to fascism is also the story of the 'non-solution' of the Catholic question. In the post-war period the Catholic question amalgamates with the question of Christian Democracy. But the two must be kept separate. To do otherwise, to put in the same basket religious ideals and political practice would have entailed the acceptance of the equation: political line (or strategy) = ideological line. To consider Catholicism on the same plane as Christian Democratic policies would be to mix up ideological level with political level, that is, to transform politics as an effect of ideology. This theoretical mistake has long been part of the Communist tradition and was also characteristic of the Second International. According to these traditions the revolutionary party was revolutionary not so much by virtue of its political line but rather by virtue of the particular theory which guided it. This theory was Marxism understood as a monolithic *corpus*, as a logic of history and, naturally, as *the* revolutionary theory, that is, an invariant truth from which any departure would be, *ipso facto*, a revision and hence a betrayal. The correctness of a political line could thus be judged in terms of the proximity of the party's position to the doctrine. The revolutionary party had to be the 'Marxist' party.

It follows that to separate Catholicism from Christian Democracy poses the question of the relation between theory and strategy. To suggest that it is perfectly possible for a Catholic not to be a Christian Democrat is in fact only the pre-condition for saying (as was said) that a Catholic can be a Communist and hence a Communist is not necessarily a Marxist. This separation between ideological forms and politics is the basis for the 'lay' conception of politics of the PCI. The struggle to 'laicize' or 'secularize' the party has the effect of 'liberating' theory from too close a relationship with politics (and vice versa).

This authentic conquest was not an easy one. From the point of view of the Party Statute it was only in 1979 that clause 5b was amended. This clause, while keeping membership open regardless of philosophical position, put the following obligation on the party member: 'to deepen his/her knowledge of Marxism–Leninism and to apply the teachings to the solution of concrete questions'. Now the clause has been deleted and so have all references to Marxism–Leninism. But well before then, even in the years of the Resistance, the only conditions imposed on the prospective member was adherence to the programme of the party, not to its ideology. The 'lay' nature of the party is not only manifested in its independence from a determinate theoretical school (which, obviously, does not mean that the political practice of the party bears no relation to theory), but also in its independence from the State and from the mass organizations which are formed in civil society. The party is not the State, it is not even the potential State of tomorrow nor is it the 'anti-State'.

In the course of this work we have often suggested that one of the differences between the PCI and the CPSU lies in the former's rejection of any identification of party and State, which is the hallmark of the Soviet conception. We should now add that, in so doing, the PCI also distinguishes itself from the Christian Democratic practice of the management of State power. This distinction appears in the period of the Resistance, that is, even before the Christian Democratic Party was to begin its own process of identification and 'take-over' of the Italian State. To illustrate how this distinction was expressed we shall use some documents dealing with the relation between the Communist trade unionist Di Vittorio and socialist and Catholic trade unionists. The documentation is made up of a number of reports addressed by Di Vittorio to the leadership of the PCI. The period in question is the first quarter of 1944. The subject is the constitution of a new Italian trade union system. It appears that the position of the Socialist trade union leader Buozzi and the Catholic leader, Giovanni Gronchi, was that the future trade union confederation would have had to obtain the legal recognition of the State, that membership in it would have to be compulsory for all workers and that all dues would have to be withheld directly from the wage packet by the employers. Buozzi, in particular, stressed the practical and technical advantages of this system:

the new trade union confederation would thus be able to penetrate 'in every small locality and in every village where before fascism there was no trade union and in which fascist unions could penetrate precisely because they were compulsory'.[5]

To this argument Di Vittorio replied proposing the following principles: 'Free trade unions; democratic basis; independence from the State and from all influences external to the working class; no compulsion in membership or in payment of dues.' And at a later meeting he explained:

A trade union whose membership is made compulsory by the State (a bourgeois state, even if democratic) is a bureacratic organism, necessarily dependent on the same State, devoid of any class content, spirit of initiative, a heavy structure, which may well have lots of money, many offices, many functionaries, but which will be despised by the working class as the fascist trade unions were despised. We, who have a *class* position, we Socialists and Communists, we must want a trade union movement which is a class organism within which can be realized the unity of the entire working class, an organism which can become a formidable instrument of struggle for the entire working class. To achieve this task the trade union must be free in the highest sense, it must be free from the State, it must be able to have freedom of initiative and of action.[6]

To Gronchi, who asked him what relations should there be between trade unions and the State, Di Vittorio answered:

In our view it must be a relation of total independence. This does not mean that the working class can be indifferent or agnostic when faced with the problems of the State or of government. Twenty years of fascism have convinced all workers – whatever their political or religious differences – that they cannot be indifferent to whether the State is democratic or reactionary.[7]

It appears here that ever since the days of the Resistance Italian Communists were constructing and defending those pluralistic elements which would be characteristics of post-war Italy. The 'new party' thus emerged from the ruins of fascism stressing in its 'lay' nature its most novel element. If, on the one hand, there can be no doubt as to the positive long-term effects of such 'conquest' not only for the PCI but for the whole of Italian society, on the other hand, one should not forget that this 'conquest', as all others, was not an easy one, nor could it be complete, nor could it be definitive. What has been called 'doppiezza' has continued to play its role in the strategy of the PCI. Moreover, 'doppiezza' is not totally absent, not even from the position of Di Vittorio. There is still a suspicion that when Di Vittorio demands autonomy from the State he thinks only of autonomy from that particular State, which he calls 'a bourgeois State, even if democratic'. What was going to become increasingly necessary was to ensure that the entire party and the masses organized by this party were fully conscious that there could not be two separate historical moments: before and after the revolution. A vision of politics as a 'two-stages' operation would in fact entail an instrumental conception of the demands of the labour movement and a renunciation of the possibility and the necessity of introducing elements of socialism in the existing social order. It would imply acceptance of the obsolete Leninist perspective which separates bourgeois democracy from socialist democracy. It would force the labour movement into a situation of 'wait and see'. Its strategy would become a series of tactical moves whose only purpose would be to maximize one's electoral chances and one's organizational capabilities in the expectation of the Great Moment, of the Decisive Phase, of the final transition from a society where everything is exploitation and oppression to that of peace, freedom and socialism.

There is no doubt that such messianic expectations and the Utopian fervour which underpins it have had a role, at times even a positive one, in the history of the labour movement. It seems to me, however, that in the present phase of the crisis of the 'enlarged State', of the 'Welfare State', this sort of mentality rather reflects the subordinate role to which, historically, the working class has been relegated. It is only in formulating a clearly political project of transition in which it is possible to think about, in the short-term as well, the elements of socialism which it is possible to introduce and which must be introduced because they are really needed (not because ideology dictates) that the working classes can reach that hegemonic position, that role of being a 'national' class that Gramsci was thinking of when, from the depths of his prison cell, he meditated on the historical defeat of the working class.

The political price to be paid is very high for those who are not able to conduct their political struggle at a level commensurate to their historical ambition (for a Communist party, the abolition of capitalist exploitation). This price is much higher than that paid by those Social Democratic Parties for whom a more just management of capitalism is now the greatest aspiration of an ever-narrowing political horizon. For these, after all, defeat is essentially electoral defeat. For a party such as the PCI the price is higher. Defeat can in fact entail the necessity to entrench itself into a 'castle of purity' which perhaps cannot be taken over but from which it is difficult to escape. This is akin to political elimination not in the physical sense, as it would be under a dictatorial regime, but in the sense that it ceases to matter as a political force. It can cease to exist as many Communist Parties have ceased to exist in many Third World countries because they have been unable to develop their own autonomous project of political transition.

But defeat can have other forms for a Communist party. Defeat can come under the guise of victory. I am thinking of the 'victories' of the Communist Parties of so many Eastern European countries. These victories were gained thanks to the external intervention of a foreign army and what that entailed was the imitation of a model of transition which was as 'external' as the Army which brought it about.

There can be yet another kind of defeat. It is a defeat which bears a resemblance to victory, for it is a formal victory. The product of a successful 'passive revolution' of the opponent, this victory consists of the acquisition of a long sought-after legitimization in exchange for becoming what used to be called 'the alternative party of the bourgeoisie'. This is the kind of 'victory-defeat' which threatens the Italian Communist Party. And it is also the kind of strategy that the opponent seems to have adopted, at least since the first half of the 1970s without, of course, giving up the possibility of using other strategies.

These considerations pose the question, amply debated in the press and in various more or less cultural circles, of the eventual social democratization of the PCI. Here we are presented with a little formula which, in spite of its superficiality, contains a basic truth: Communist Parties have come about through a fundamental choice on a historical event of enormous magnitude: the Bolshevik revolution and the Leninist principles which inspired it. To abandon Leninism is tantamount to putting into question this choice and returning along the road which had been abandoned when the Third International was created. It means, in other words, to return to the arms of social democracy.

It is, as we have said, a superficial formula because it does no more than pose once again the old question of the obligatoriness of the alternative between Soviet model and social democracy. This question can be brutal: Lenin or Kautsky?

One could simply answer by saying that the Italian Communist Party is well beyond both Kautsky and Lenin, if for no other reason than that the international political system and the modern state cannot be understood simply by using the cultural reference points of the two greatest theoreticians of the working class movement of the first twenty years of this century. There remains the question, which cannot be avoided, of whether the PCI and its intellectual tradition as it appears at the beginning of the 1980s bears more affinity to the Leninist tradition even while it recuperates some aspects of the social democratic tradition. A hurried answer could point out that the crux of Leninism, the central element which demarcates it from the entire Kautskyist tradition and from social democracy as it has evolved, lies in the question of the State. Even in *State and Revolution*, a text where the instrumental conception Lenin had of democracy appears in its most accomplished and vivid form, the theoretician of Communism posed as the central element of Marxism the notion that the phase of socialist transition can only be entered into by elaborating a new form of state. This notion does not exist in Kautsky. And it does not exist in any of the Social Democratic Parties (nor does it exist in many European Communist Parties, particularly among those who stress their commitment to the 'Leninist oath'). For Kautsky and European social democracy the road towards socialism is entered into not by elaborating a new form of state but by the conquest of a majority in Parliament and by giving a socialist content to parliamentary legislation. Socialism comes from the State, it does not change it. The struggle for democracy is reduced to a struggle to maintain the parliamentary form of democracy. The 'Kautskyian' way to socialism means possession of the state apparatus through Parliament and socialist leglislation. Thus in Kautskyism democracy means parliamentary democracy and socialism means socialist legislation or, and that is the same thing, the socialist will of the parliamentary representatives of the socialist party. Thus, in Kautsky, the intimate connection between socialism and democracy is broken. We are faced with two different levels. The first level — that of democracy — refers to the state-apparatus. The second level — that of socialism — refers to the political contents of the laws.

It seems to me that Communist politics in the period we have examined has not much to do with this narrow vision of the transition to socialism. The themes of structural reforms, progressive democracy, elements of socialism and historic compromise (at least in Berlinguer's interpretation) have not much to do, except perhaps from the formal point of view, with Kautsky's vision. But it is here necessary to clarify one final point: the question ('Lenin or Kautsky'?) as it is posed is a highly formalistic one. In fact there is no such a thing as a Leninist model or a Kautskyist one. It is not possible to take texts which are the product of a determinate historical process and the result of a determinate political struggle and then, through a process of abstraction, raise them to the level of 'models' and use them to judge the politics of another party, of other leaders, of another country, in different conditions and in a different epoch. This theoretico-political 'Supreme Tribunal' treats theory not as if its task were to enable us to understand the world, but as if it should permit us to give a moral judgement. In this way theory loses all autonomy. It is used only as a 'control instrument' of politics: its purpose, in this case, is that of enabling us to decide whether a political strategy is correct or erroneous according to how far it situates itself from the theoretical model we have, *a priori*, adopted.

We could add that this view of the relation between theory and politics is not that far removed from a Stalinist practice, if behind all that there were not a historicist practice which precedes by a long stretch Stalin's Russia.

Notes

1. P. Togliatti, *Opere scelte*, pp. 1071–2.
2. V. I. Lenin, *Collected Works*, vol. 33, pp. 421–2.
3. Ibid., p. 428.
4. A. Gramsci, *Selections from the Prison Notebooks*, London, 1971, p. 144.
5. M. Pistillo, *Di Vittorio 1924–1944*, Rome, 1975, p. 235.
6. Ibid., pp. 235 and 249.
7. Ibid., pp. 240–1.

Bibliography

International Meeting of Communist and Workers Parties, Moscow, 1969.

'La politica di Corbino', *Rinascita*, No. 8, August 1946.

'Nuovo corso', *Rinascita*, No. 9, September 1946.

'Sulla nostra politica', *Rinascita*, No. 9–10, September–October 1948.

'Panorama dell'VIII Congresso', *Rinascita*, No. 12, December 1956.

'Problemi del dibattito tra i partiti comunisti', *Critica Marxista*, No. 4, July–August 1963.

AA.VV., *Trent'anni di vita e di lotte del PCI, Quaderno No. 2 di Rinascita*, Rome, Riuniti, 1952.

AA.VV., *Documenti della conferenza di 81 partiti comunisti e operai*, Rome, Riuniti, 1960.

AA.VV., *Il Partito comunista italiano e il movimento operaio internazionale*, Rome, Riuniti, 1968.

AA.VV., *Problemi di storia del PCI*, Rome, Riuniti, 1971.

AA.VV., *Italia 1945–1950, Ricostruire, ma come?, Giovane Critica*, No. 34, 35, 36, Spring 1973.

AA.VV., *I comunisti a Torino, 1919–1972*, Rome, Riuniti, 1974.

Allum, P. A., *Politics and Society in Post-War Naples*, Cambridge, CUP, 1973.

Amendola, G., 'Cause e pericoli dei legami unitari tra comunisti e socialisti', *Rinascita*, No. 1, January 1958.

Amendola, G., *Lotta di classe e sviluppo economico dopa la Liberazione*, Rome, Riuniti, 1962.

Amendola, G., 'Unità e autonomia della classe operaia', *Critica Marxista*, No. 1, January–February 1963.

Amendola, G., 'Movimento e organizzazione delle masse', *Critica Marxista*, No. 5–6, September–December 1963.

Amendola, G., 'Il monopolio nemico principale nel quadro della azione anticapitalista', *Rinascita*, No. 12, 21 March 1964.

Amendola, G., 'Il socialismo in Occidente', *Rinascita*, No. 44, 7 November 1964.

Amendola, G., 'Ipotesi sulla riunificazione', *Rinascita*, No. 47, 28 November 1964.

Amendola, G., 'Insegnamenti del VII Congresso dell'Ic (Rileggendo Dimitrov)', *Critica Marxista*, No. 4, July–August 1965.

Amendola, G., 'L'avvento della repubblica', *Critica Marxista*, No. 2, March–April 1966.

Amendola, G., 'Analisi e prospettive politiche in un documento del 1941 riveduto da Togliatti', *Critica Marxista*, No. 1, January–February 1968.

Amendola, G., 'Venticinque anni dopo lo scioglimento dell'internazionale comunista', *Critica Marxista*, No. 4–5, July–October 1968.

Amendola, G., 'Il balzo nel Mezzogiorno (1943–1953)', in *Quaderno No. 5 di Critica Marxista, Storia, politica, organizzazione nella lotta dei comunisti italiani per un nuovo blocco storico*, 1971.

Amendola, G., *Lettere a Milano*, Rome, Riuniti, 1973.

Amendola, G., 'Il limiti dell'antifascismo' in *Quaderno No. 7 di Critica Marxista, Il 1943 — Le origini della rivoluzione antifascista*, 1974.

Amendola, G., 'La rottura della coalizione tripartita', *Il Mulino*, No. 235, September–October 1974.

Amendola, G., 'Riflessioni su una esperienza di governo del PCI (1944–1947)', *Storia Contemporanea*, No. 4, December 1974.

Amendola, G., *Intervista sull'antifascismo*, Rome–Bari, Laterza, 1976.

Amendola, G., *Una scelta di vita*, Milan, Rizzoli, 1976.

Amendola, G., *Il Rinnovamento del partito*, Rome, Riuniti, 1978.

Anderson, P., 'Introduction to the Debate of the CC of the Italian Communist Party on the 22nd Congress of the CPSU', *New Left Review*, No. 13–14, January–April 1962.

Apter, D., and Eckstein, H. (eds.), *Comparative Politics*, New York, The Free Press, 1963.

Barca, L., 'Per un programma di sviluppo economico', *Rinascita*, No. 6, June 1959.

Barca, L., 'I partiti e la programmazione', *Critica Marxista*, No. 2, March–April 1964.

Barca, L., Botta, F., and Zevi, A., *I comunisti e l'economia italiana 1944–1974*, Bari, De Donato, 1975.

Berlinguer, E., 'Lo studio del partito in rapporto alla modificazioni della società italiana', *Critica Marxista*, No. 5–6, September–December 1963.

Berlinguer, E., 'Reflections after the Events in Chile', *Marxism Today*, February 1974.

Berlinguer, E., *La Questione Comunista*, 2 vols., Rome, Riuniti, 1975.

Bertolo, G., Curti, R., Guerrini, L., 'Aspetti della questione agraria e delle lotte contadine nel secondo dopoguerra', *Italia Contemporanea*, No. 117, October–December 1974.

Blackmer, D. L. M., *Unity and Diversity: Italian Communism and the Communist World*, Cambridge, Mass., and London, M.I.T. Press, 1968.

Bocca, G., *Palmiro Togliatti*, Rome–Bari, Laterza, 1973.

Bocca, S. (ed.), *Le baronie elettriche*, Bari, 1960.

Braunthal, J., *History of the International 1914–1943*, London, Thomas Nelson and Sons, 1966.

Brewster, B., 'Communication', *New Left Review*, No. 70, November–December 1971.

Broadhead, H. S., 'Togliatti and the Church 1921–1948', *The Australian Journal of Politics and History*, No. 1, April 1972.

Caforno, G. (ed.), 'Il dibattito al X Plenum della Terza Internazionale sulla social democrazia, il fascismo e il social-fascismo', *Critica Marxista*, No. 4, July–August 1965.

Caracciolo, A., 'Il centralismo democratico e la vita interna dei partiti operai', *Società*, No. 6, November–December 1956.

Chiarante, G., 'Possibilità e limiti della "sinistra cattolica" ', *Rinascita*, No. 4, April 1959.

Chiarante, G., 'Limiti e equivoci nel dibattito sulla programmazione', *Critica Marxista*, No. 2, March–April 1963.

Chiarante, G., 'L'Enciclica, i comunisti e il laicato cattolico', *Critica Marxista*, No. 3, May–June 1963.

Chiarante, G., 'La crisi di egemonia riversata sul potere', *Rinascita*, No. 21, 25 May 1973.

Claudin, F., *The Communist Movement. From Comintern to Cominform*, Harmondsworth, Penguin, 1975.

Colletti, L., 'Antonio Gramsci e la rivoluzione in Italia', *La Sinistra*, No. 1, October 1966.

Colletti, L., 'The Question of Stalin', *New Left Review*, No. 61, May–June 1970.

Coppola, A., 'Profilo di Fanfani', *Rinascita*, No. 25, 22 June 1973.

Cortesi, L., 'Alcuni problemi della storia del PCI', *Rivista Storica del socialismo*, No. 24, 1965.

D'Agostini, F., 'Il rapporto partiti-sindacati', *Rinascita*, No. 1, 3 January 1975.

250   *Bibliography*

Daneo, C., *La politica economica della ricostruzione 1945-1949*, Turin, Einaudi, 1975.

Daniels, R. V., *A Documentary History of Communism*, 2 vols., New York, Vintage, 1960.

D'Antonio, M., *Sviluppo e crisi del capitalismo italiano (1951-1972)*, Bari, De Donato, 1973.

De Clementi, A., 'La politica del PC d'I nel 1921-22 e il rapporto Bordiga–Gramsci', *Rivista Storica del Socialismo*, No. 28 (Part I) and No. 29 (Part II), 1966.

De Felice, F., *Serrati, Bordiga, Gramsci e il problema della rivoluzione in Italia 1919-1920*, Bari, De Donato, 1971.

De Felice, F., 'Togliatti e la costruzione del paritto nuovo nel Mezzogiorno', paper presented at the *Convegno di studi su Togliatti e il Mezzogiorno*, Bari, 2-4 November 1975 (*mimeo*).

Degas, J. (ed.), *The Communist International 1919-1943*, vol. 3., London, R.I.I.A. 1965.

Degli Espinosa, A., 'Sviluppi e prospettive del Piano del Laboro', *Società*, No. 3, 1950.

Del Carria, R., *Proletari senza rivoluzione*, Milan, Edizione Oriente, 1965.

Della Volpe, G., 'Sulla dialettica. Una risposta a compagni e agli altri', *Rinascita*, No. 19, 15 September 1962.

De Rosa, G., *Il Partito popolare italiano*, Rome–Bari, Laterza, 1972.

Dimitrov, G., *For the Unity of the Working Class Against Fascism*, London, Red Star Press, 1973.

Di Vittorio, G., 'L'industria italiana e il piano del lavoro', *Rinascita*, No. 6, June 1950.

Di Vittorio, G., 'Nuovo prospettive della unità sindacale in Italia', *Rinascita*, No. 10, October 1956.

Djilas, M., *Conversations with Stalin*, Harmondsworth, Penguin, 1962.

Faenza, R., and Fini, M., *Gli americani in Italia*, Milan, Feltrinelli, 1976.

Ferrara, M., and Ferrara, M., *Conversando con Togliatti,* Rome, Edizioni di Cultura Sociale, 1953.

Ferrara, M., 'A un anno dal XX Congresso. Ricerche e discussioni nel movimento operaio internazionale', *Rinascita*, No. 4, April 1957.

Ferrara, M., 'Dagli appunti di lavoro del direttore di "Rinascita" ', *Rinascita*, No. 27, 5 July 1974.

Fuà, G., *Notes on Italian Economic Growth 1861-1964*, Milan, Giuffrè, 1965.

Fuà, G., and Sylos-Labini, P., *Idee per la programmazione economica*, Bari, Laterza, 1963.

Galante, S., (ed.), *La politica del PCI e il Patto Atlantico*, Padua, 1973.

Galli, G., 'The Italian CP. The Road Toward a Dilemma', *Problems of Communism*, No. 3, 1956.

Galli, G., *La Sinistra italiana nel dopoguerra*, Bologna, Il Mulino, 1958.

Galli, G., *Storia del PCI*, Milan, Ed. Il Formichiere, 1976.

Gambino, A., *Storia del Dopoguerra. Dalla Liberazione al potere DC*, Rome–Bari, Laterza, 1975.

Gavarini, S., 'Gli anni '50 alla FIAT: un'esperienza storica', *Politica e economia*, No. 2, September–October 1970.

Gavarini, S., 'La Restaurazione capitalistica (1948-1955)', in AA.VV. *I Comunisti a Torino 1919-1972*, Rome, Riuniti, 1974.

Gerratana, V., 'La teoria marxista dello Stato e la via italiana al socialismo', *Rinascita*, No. 8-9, August–September 1956.

Gerratana, V., 'Forme e contenuti della democrazia nei partiti politici italiani', *Critica Marxista*, No. 5-6, September–December 1963.

Ghini, C., *Il voto degli italiani 1946-74*, Rome, Riuniti, 1975.

Giolitti, A., *Riforme e rivoluzione*, Turin, Einaudi, 1957.

Giolitti, A., *Un socialismo possibile*, Turin, Einaudi, 1967.

Gramsci, A., *Scritti giovanili 1914-1918*, Turin, Einaudi, 1958.

Gramsci, A., *La quistione meridionale*, Rome, Riuniti, 1970.

Gramsci, A., *Selections from the Prison Notebooks*, London, Lawrence and Wishart 1971.

Gramsci, A., *Selections from Political Writings 1910-1920*, London, Lawrence and Wishart, 1977.

Grieco, R., 'Prospettive della riforma agraria', *Rinascita*, No. 11-12, November–December 1947.

Grieco, R., *Introduzione alla riforma agraria*, Turin, Einaudi, 1949.

Grieco, R., *I comunisti e la lotta per la riforma agraria*, Rome, Centro di documentatione sociale, 1949.

Grieco, R., *Problemi di politica agraria*, Rome, 1950.

Gruppi, L., 'Un nodo: il 1947', *Rinascita*, No. 5, 29 January 1971.

Gruppi, L., *Il concetto di egemonia in Gramsci*, Rome, Riuniti, 1972.

Gruppi, L., *Togliatti e la via italiana al socialismo*, Rome, Riuniti, 1974.

Gullo, F., 'Suggerimenti per una riforma agraria', *Rinascita*, No. 12, December 1945.

Hobsbawm, E. J., 'Forty Years of Popular Front Government', *Marxism Today*, July 1976.

Hongqi editorial board (Red Flag), *More on the Differences Between Comrade Togliatti and Us*, Peking, 1963.

Ingrao, P., 'La democrazia interna l'unità e la politica dei comunisti', *Rinascita*, No. 5-6, May–June 1956.

Ingrao, P., 'Il problema dell'unità della classe operaia nella attuale situazione politica', *Rinascita*, No. 5, May 1958.

Ingrao, P. 'La crisi degli istituti rapprensentativi e la lotta per una nuova democrazia', *Critica Marxista*, No. 3, May–June 1963.

Ingrao, P., 'Democrazia socialista e democrazia interna di partito', *Rinascita*, No. 17, 25 April 1964.

Ingrao, P. 'Risposta a Lombardi', *Rinascita*, No. 21, 23 May 1964.

Ingrao, P., 'Discussione e ricerca dell'unita', *Rinascita*, No. 27, 4 July 1964.

Ingrao, P., 'Sistema di potere e tipo di sviluppo economico industriale', *Rinascita*, No. 21, 25 May 1973.

Ingrao, P., *Masse e potere*, Rome, Riuniti, 1977.

Istituto Gramsci, *Tendenze del capitalismo italiano, Atti del Convegno del 23-25 Marzo 1962*, Rome, Riuniti, 1962.

Istituto Gramsci, *Programmazione economica e rinnovamento democratico, Atti del Convegno del 14-15 Marzo 1963*, Rome, Riuniti, 1963.

John XXIII, *Mater et Magistra*, Rome, 1961.

John XXIII, *Pacem in Terris*, Rome, 1963.

Jotti, N., 'Il nostra incontro con i cattolici sui principi base della Costituzione', *Critica Marxista*, No. 4-6, September–December 1966.

Kirchheimer, O., 'The Party in Mass Society', *World Politics*, October 1957–July 1958.

Khruschev, N. S., 'Rapporto al XX Congresso del PCUS', *Rinascita*, No. 2, February 1956.

Kogan, N., 'National Communism vs. National Way to Communism – An Italian Interpretation', *Western Political Quarterly*, No. 3, September 1958.

Kogan, N., *A Political History of Post-War Italy*, New York, Praeger, 1966.

Lanzardo, L., *Classe operaia e partito comunista all FIAT La strategia della collaborazione, 1945-1949*, Turin, Einaudi, 1971.

La Palombara, J., 'Left-Wing Trade Unionism: the Matrix of Communist Power in Italy', *Western Political Quarterly*, No. 2, June 1954.

Ledda, R., 'La riunificazione: come e per che cosa', *Rinascita*, No. 48, 5 December 1964.

Lenin, V. I., *Collected Works*, London, Lawrence and Wishart, vol. 33.

Leonardi, S., 'Schema di interpretazione dello sviluppo italiano in questo dopoguerra', *Critica Marxista*, No. 4–5, July–October 1968.

Lepre, A., *Dal crollo del fascismo alla egemonia moderata*, Naples, Guida, 1974.

Longo, L., 'Costruendo il socialismo si son fatti degli errori, ma la vostra non è democrazia', *Rinascita*, No. 3, March 1956.

Longo, L., *Revisionismo nuovo e antico*, Turin, Einaudi, 1957.

Longo, L., 'Osservazioni sulle alleanze della classe operaia nella lotta contro i monopoli', *Rinascita*, No. 4, April 1957.

Longo, L., 'La nostra lotta per l'unità della classe operaia e delle forze socialiste', *Rinascita*, No. 50, 1964.

Longo, L., *I centri dirigenti del PCI nella Resistenza*, Rome, Riuniti, 1973.

Longo, L., 'Dal dialogo tra Roma e Milano alla insurrezione', *Rinascita*, No. 35, 7 September 1973.

Lutz, V., *Italy – A Study in Economic Development*, London, OUP, 1962.

McKenzie, R. T., *British Political Parties*, London, Mercury Books, 1963.

Magri, L., 'Problemi della teoria marxista del partito rivoluzionario', *Critica Marxista*, No. 5–6, September–December 1963. English translation: 'Problems of the Marxist Theory of the Revolutionary Party', *New Left Review*, No. 60, 1970.

Magri, L., 'Unificazione: su quale linea?', *Rinascita*, No. 10, 6 March 1965.

Magri, L., 'Il valore e i limiti delle esperienze frontiste', *Critica Marxista*, No. 4, July–August 1965.

Napoleoni, C., and Rodano, F., 'Significato e prospettive di una tregua salariale', *Rivista trimestrale*, No. 10, June 1964.

Natoli, A., 'Il dibattito sul XX Congresso nella federazione di Roma', *Rinascita*, No. 5–6, May–June 1956.

Natoli, A., 'Potere operaio e libertà democratiche', *Rinascita*, No. 10, October 1956.

Natta, A., and Pajetta, G. C., 'Il centralismo democratico nella elaborazione e nell' esperienze dei comunisti italiani', *Critica Marxista*, No. 5–6, September–December 1963.

Onofri, F., 'In terma di conquista della maggioranza e di alleanze di classe', *Rinascita*, No. 11–12, November–December 1954.

Onofri, F., 'Un innamissibile attacco alla politica del PCI', *Rinascita*, No. 7, July 1956.

Onofri, F., *Classe operaia e partito*, Bari, Laterza, 1957.

Orfei, R., *L'occupazione del potere. I democristiani'45/'75*, Milan, Feltrinelli, 1976.

Pajetta, G. C., 'Alle origini del partito nuovo', *Rinascita*, No. 35, 7 September 1973.

PCI, *La politica dei comunisti dal quinto al sesto congresso*, Rome (n.d.).

PCI, *Documenti per il VI Congresso nazionale del PCI*, Rome, 1947.

PCI, *Il VII Congresso del PCI. Resoconto*, Rome, 1951.

PCI, *VII Congresso nazionale del PCI. Documenti politici di organizzazioni democratiche di massa*, Rome, 1954.

PCI, *Documenti per l'VIII Congresso del PCI. Un partito più forte e rinnovato*, supplement to *Voce comunista*, No. 38, 4 October 1956.

PCI, *VIII Congresso del Partito comunista italiano. Atti e risoluzioni*, Rome, Riuniti, 1957.

PCI, *Risoluzione del comitato direttivo della federazione Milanese*, 15 October 1956.

PCI, 'Debate of the CC of the Italian CP on the XXII Congress of the CPSU', in *New Left Review*, No. 13–14, January–April 1962.

PCI, *X Congresso. Atti e risoluzioni*, Rome, Riuniti, 1963.

PCI, *La politica economica italiana 1945-1974. Orientamenti e proposte dei comunisti*, Rome (n.d.).

PCI, XIII Congresso, *Atti e risoluzioni*, Rome, Riuniti, 1969.

Pecchiolo, U., 'Le forze democratiche e l'Europa del Mec', *Critica Marxista*, No. 3, 1966.

Peggio, E. 'Aspetti della politica economica italiana dal 1961 ad oggi', *Critica Marxista*, No. 4–5, July–October 1964.
Peggio, E., *Capitalismo italiano anni '70*, Rome, Riuniti, 1970.
Pepe, A., 'La CGIL dalla ricostruzione alla scissione (1944–48)', *Storia contemporanea*, No. 4, December 1974.
Pesenti, A., 'Sul "capitale finanziario" ', *Critica Marxista*, No. 3, May–June 1963.
Pillon, C., *I comunisti e il sindacato*, Cinisello Balsamo, Palazzi, 1972.
Pinzani, C., 'Togliatti e l'Unione sovietica', *Rinascita*, No. 15, 11 April 1975.
Pistillo, *Di Vittorio 1924–1944*, Rome, Riuniti, 1975.
Portelli, H., *Gramsci et la question réligieuse*, Paris, Editions Antropos, 1974.
Poulantzas, N., *Fascism and Dictatorship*, London, New Left Books, 1974.
Pozzolini, A., *Che cosa ha veramente detto Togliatti*, Rome, Ubaldini, 1970.
Quercioli, E., 'Validità e attualità del decentramento organizzativo del PCI', *Critica Marxista*, No. 1, January–February 1969.
Ragionieri, E., *Palmiro Togliatti, aspetti di una battaglia ideale e politica*, Rome, Riuniti, 1966.
Ragionieri, E., 'Dalla "Grande alleanza" alla "guerra fredda" ', *Critica Marxista*, No. 2, March–April 1968.
Ragionieri, E., 'Il PCI nella Resistenza: la nascita del "partito nuovo" ', *Studi Storici*, No. 1, January–March 1969.
Ragionieri, E., 'I comunisti nella Resistenza' in L. Valiani, G. Bianchi, E. Ragionieri, *Azionisti cattolici e comunisti nella Resistenza*, Milan, Franco Angeli, 1971.
Ragionieri, E., *Palmiro Togliatti*, Rome, Riuniti, 1973.
Ragionieri, E., *Palmiro Togliatti e il VII Congresso dell'Ic*, pamphlet of the educational division of the PCI, Rome, 1973.
Ragionieri, E., Pinzani, C., *La Storia d'Italia*, vol. 4, tome 3, Turin, Einaudi, 1976.
Ravera, C., *Diario di Trent'anni 1913–1943*, Rome, Riuniti, 1973.
Reale, E., *Nascita del Cominform*, Milan, 1958.
Reichlin, A., 'Legame organico tra L'integralismo clericale e l'odierno capitalismo italiano', *Rinascita*, No. 10–11, November–December 1957.
Reichlin, A., 'Il "riformismo" integralista di Fanfani, prodotto di una crisi della politica D.C. e strumento di un regime clericale', *Rinascita*, No. 8, August 1958.
Reichlin, A., 'Puo la DC mantenere l'attuale base di massa?', *Rinascita*, No. 4, April 1959.
Reichlin, A., 'Aspetti della politica unitaria col Psi', *Critica Marxista*, No. 4, July–August 1963.
Reichlin, A., 'Il Pci e l'Europa', *Rinascita*, No. 30, 25 July 1975.
'Remin Ribao' (People's Daily) editorial, *The Differences between Comrade Togliatti and Us*, 31 December 1962, Peking, 1963.
Rodano, F., 'Il "nuovo corso" ', *Rinascita*, No. 10, October 1946.
Rodano, F., 'Il piano Marshall e l'Italia', *Rinascita*, No. 3, March 1948.
Rossanda, R., 'Note sul rapporto riforme–rivoluzione nella elaborazione del PCI', *Critica Marxista*, No. 2, March–April 1963.
Rossanda, R., 'Appunti per una discussione sugli intelletuali e il partito', *Rinascita*, No. 11, 14 March 1964.
Salvati, M., 'The impasse of Italian Capitalism', *New Left Review*, No. 76, November–December 1972.
Sansone, V., 'La prima testimonianza diretta sui sanguinosi episodi', *L'Unità*, 1 July 1956.
Saraceno, P. (ed.), *L'economia italiana dal 1861 al 1961*, Milan, Giuffrè, 1961.
Saraceno, P. (ed.), *L'Italia verso la piena occupazione*, Milan, Giuffrè, 1963.
Sassoon, D. (ed.), *The Italian Communists speak for themselves*, Nottingham, Spokesman, 1978.
Scoccimarro, M., 'Dottrina marxista e politica comunista', *Rinascita*, No. 5-6, 1945.

Scoccimarro, M., 'Nazionalizzazione e controllo democratico', *Rinascita*, No. 3, March 1959.

Scoppola, P., 'De Gasperi e la svolta politica del maggio 1947', *Il Mulino*, No. 231, January–February 1974.

Secchia, P., 'L'organizzazione, la voce, il volto del partito comunista nel nostro paese', *Rinascita*, No. 11–12, November–December 1954.

Secchia, P., 'La Resistenza: grandezza e limiti oggettivi', *Rinascita*, No. 8, 19 February 1971.

Secchia, P., *Il Partito comunista italiano e la guerra di liberazione 1943–1945*, Milan, Feltrinelli, 1973.

Sereni, E., 'Nuovi obiettivi e forme di lotta', *Rinascita*, No. 11–12, November–December 1947.

Sereni, E., *Il Mezzogiorno all' opposizione*, Turin, Einaudi, 1948.

Sereni, E., 'Democrazia e socialismo nella rivoluzione italiana', *Rinascita*, No. 3, March 1957.

Sereni, E., 'Gli obiettivi di lotta dei contadini italiani contro il "blocco rurale" conservatore', *Rinascita*, No. 3, March 1958.

Sereni, E., 'La scelta del 1943–1945', *Rinascita*, No. 5, 29 January 1971.

Sereni, E., 'Fascismo, capitale finanziario e capitalismo monopolistico di stato nelle analisi dei comunisti italiani', *Critica Marxista*, No. 5, September–October 1972.

Sereni, E., *Capitalismo e mercato nazionale*, Rome, Riuniti, 1974.

Silone, I., 'Invito a un esame di coscienza', *Tempor presente*, No. 9, December 1956.

Spano, V., 'I comunisti e il Congresso di Bari del 1944', *Cronache meridionali*, No. 4, 1964.

Spezzano, F., 'Vogliamo una finanza locale conforme alla Costituzione e democratica', *Rinascita*, No. 3, March 1956.

Spriano, P., *Storia del Partito comunista italiano*, 5 vols., Turin, Einaudi, 1967–75.

Tarrow, S. G., *Peasant Communism in Southern Italy*, New Haven, Yale University Press, 1967.

Togliatti, P., 'Che cosa deve essere il partito comunista', *Rinascita*, No. 1, June 1944.

Togliatti, P., 'Che cosa è il partito nuovo', *Rinascita*, No. 4, October–December 1944.

Togliatti, P., 'Principi dei rapporti sociali', *Rinascita*, No. 9, September 1946.

Togliatti, P., 'Piano del Lavoro', *Rinascita*, No. 2, February 1950.

Togliatti, P., 'La via italiana verso il socialismo', *Rinascita*, No. 2, Feburary 1956.

Togliatti, P., 'La realtà dei fatti e la nostra azione rintuzza l'irresponsabile disfattismo', *Rinascita*, No. 7, July 1956.

Togliatti, P., 'Per un congresso di rafforzamento e rinnovamento del Partito comunista', *Rinascita*, No. 8–9, August–September 1956.

Togliatti, P., 'Congresso democristiano e unificazione socialista', *Rinascita*, No. 10, October 1956.

Togliatti, P. 'Invito ai socialisti', *Rinascita*, No. 1, January 1959.

Togliatti, P., 'Alcuni problemi della storia dell'internazionale comunista', *Rinascita*, No. 7–8, July–August 1959.

Togliatti, P., 'Sugli orientamenti politici del nostro partito (Intervento alla riunione dei 64 partiti comunisti e operai, Novembre 1957)', *Rinascita*, No. 11, November 1959.

Togliatti, P., 'Commenti alla conferenza di Mosca degli 81 partiti', *Rinascita*, No. 1, January 1961.

Togliatti, P., 'Tesseramento e reclutamento', *Rinascita*, No. 4, April 1961.

Togliatti, P., 'Obtorto collo', *Rinascita*, No. 19, 30 June 1962.

Togliatti, P., *Problemi del movimento operaio internazionale 1956–61*, Rome, Riuniti, 1962.

Togliatti, P., *Nella democrazia e nella pace verso il socialismo*, Rome, Riuniti, 1963.

Togliatti, P., 'Viaggio in Jugoslavia', *Rinascita*, No. 5, 1 February 1964.

Togliatti, P., 'Ceto medio e Emilia rossa', *Critica Marxista*, No. 4–5, July–October 1964.
Togliatti, P., *La via italiana al socialismo*, Rome, Riuniti, 1964.
Togliatti, P., *Sul movimento operaio internazionale*, Rome, Riuniti, 1964.
Togliatti, P., *Gramsci*, Rome, Riuniti, 1967.
Togliatti, P., 'La situazione economica e politica sociale dell'Italia' (1941), *Critica Marxista*, No. 1, January–February1968.
Togliatti, P., *La politica di Salerno aprile-settembre 1944*, Rome, 1969.
Togliatti, P., *Il Partito comunista italiano*, Rome, Riuniti, 1971.
Togliatti, P., *Il partito*, Rome, Riuniti, 1973.
Togliatti, P., *Opere* (E. Ragionieri, ed.), vol. 2, Rome, Riuniti, 1973.
Togliatti, P., *Comunisti socialisti cattolici*, Rome, Riuniti, 1974.
Togliatti, P., *Momenti della storia d'Italia*, Rome, Riuniti, 1974.
Togliatti, P., *Da Radio Milano-Libertà*, Rome, Edizione Rinascita, 1974.
Togliatti, P., *Politica nazionale e Emilia rossa*, Rome, Riuniti, 1974.
Togliatti, P., *Opere scelte*, Rome, Riuniti, 1974.
Togliatti, P., *Discorsi alla Costituente*, Rome, Riuniti, 1974.
Togliatti, P., *Lectures on Fascism*, London, Lawrence and Wishart, 1976.
Trentin, B., 'Politica dei redditti e programmazione', *Critica Marxista*, No. 1, January–February 1964.
Turone, S., *Storia del sindacato in Italia 1943-1969*, Rome–Bari, Laterza, 1973.
Vacca, G., 'La logica dei blocchi', *Rinascita*, No. 41, 17 October 1969.
Vacca, G., 'Il contrastato approccio dei giovani a Togliatti', *Rinascita*, No. 33, 24 August 1973.
Vacca, G., *Saggio su Togliatti*, Bari, De Donato, 1974.
Vlahovic, V., 'A Mosca nel 1943: prima formulazione del policentrismo', *Rinascita*, No. 34, 1965.
Woolf, S. J. (ed.), *The Rebirth of Italy 1943-1950*, London, Longman, 1972.

Index